"Mother Loyola's name is is an endorsement of every book careful use of Mother Loyola's work will be productive of the best results."

--Rosary Magazine, November 1901

About Mother Mary Loyola:

Most Catholics today who have heard the name Mother Mary Loyola know her as the author of *The King of the Golden City*, which has enjoyed a resurgence in popularity in recent years. But few know that she wrote over two dozen works, and that she was once a household name among Catholics of her era. What made her unique among Catholic authors was her ability to draw in her listeners with story after story—and not just any stories, but ones that incorporated current events and brand new inventions of the time. Despite the fact that those events are no longer current, and those inventions no longer brand new, her books scintillate with the appeal of an active mind that could find a moral in the most unusual places. And while the printed word lacks the animated facial expressions and vocal inflections which reveal a gifted storyteller, hers convey her enthusiasm so capably that the reader can easily imagine sitting at the feet of this wise old nun.

About *Home for Good*:

The unassuming title "Home for Good" and the original motivation Mother Loyola had in writing this book—that is, to help young ladies who were finishing boarding school to make the right choices in life—both utterly belie the groundbreaking significance of its content. While *King of the Golden City* is charming and entertaining; while Mother Loyola's catechesis books are both informative and inspiring; and while her devotional works are unparalleled in their ability to reach the hearts of their readers, *Home for Good* is a rock on which an unshakable faith can be built amidst the storms and calms of everyday life. Readers of all ages, both male and female, have equally to gain by reading from this book regularly.

To learn more about Mother Mary Loyola, visit our website at
www.staugustineacademypress.com.

The Old and the New

Here's what a Jesuit review said of <u>Home for Good</u> in 1907:

"Mother Mary Loyola is unwearied in providing the very practical species of instruction which in so special a manner she has made her own. In this her latest volume she addresses herself to supply...a great and urgent need. Young persons, youths and maidens alike, who finish their school course...settle down to a mere aimless pursuit of pleasure and amusement, which, if once adopted as a rule of life, will make it very difficult for them ever to become what they ought to be—strenuous workers in the cause to which all Catholics are called to devote themselves...

...It need not be added that in her hands the old substantial truths which have ever been the burden of Catholic instruction, run no danger of seeming trite or hackneyed, but in the ingenious setting which she knows how to give them, become thoroughly 'up-to-date.' "

-- *The Month*, September 1907

Here's what a modern reader had to say in 2011:

"This is one of the very few advice books still relevant after a century. Mother Mary Loyola's *Home for Good* was originally written for boarding school girls about to return home after graduation. She is unapologetically--in fact, gloriously--Catholic and liberally sprinkles doctrine and Biblical quotes throughout her lessons. Occasionally, the wise nun reveals her century, like when she reminds her students that girls should not participate in "...the indiscriminate reading of Encyclopedias and newspapers..." Mostly, however, she dispenses sound, practical, and timeless advice about self-discipline, scheduling, hobbies, chores, volunteerism, priorities, friends, and family. "We cannot know at the outset of life what our life's task is to be. But we know there is a vocation for every one of us." Each Catholic girl between the ages of ten and twenty-five should own and read this book!

--T. L. Kleck

Home for Good

The Visitation

"And Elizabeth was filled with the Holy Ghost: and she cried out with a loud voice, and said: '. . . And whence is this to me, that the mother of my Lord should come to me?'"—*St. Luke.*

HOME FOR GOOD

BY
MOTHER MARY LOYOLA

EDITED BY
REV. HERBERT THURSTON, S.J.

"I can devote myself: I have a life to give."
Browning, *Paracelsus*

2012
ST. AUGUSTINE ACADEMY PRESS
LISLE, ILLINOIS

This book is newly typeset based on the 1915 edition by Burns & Oates.
All editing strictly limited to the correction of errors in the original text
and minor clarifications in punctuation or phrasing.
Any remaining oddities of spelling or phrasing are as found in the original.

Nihil Obstat
Herbertus Thurston, S.J.
Censor Deputatus

Imprimi Potest
✠ Gulielmus
Episcopus Arindelensis
Vicarius Generalis

Westmonasterii
die 7 Junii 1907

This book was originally published in 1907 by Burns & Oates.
This edition ©2012 by St. Augustine Academy Press.
Editing by Theresa Kleck and Lisa Bergman.

ISBN: 978-1-936639-12-0
Library of Congress Control Number: 2012930117

Unless otherwise noted, all illustrations in this book, including the cover,
are either the original illustrations as found in the book,
or are public domain images.

TO
THE MAIDEN OF NAZARETH
SO YOUTHFUL YET SO VENERABLE
SO HIGHLY EXALTED YET SO LOWLY
WHOM FOR HER GENTLE COURTESY
HER TENDER SYMPATHY AND TIMELY HELP
WE LOVE TO CALL
OUR LADY

Contents

	Preface	ix
I	What Mother Juliana Saw	1
II	"Make Haste and Save Thyself"	7
III	The Two Roads	19
IV	Why Sin Is So Bad	29
V	Temptation and How to Meet It	38
VI	"You Romans"	54
VII	"I Am a Child of the Church"	70
VIII	Is Seeing Believing?	75
IX	"Mother Says So"	85
X	Does it Matter?	94
XI	About Friends	104
XII	About Books	112
XIII	A Traitor	123
XII	"Work Your Work Before the Time."	134
XV	Joan	144
XVI	Home and Homemakers	154
XVII	Coming Out	168
XVIII	About a Jelly-fish	179
XIX	"Trade Till I Come"	185
XX	"Lord, When did we see Thee Hungry?"	193
XXI	"God's Coadjutors"	202
XXII	About a Bishop and a Time-Table	214
XXIII	Books Again	225
XXIV	"In Him was Life, and the Life was the Light of Men"	236
XXV	Charity Begins at Home	240
XXVI	Home-makers and their Difficulties	247
XXVII	Home: The First Field of Work	254
XXVIII	Wider Fields	260
XXIX	"Noblesse Oblige"	268
	Alphabetical Index	283

Editor's Note

I have endeavored in this new revised edition of Mother Mary Loyola's *Home for Good* to be as faithful as possible to the original text as printed in the 1915 edition by Burns & Oates. However, I have, in a few cases, judiciously corrected punctuation and spelling where the change significantly enhanced the clarity of the passage. I have also augmented the text with additional footnotes, in the hopes of shedding some light on personages and events which were well-known to readers at the time, but are no longer so. Therefore the reader should understand that though this text is considered revised due to these facts, the majority of the material found herein is exactly as it was written over a century ago.

Lastly, I would point out that all Scriptural references found in this book are from the Catholic Douay-Rheims version, and thus they often do not align in chapter and verse with modern bibles, which conform more closely to the chapter and verse structure of the Protestant King James Version.

In Christ,
Lisa Bergman
St. Augustine Academy Press
April 2012

Preface

The time of leaving school, as all will agree, is a critical period for both girls and boys, and it is often a period of great difficulty for their fond and anxious parents. The old home relations of the nursery have long been broken through. For six years, seven years, or even longer, these growing lads and maidens have appeared only as visitors in their father's house. Even in the best regulated families, the child home for the holidays is a privileged being, while in those that are less well-regulated he develops too often into a sort of chartered libertine, the short duration of whose period of freedom is made the excuse for every kind of irregularity. Moreover, under modern conditions, the longer vacations are constantly spent in some hotel or temporary residence by the seaside, where every detail of daily life militates against even the mildest form of discipline. This is not always a good preparation for the final home-coming, which in the case of most girls and not a few boys, follows immediately upon the end of their school-days. The child, in many instances, looks forward to this time as to an emancipation, which is again to be altogether of the nature of a holiday—only more so. The parent is constantly apprehensive that home will be dull after the varied *agréments* of an expensive and well-appointed modern school. A child exacting, bent on amusement and threatening revolt at the least rebuke; a parent weak, vacillating and almost apologetic for any rare exercise of authority—these are elements that offer but a poor promise of ultimate happiness for either of the parties concerned. And yet it is precisely during this first year or first six months at home that, in a large number of cases, the great decision of life is made. It is then, more than at any other time, that the girl consciously or unconsciously frames her answer to the vital question of *what she is going to be*—a frivolous pleasure-seeker or one who, in Christ's name, is resolved as cheerily as may be to accept her share of the burdens of life.

Mother Mary Loyola has surely done well to emphasise the importance of this critical time, and to encourage children who are yet at school to look forward to it and to prepare for it. In these days of examinations for girls as well as boys the busy round of school tasks and school amusements is more absorbing than ever, and the sort of back-water in which many a girl finds herself in a quiet country home after the excitements she has grown accustomed to is apt to prove not a little disconcerting if principle does not come to her aid. All who know Mother Loyola's other books will be familiar with her happy touch in facing practical difficulties of conduct and suggesting remedies. They will be prepared for the insistence with which she waives aside pretences and concentrates the attention of her auditors in these imaginary conversations upon the sense of responsibility and the solid formation of character. Even from early years she cautions them wisely against the false promises and self-assertive allurements of pleasure and excitement and popularity. It will not be her fault if they do not learn to appreciate what is best and highest. "Are there not," she seems to ask with Clough,

> "Are there not, then, two musics unto men?—
>   One loud and bold and coarse,
>   And overpowering still perforce
>   All tone and tune beside;
>   Yet in despite its pride
> Only of fumes of foolish fancy bred
> And sounding solely in the sounding head."

And very skilfully she pleads with her youthful hearers to try to open their minds and hearts to the subtler charm, to that higher life of unselfishness and well-doing whose appeal is so much more difficult to catch.

> "The other soft and low
>   Stealing whence we not know,
> Painfully heard, and easily forgot,
> With pauses oft and many a silence strange
> (And silent oft it seems when silent it is not),
> Revivals too of unexpected change:
> Haply thou think'st 'twill never be begun,
> Or that 't has come and been and passed away:
>   Yet turn to other none,—
>   Turn not, oh, turn not thou!
> But listen, listen, listen—if haply be heard it may,
> Listen, listen, listen,—is it not sounding now?"

It is to the counsels and the ideals of such educators as Mother Loyola that we have to look for the hope that this second music will never lose its charm, and that the bright example of the Christian life may still kindle and attract the hearts of brave and generous youth in generations yet unborn.

HERBERT THURSTON, S.J.
FEAST OF THE ASCENSION,
MAY 2, 1907

HOME FOR GOOD

I

WHAT MOTHER JULIANA SAW

LONG, long ago—it was at the close of the reign of Edward III—there lived in the ancient city of Norwich a holy solitary named Juliana. She lived alone within four narrow walls, spending her time in prayer and manual work.

This kind of life seems strange to us in these days, and perhaps we cannot quite see the use of it. We wonder why she did not nurse the sick, or teach children, or take care of the aged poor—help her neighbour, in short, in one of the many ways in which we are used to see nuns spend their lives nowadays. One reason is that the active Orders, as they are called, did not then exist in the Church. But we must not think that this active service of our neighbour is the only way in which to serve God. Even before our Lord came there were men and women devoted altogether to the worship and praise of their Creator, though these solitaries have always helped their neighbour at least by prayer.

In the Book of Exodus, we learn how great is the power with God which His special servants possess. When the Israelites in the desert were nearing the Promised Land, the Amalekites came out to fight them. What did Moses, the leader of the people, do? Did he take a sword and go with them into the fray? No, this he left to the warlike Josue: "And Moses said to Josue: Choose out men, and go out and fight against Amalec: tomorrow I will stand on the top of the hill having the rod of God in my hand. Josue did as Moses had spoken, and he fought against Amalec; but Moses and Aaron and Hur went up upon the top of the hill. And when Moses lifted up his hands, Israel overcame; but if he let them down a little, Amalec overcame. And Moses' hands were heavy; so they took a stone and put under him, and he sat on it, and Aaron and Hur stayed up his hands on both sides. And it came to pass that his hands were not weary until sunset. And Josue put Amalec and his people to flight by the edge of the sword." (Exod. xvii)

When, later on, God was angry with the people for their worship of the golden calf, so that He said to Moses: "Let Me alone, that My wrath may be kindled against them and that I may destroy them," Moses prayed. "And the Lord was appeased from doing the evil which He had spoken against His people."

We see, then, that it would be a great mistake to think that prayerful lives are useless. The Church has approved them from the beginning. The deserts of Egypt were at one time peopled by holy solitaries, and for about four hundred years there were to be found, even in great cities, anchorets and anchoresses living in cells or tiny houses adjoining a church, into which they could look through a little window. Their chief employment was meditation on eternal things. When not in prayer, they worked with their hands at basket-making or needle-work, either for their own support or for the relief of the poor.

So far were the townsfolk of those days from looking upon these solitaries as "lazy drones," or useless citizens, that they counted much on their prayers, and believed many blessings came through their means, so that they were glad to help them and provide them with the few things they needed.

Mother Juliana of Norwich was one of these anchoresses. God made known to her many wonderful secrets concerning, for the most part, His tender love for men. He told her that these revelations were not for herself alone. She was to write them down that men and women who were to come after her might know how dearly He loves them—every one, one by one. Much of what she heard and saw has come down to us in her own words, and in the quaint language and spelling of the time, which makes it doubly interesting. Let us hear what she says:—

"One day He showed a little thing, the quantitie of a hasel-nutt, lying in the palme of my hand, as me seemed; and it was as round as a ball. I looked with the eie (eye) of my understanding and thought: What may this be? And it was answered generally thus:

" *'It is all that is made.'* I marvelled how it might last; for me thought it might suddenly have fallen to naught for litleness. And I was answered in my understanding: *'It lasteth and ever shall: for God loveth it.'*"

"In this litle thing I saw three properties:

"The *first* is, that God made it.

"The *second* is, that God loveth it.

"The *third* is, that God keepeth it."[1]

Now here, as is usual in the revelations of the Saints, there are things too high for us to understand, and things which it will help us much to try to understand. For us they were shown by God to His favoured servants, and if we pass them by as no business of ours we shall miss much that He means us to have.

Think, now, if you know anything so small that it might "sodenlie fall to naught for litleness, but it lasteth and ever shall, for God loveth it."

"Would it be me?"

---

1 "Revelations of Divine Love showed to Mother Juliana of Norwich," p. 13. (Kegan Paul, Trench, Trübner & Co.)

To be sure it would. And now let us see how dearly God loves this little thing, that it may love Him back. For this is what He wants. If He makes known to us His love for us, it is that we may return Him love for love. "Wouldst thou wit (understand) thy Lord's meaning in this?" she asks. "Wit it well: Love was His meaning."

All the message she had to give us is in these words. All the great and the tender things she tells us about God are to bring home to us this one truth—that we are each and every one of us very dear to the great God who made us. She wants us to see what she saw clearly, that whatever He gives is out of love; whatever He does not give, is out of love. Why I have many joys, and some difficulties and troubles—"Wit it well: Love is the meaning" of it all.

We make things either because we cannot do without them, or because, though not necessary, they will be useful or pleasant. God needs nothing. From all eternity He was perfectly happy by Himself. If He creates intelligent beings, such as the Angels and men, it is out of love, that He may share His happiness with others. True, it is for His own glory, for God, like us, must have an end in what He does, and He could not have a lower end than Himself. But His Will is that His glory should come out of the happiness of the creatures He makes, as a father's joy is in the joy of his little ones when they crowd round the Christmas tree to see all he has got ready for them. And so, whilst it is true that God needs no one, we can say each and all of us: "God made me because He wanted me, and He wanted me because He loved me."

He made us, then, out of love. Think as far back as you can go, millions upon millions of years, when there was no world of ours at all, nor one of the multitudes of worlds we see glittering over our heads at night; no Angels—nothing but God. Go back as many millions of years as there are leaves on the trees and sands on the seashore—what will you find existing then? Only God. Not lonely, quite happy, yet looking forward to the time when we too should exist; when, straight from His hand, our soul would come; when it would begin its pilgrimage through this world, and after a little, a very little while, return to Him to enjoy all the delights He has made ready for it. If this is not love, what shall we call love?

But there is more than this. It cost Him nothing to create us. But—oh! what it has cost Him to keep us, to win us back when we had wandered away from Him and lost ourselves. We spoilt His beautiful plan. From being His dearest children we made ourselves slaves of the devil. From having a right to His company for ever, we deserved a place among His enemies in hell. He might have left us in our misery, and made other creatures in our place who would have been grateful and faithful to Him. But His love would not let Him do this. He could not let us go. And see what He did.

If He had determined to keep us, He might have forgiven us without requiring any reparation; or, if there were to be cost in order to show how hateful a thing sin is, and it had been possible for Him to entrust the work of suffering for us to an Angel, this would have shown love indeed, but infinitely less love than if He were to come Himself to undertake the painful work of our Redemption. Besides, how we should have loved this Angel-Saviour! And He, the Lord of Angels, wanted our love. "So He became their Saviour…in His love and in His mercy He redeemed them," says the prophet Isaias.

"Wit it well: Love was the meaning" of the Incarnation, of the hardships of Bethlehem and Egypt, of the long Hidden Life, of the journeyings to and fro among the poor and the suffering, of the tortures of the Agony in the Garden, and the Scourging, and the Crowning with thorns, of the Way of the Cross and the Crucifixion—Love was the meaning of it all.

Not only, then, has God loved this "litle thing" by "making it," but He has done all He can to "keep it," that it may not wander from Him any more, and lose itself by losing Him. Some one else, however, has to help Him here. Let us see who it is.

II

"Make Haste and Save Thyself"[1]

We all know the story of the destruction of wicked Sodom; how two Angels were sent to save Lot who lived there; and how eager they showed themselves on their charitable errand. "And the Angels pressed Lot, saying: Arise, save thy life; look not back, but save thyself in the mountains.... And as he lingered, they took his hand, saying: Make haste and be saved."

Our good Angel says the same to us to-day and every day. "Make haste, dear child, and save yourself—not from the fire which destroyed Sodom, but from one more terrible by far: a fire compared with which the fiercest furnace of earth is but painted fire. You who cannot bear a spark on your hand, save yourself from the flames that burn without destroying, that torment both soul and body, that can never, never be extinguished.

"But to save yourself means more than this. It is not only escaping eternal pain, it is securing eternal joy, such joy as you have never dreamed, the joy for which God made you, a joy so great that eye has not seen, nor ear heard, nor heart imagined it; the very same joy that the Angels and Saints, and our Lady, and our Lord Jesus Christ, and God Himself enjoy. It is a happiness that will quite satisfy you, and it is the only happiness that can.

---

1 Gen. xix 17, 22.

It is promised to you by God, who can neither deceive nor be deceived; if you will you can reach it—dear child, make haste, make haste!"

To save our soul is the work for which we were sent into this world. We must try to understand how important, how necessary it is, how great is the value of our soul. If you want to know the worth of a precious stone, you take it to a jeweller, you ask what he would give for it. If you want to know the worth of your soul, see what God who made it thinks of it, what He has given for it.

God the Father has had it in His mind from all eternity. As long as He has been God He has loved it, and provided everything it will need to bring it to the happiness He has prepared for it. Because it is the work of His hands it must be something very grand. People go a long way to see a painting by a great artist. What must the soul be like on which God has stamped the image of Himself. Your soul in the state of grace is so beautiful in His sight that He would give all the precious things in this world for it, nay, He has actually given all the Blood of His only and well-beloved Son to keep it from harm.

To save it, Jesus Christ came down from Heaven, and suffered, and died. He did not think His Precious Blood, poured out to the last drop, too much to give for it. The Church says He did not hesitate a moment when He had to choose between the torments of the cross and the salvation of your soul. How He must love it!

At your Baptism the Holy Ghost came to dwell in your soul as in His temple. We adorn a church with rich ornaments because it is the temple of God; but no richness of gold and silver, and marbles, and carving, and jewelled monstrance, and windows glowing with many colors, can be compared with the splendors of grace with which God has enriched your soul in Baptism and

Confirmation. This is a living temple which can know and love Him who has made and adorned it. And so He loves to dwell in it, and perfect it more and more. He is continually speaking to you by His holy inspirations, putting good thoughts into your mind and helping you to do what is right.

It is not enough to say that to save your soul is the most important, the most necessary work you have to do. Our Lord says it is the "one thing necessary," and that nothing else will be of any use to you if you fail in this. What do we mean by a thing being necessary? That we cannot do without it; that we *must* have it at any cost. Air is necessary, food is necessary. But compared with the salvation of my soul these are not necessaries at all. Without air and food I shall die of course, but the life of my body is not necessary. It is the soul that matters. To keep it safe for eternal life—this is necessary, this I must secure at any price.

"Save thyself," the Angels said to Lot. Because no one could get him out of Sodom unless he bestirred himself, and set out for the high mountain where he would be safe. So is it with us. Neither our parents nor our teachers, nor God Himself, can save us unless we make efforts ourselves. The Angel took Lot by the hand and led him along the right road. Our good Angel will lead and help us, but we must go with him, we must take the necessary steps. This brings us to the study of a very important word, perhaps there is not one more important in the language. Kings and crossing-sweepers, learned and unlearned, fathers and mothers and children, must grasp its meaning well.

"I know—God."

"The Catechism."

"Being fair to everybody, not being a sneak and mean."

It has to do with all these, but I am afraid it is too hard for you to guess; the word is—*Responsibility*.

"Responsibility! why, there's not much in that; every one knows what that is."

Tell us, then.

"Well, when you've got a canary or anything to look after, you mustn't leave it without seed or water. And if any one has lent you a bicycle or a book and you spoil it, you'll have to get it mended or make it good somehow, because it isn't your own."

Exactly. Responsibility, as you Latin scholars know, comes from *respondeo*, I answer. It means, then, the obligation of having to account or answer to another for something entrusted to us. We have to account to God for the immortal soul He has given us. This responsibility began as soon as we were able to tell right from wrong. It increases as the powers of our soul unfold and strengthen, as the light of reason and the light of faith grow through the instructions, the graces, the inspirations, the Sacraments we receive. We cannot shirk it or shift it on to another. What we must do is to look it steadily in the face and square our conduct by what it requires of us.

We are responsible to God for our souls. It is a grand thing to have so noble a charge, to be trusted with the guardianship of this royal child and its training for the Kingdom of Heaven.

"But if you don't do it properly it will be the worse for you. I think sometimes I'd rather not have the charge."

"Oh, I wouldn't. Why, we shouldn't be any better than beasts if we had no soul."

Would it be very grateful, do you think, to wish we had not this responsibility, or would it be rather selfish? Suppose your mother were to trust you with your youngest brother or sister, who had to be got safe to school every day through the streets of a big town, would you find it in your heart to grumble, or would you be proud that the pet of the family was trusted to your care?

But there is no use discussing likes and dislikes here. We were not consulted on the subject, we could not have been. "Wit it well: Love was His meaning" in giving you to yourself, a love that now bids you bring yourself safely with its help to the eternal happiness in store for you.

"Save *yourself*," your Angel says. No one can do this for you, not even God Himself, for "He who made you without you will not save you without you," says St. Augustine. God's rule is that all His creatures to whom He has given understanding and will, shall use these grand powers in His service, and by so doing gain Heaven for themselves. He holds out Heaven as a prize and says: "See what I have ready for you when your short time on earth is over, if you show yourself worthy of it and do what I tell you to save your soul. I call it yours, but remember it is Mine much more than yours, because I made it. I love it dearly, more, much more than you do. I am angry with any one who hurts it or spoils its beauty. I have trusted it to you and you will have to give Me an account of it. Take care of it, then. It is the most precious thing you have; it is the only thing that is really yours; you must lose everything else. How foolish it would be for the sake of a pleasure that is gone directly to risk losing this treasure. Watch it, guard it well. Do not let its companion, the body, have all it cries for. It often wants what would hurt the soul. Where the soul goes after death the body will go too some day. If you save the soul, the body will go bright and beautiful with it to Heaven. If you lose your soul, the body, like a hideous mask, will be with it in hell for all eternity. Therefore think of your soul first, and say a resolute "No" to the body when it asks what would harm the soul. If you could see your soul as I see it, you would think no trouble too great to prevent its being spoilt by sin. If you knew the happiness of those who have saved their soul, the despair of those who have lost it, you would fear sin above all other evils, so as to be resolved never to commit a wilful sin for the love or fear of anything whatsoever."

The devil who hates you would do anything to get your soul and prevent it from gaining the happiness he has lost. He does not mind trouble. He lays plots for the ruin of every one; he dared to tempt Jesus Christ Himself.

Learn, then, the worth of your soul from those who know its value—from the God who made it; from its great enemy, the devil; from the blessed in heaven, who have saved their souls; from those in hell who, having lost their souls, have lost all.

I see how God and all creatures able to judge value my soul. Let me see if I really value it. I can find out what I think of a thing by seeing how much I am ready to give for it or to suffer for it. If I am very keen on tennis I shall not think a guinea too much to give for a racquet. If I care for my bodily comfort I shall be willing to have a bad tooth drawn, or a gathered finger lanced. Yet the body is a very poor concern after all. It is made from the dust, as the Church reminds me every Ash Wednesday, and in a very short time it will be dust again. But my soul that will never die, that is made for eternity, to see, love, and enjoy God for ever—how do I prize this?

Perhaps I scarcely ever think of it. Perhaps everything I am asked to do for it seems too much trouble. May be I am not afraid of losing it by mortal sin. Oh, how can I be so foolish as to neglect the one thing that is really my own, which if I lose once is lost for ever! Our Lord says it is wrong to call any one a fool, but He Himself uses this word of contempt for one who cares only for the corruptible body and neglects the immortal soul. "Thou fool," He said to the rich man, who was going to pull down his barns and build greater that there might be room to hold all his corn and that he might have plenty for many years. "Thou fool, this night do they require thy soul of thee, and whose shall those things be which thou hast provided?" That very night he was to be called away from all his riches. He was to leave everything he had in this world, and to appear alone before his Judge to give an account of his soul! If he had lost that, what good to him was all he had left behind? Oh, "What does it profit a man," as our dear Lord so earnestly reminds us, "if he gain the whole world and lose his soul?" What does Herod think now of the crown for the sake of which he sacrificed so many innocent lives? What does Judas think of the thirty pieces of silver that were to make him so happy? And what should I think of my past pleasures and amusements if I were to die in mortal sin and lose my soul?

We shall not be in this world very long; it is only a passage to the world in which we are to stay for ever. Our chief business here is to see to the salvation of our soul. We must make a *business* of it. "Business before pleasure," we hear men say. They do not deny themselves all pleasure, but it must not interfere with work. Are we people of business? Do we bring to our great work the punctuality, industry, determination, perseverance, that make men successful in their pursuits? They must be at their office at a specified hour. Liking has nothing to do with it. Whether they feel inclined or not, they turn out into the fog or the cold, and are at their desk as the clock strikes.

We have to say our morning and night prayers at a certain time, to go to confession on a fixed day. Can it be said of us that when the time comes—there we are? Business men work hard, not by fits and starts, but steadily year after year, losing here, gaining there, but never discouraged by their losses, never thinking they have done enough. Are we like them? They do not trust to clerks however trustworthy, nor even to partners. They have an eye to all themselves; they look over accounts, they clear up difficulties, they take trouble—because they are business men.

Let us beware of leaving our great work to the care of others, least of all to that most unreliable partner—the body. It would cheat us frightfully. It has no scruple about ruining the soul and itself too for the merest trifle, for a little passing pleasure; we must keep a sharp eye upon it! When companions, reading, amusements, sloth, greediness—self-indulgence in any shape, tries to make us lose sight of the work for which we were sent into this world, let us say with the boy Stanislaus: "I was born for something greater than to be a slave to my body." Or with Aloysius: "How will this look in eternity?" Or with our Lord Himself at the age of twelve: "Did you not know that I must be about My Father's business?"

"Our Lord was quite perfect when He was only twelve. And the Saints—well, they were Saints, but it's different with us, of course."

Why "of course"?

"I mean—but it seems horrid to say it, and I'm sure no one else thinks things like I do."

And I'll be bound plenty of us do. If we were less afraid of coming out with our difficulties there would be a chance of getting rid of them. Many and many a child grows up with real puzzles and troubles which could have been set right at once had they been brought to light when they began. But we are afraid of shocking those who hear us, or of being thought silly, so we let our difficulties grow up with us and be perhaps a real hindrance in our path through life. Now what is it you think about the Saints?

"Well, I can't help being aggravated when people say we ought to be like them, because, you know, it wasn't so hard for them to be good. If our Lady had put the Infant Jesus into my arms, or if He would sit by me at class, like St. Edmund, or come and stand on my book as He did on St. Antony's, I'm sure I could do anything."

"Yes, that's just what I think."

"And so do I."

And—would you believe it—I have thought the same. So we are all in the same boat and can feel for one another. But let us examine our thought.

Suppose we allow that God *has* His favourites, that He does give special graces and favours to some—well, what of that! Do we count it a hardship to be Catholic children, well cared for and taught how to save our souls, when there are so many little pagans who have never even heard of the Infant Jesus and His Blessed Mother?

"Oh, I never thought of that!"

And does it follow that these favourites of God have no troubles or struggles? Is it smooth sailing with them always?

"Of course not. But I do think when God was so very good to them it must have made a difference."

No doubt. Just as there must be all the difference in the world between Catholic children and those who have not their helps. But what I want to find out is whether all of us, not excepting these special favourites, have to deny ourselves, that is "to go against our own humours, inclinations, and passions" in order to save our souls?

"I suppose so, but I should say some have to do it more than others."

And what if it is just these favoured children of God who have to suffer most, to overcome most! What if some of them have to struggle against stronger passions than we have, against bad example, temptation, and trials which we are afraid even to think of! It is true some seem to be Saints from the cradle, but it is never true that even the most innocent have no need to fight and to fight hard. They are of the same nature as you are;

do you suppose they enjoy any more than you do the pain of self-denial, the going against their own humours, inclinations, and passions?

"I wonder if there are any Saints now?"

"Real live Saints. I should love to see a live Saint."

To be sure there are—passing us in the streets, going by the same trains, using the same books, praying in the same church; only praying and studying better than we do, bearing their cross better, and—which is much to our present purpose—rising more quickly and more courageously after their falls.

"Do they have falls if they are Saints?"

There are none altogether faultless. If we could know the secret story of their lives day by day, we should see that it is no unwavering upward course, such as we imagine, but a zigzag of ups and downs. When we are able to hear from their own lips a true account of themselves, we shall say: "Oh, how I wish I had known that you were like that—that you were weak and failing like me; it would have helped me ever so much more!"

"I should think they write their lives best themselves."

They do. And we find there, side by side with the marvellous consolations which excite our envy, trials so heavy that only their burning love of God and desire to be like Christ Crucified, sustained them on their difficult path. St. Francis of Assisi goes so far as to say: "No man should deem himself a true friend of God, save in so far as he has passed through many temptations and tribulations." Were we offered the privileges of the Saints at the price they paid for them, I expect many of us would draw back and prefer to travel on a lower and less painful road.

"Do you think so?"

I judge by what daily experience proves. We know quite well that greater care in the way we say our prayers or prepare for the Sacraments, more generous efforts to check our temper or our self-will, or our unkind thoughts of others, would make us dearer to God, and win for us more grace here and glory hereafter. Yet such knowledge does not spur us on to make these efforts.

It is clear, then, that the Saints who have the same nature as ourselves, have, like us, to conquer their nature when it would lead them astray. And that it is because they are more generous than we are in their work of self-conquest, that they deserve the rewards of generosity.

Mind, I am not saying that God would be sure to give us all He has given them if we did our best. He is Lord and Master and can do as He wills. He treats no two of us alike, because no two of us are meant for the same place in Heaven. But to each and all of us He holds out His helping hand. To each He gives those special gifts which are to fit us for our place. Because such and such favours will help, they are given. Because others would not help, they are not given. "Wit it well: Love is His meaning" in all this. How much better it will be for us to thank Him for what He has done and for what He wants to do for us, to trust to His Fatherly goodness, and beg we may not be wanting on our part, than to be peevishly comparing His gifts to us with what He has given to others.

"I think I see that now."

When we get to Heaven and behold our past life as in a picture, we shall wonder, and wonder for all eternity, why God has been so good to us, why He has given us so much—not why He has not thought good to give us more. We have to train ourselves to think now as we shall think when we get there and see all things clearly.

In the meantime it is plain that favourites are expected to give as well as take, to show extra devotedness, to pay for their privileges, as it were. Sometimes they pay dearly.

Not long ago a fire broke out at night in a house in which there were many little children. The flames spread rapidly, and when at length the alarm was given to the sleeping household, there was barely time to get the children into the street, before the building was wrapped in a sheet of fire. The father was the last to leave the house. Looking round upon his terrified little ones, he missed the youngest, Ray. Had any one seen him? Was he anywhere in the fast gathering crowd? No. The poor father was going to rush back into the house, but people held him fast. It was too late; the staircases had given way, it would be madness, and the loss of another life. "Let me go! Let me go!" he cried; "I must, I will save my child! Ray, Ray!" and he waved his arms frantically towards the nursery windows. He was answered by a bark from Fritz, the big Newfoundland, and Ray's special pet. That sound brought hope: "Good dog, fetch Ray, fetch Ray!" A short bark, a toss of his head, and Fritz darted forward and disappeared. In three minutes he was back, his coat singed, his ears burnt, but—he was alone. He raced this way and that, barking furiously at the flames. "Fetch Ray, fetch Ray," shouted his master, and again the dog sprang forward into the burning pile. After some minutes he was seen coming painfully through the smoke, a precious burden in his mouth. He dropped it at his master's feet, and tore off howling into the adjoining stables. They followed and had to shoot him, poor fellow, to put him out of his agony. But he had saved the child.

We have made a long digression, and must put off till to-morrow the important question we have to ask ourselves: "Am I quite in earnest about saving my soul?"

"I like digressions, about dogs especially. Was Ray burnt, and did he cry when they told him Fritz had had to be shot?"

III

THE TWO ROADS

What men will do for gain! When it was spread abroad that gold had been discovered at a point on the Klondike, a small tributary of the great Yukon River in British Columbia, there was a rush for the gold-field, which was believed to be thirty miles square. From the United States, from Canada, miners poured to the diggings. Nothing frightened them. Not the terrors of an arctic winter, with the prospect of eight months of semi-darkness in a miserable hut. Not hard, dirty, uninteresting work. Not the knowledge that food was scarce and sold to the highest bidder, and that those who could not bid high must starve. No, nor the terrifying story of two men who, returning from the gold-fields, one with £16,000, the other with £18,000, had died of hunger on the way home. Nothing of all this kept them back. There was gold at Klondike, and just a chance of making a fortune. For the sake of that chance it was worth while running any risks, so in the course of a few months 30,000 miners had left for the diggings.

Is it not a pity that we cannot bring ourselves to take a little pains for "a treasure in Heaven which faileth not"? God is faithful. He will not let us labour in vain, as so many of the poor miners did. He will most certainly give us the riches of Heaven with all the delights there that we can desire or imagine, if we will take the trouble to go in search of them. How is it we care so little about it?

"I think it is because gold seems a more real thing, somehow, than our souls. It's awfully hard to be always thinking about a thing you can't see or feel."

We cannot see our soul, certainly, but I am not so sure about the feeling. It is my soul that is joyful, or sad, or frightened. When the little voice I call conscience tells me to do this, or not to do that, it is God speaking to my soul, and my soul obeys or disobeys that voice. Which of us does not feel this every day and many times a day?

It is just possible that we might be more willing to work for our soul if we could see what we do when we help it or harm it. But where then would be the Faith to which such glorious things are promised? "Blessed are they who have not seen and have believed," says our Lord.

If you look at the 11th chapter of St. Paul's Epistle to the Hebrews, you will find quite a litany of the praises of Faith. He shows how it was by this noble virtue that all the Saints from the beginning have done their glorious deeds and won their crowns. Why should we think it hard to gain ours in the same way?

> "Faith for all defects supplying
> Where the simple senses fail,"

we sing in the *Tantum ergo* whenever we go to Benediction. We must be content for a little while to believe what Faith teaches us and to act by Faith, which means behaving as we should do if we could see. The day will come when the veil of Faith will drop. We shall not be asked any more to believe, but our Lord will say to us what He said once to Andrew and John: "Come and see."

There is no middle place between Heaven and Hell. I must either be perfectly and eternally happy, or eternally miserable.

"There's Purgatory."

For those who have saved their souls. For those who have done their work in this world and deserve Heaven, but are not quite ready for their reward. But in the moment of death, when we stand before our Lord to be judged, the sentence is for Heaven or for Hell. Can we afford, then, to be careless? In this world Heaven is above us, Hell beneath us; we are between the two—and we have to choose.

"I thought our godfathers and godmothers chose for us long ago."

They did, because the Church says we are to be made children of God as soon as ever we can be brought to the font to be baptized. And as we cannot answer ourselves the questions she asks of us, or make the promises she requires, our godparents speak in our name. But when we come to the use of reason and are able to understand what has been done, we must make these promises for ourselves and confirm by our own freewill what was done for us as babies.

We must not wait till we grow up to do this. "Make haste to save thyself." There is no time to lose. Who knows whether we shall grow up to be men and women? Only God. And He knows that many a boy and girl who are now looking forward to having "a good time" at Midsummer or Christmas, will be in eternity before then—the eternity they are choosing now. Our Lord tells us He will come like a thief in the night, like the lightning. These give no warning. "At the hour when you think not, the Son of Man will come." We must be always ready.

What care we take of a treasure which if lost or spoilt cannot be replaced. See the anxiety of parents for an only child. My soul is my only one—what am I doing for it? It is no great matter whether I am rich or poor, whether I have many pleasures or few, for these things concern the body only, and will come to an end when I die. The soul that will never die must be my chief concern. To keep it in God's grace, to make it more and more pleasing to Him—this is worth any pains.

"We can tell the price of our soul," says the holy Curé of Ars, "by the efforts God makes to save it and the devil to ruin it. Heaven leagues together for it; Hell against it—oh, how great it must be!"

Before we go on, I want you to take a good look at two well-trodden roads, on one or other of which our feet are at this very moment standing.

There are two great thoroughfares leading through this world to the next. You know them by the gates at the entrance. One gate is high and wide, and above is written: *The Broad Way*. It opens upon a sunny road bordered by flowers. These flowers soon fade and many of them are poisonous, but they are gaudy and attractive while they last. The highway is full of people, men, women, and children. Some of them with hard, stern faces are hurrying forward, looking neither right nor left, too full of their business to give a thought to anything else. Others, on the contrary, saunter along, stopping at everything that takes their fancy. They bask in the sunshine or lie down under the shady trees. They stop or go on, sleep or play, just as their whims lead them. You would never think they were on a journey, but you would suppose they were going to loiter on this pleasant road always, or that it led to some place more pleasant still. And you would never guess that all on the highway are servants sent on an errand by their Master, and bound at a fixed time to return to him with their work done. Some of them, I have said, are full of business, but it is not the business on which they were sent. It is one of their own choosing and takes up all their thoughts, so that they have no

time to give to their Master's work. As to the others, they do no real work of any kind, but dawdle along the way, thinking only how to get as much pleasure as they can out of everything they pass, and how to keep clear of everything troublesome or disagreeable. One thing none of them considers—where this road leads. If they could see it, how terrified they would be. For suddenly it stops quite short on the brink of a frightful precipice and—a pool of fire!

Turn now and look at the other road. The gate is low, and you must bow your head to pass beneath. It opens on to a narrow way, steep and often rough. You notice that all the travellers on this road, even the children, bear a cross more or less heavy on their shoulders. Yet there is a peaceful look on their faces even when their feet are weary or bleeding from the stones by the way. Unlike those on the broad road, they are not always looking out for what is easy and pleasant. When these things fall to their lot they are glad and grateful, but when a painful bit of road has to be passed, or the day is dull and gloomy, they trudge on still. They know they are servants sent out on their Master's business, pilgrims and travellers in a foreign land. When trouble comes they are not surprised, but lift their eyes to the distant hills of the Home Country which they are nearing, and which is not so distant as it looks. For suddenly, like the other road, this narrow way ends. Outstretched beyond is a vast and beautiful plain. And coming to meet them, are those who have trodden the narrow way before them, and the Master who will say to them: "Well done!"

"But you are only pretending, there are not really those two roads anywhere."

Indeed I am not pretending. It is our Lord Himself who tells us of them. Every man and woman and child you meet is walking on one or other of these ways. Each one has to choose which he will take, and our Lord wants us to think well what we are about before we choose. Not that we are free to take which course we like and lose our souls if we will. Our godfathers and godmothers chose for us long ago, as one of you said, and made promises for us which we have renewed again and again since we came to the use of reason. But because the enticements of the broad road lead many who have begun to walk in the narrow way to leave it at length for the other, and because as long as we are in this world we are always able to choose evil, we should strengthen our will in good by thinking seriously what comes of a wrong choice, and what a reward is in store for those who persevere on the narrow way to the end.

"Is it always nice on the broad way and always rough on the other?"

No; I should have told you that the people on the wide road have not everything their own way. Far from it. Though the road is broad, they cannot help knocking up against persons and things. This makes them angry, and what with vexation at actual mishaps, and fear of those that may come, they have anything but a peaceful time. You see they are at the mercy of everything they meet, and because they have not learned, and do not mean to learn, how to submit and how to suffer, they cannot be long in peace, for one thing or another on the road is sure to put them out of their way.

Those on the other road, too, jostle one another and run against obstacles.

"More than the others, I should think, as the road is so narrow."

But as they have made up their minds to bear patiently whatever has to be borne, and know the way is not very long and they will never have to pass it again, they keep up their hearts. They have brave companions, too, who cheer them on, and, more than all, they have the sight of the Master walking on in front. So they manage to trudge along cheerily, and really suffer less than those whose whole time is spent in hunting after pleasant things and shunning everything disagreeable.

There are two kinds of people who are in danger of missing their way to Heaven—those who say that all is sure to come right, and so they take no trouble, and those who say it is sure not to come right—the road is too difficult, they cannot keep all the Commandments, give up every pleasure, persevere to the end. And so they will not give up anything or even make a beginning. It is the "father of lies," as our Lord calls him, who deceives these faint-hearted ones. The road to Heaven is not so difficult. It is levelled and smoothed by the feet of multitudes who have gone before us. God is too good to require what is too hard. We are His "most dear children." He desires all to be saved. He helps us. If it depended only on Him, we should all most certainly reach Heaven in safety. It depends on ourselves too, but on ourselves only, not on those about us. If it were in the power of any one or of anything to prevent us, we might well be afraid. But nothing can hurt us against our will, neither the devil, nor temptation, nor bad example. Mortal sin alone can rob us of Heaven, and that we can only fall into by our own free will. Every one in hell has to own that it is entirely by his own free will that he is there.

"I know all that, but it is just myself that I am afraid of. How do I know that I shall always want to go on being good. I might get bad and do a mortal sin and die."

That very fear of yourself will keep you safe. For it will make you distrust yourself and put all your confidence in God. It will make you determine never to give up prayer, and if you persevere in prayer you are sure to save your soul.

Another thing. Do not let the enemy persuade you that to walk along the narrow way you must give up every kind of pleasure. Our Lord has never said this. He likes to see us bright and happy, and it is to keep us so that He guards us by His Commandments from what might please us for a moment and like a poisonous sweet leave a bad taste behind. If you try in earnest to save your soul, you will be happy in this world as well as in the next. If you are not in earnest, if you think little of venial and even of mortal sin, and are careless about prayer and the sacraments, you will be miserable and always in fear during your life here, and be preparing for yourself a miserable eternity. Even in this world the good are really happiest, and when at the Last Day the wretched ones on our Lord's left hand see the blessed on His right, they will own in rage and despair that these have suffered less in saving their souls than the wicked have done in losing theirs. Let us not be afraid, then, but like our Blessed Lord set our face steadfastly to go to Jerusalem. He will be with us all the way, and when the road is a bit steeper or rougher than usual, His grace will be stronger and bear us over it.

"I wish we could just choose the right road once for all as we do when we are going home for the holidays, and then be sure of getting safe to Heaven."

Ah yes! we should all like that. But it is something at any rate to be well started on the right road.

"I suppose you mean because we're Catholics. But plenty of Catholics go wrong."

You wish the way to Heaven were as straight as that to your home. Are there no lanes branching off from that well-known road?

"Lots, and some of them very pretty ones; no end of blackberries and nuts there in autumn."

Yet they never tempt you to leave the road?

"They're ever so much nicer, but they don't go my way, and of course I want to get home as fast as I can."

To be sure, your heart has gone on before and is drawing you there. Now, only put your heart in Heaven, and it will draw you safely there past all the bye-lanes that might have lured you out of your course.

"It would be splendid if we could be like the Martyrs; they had their heads chopped off and there was an end of it."

Yes, but it was not the beginning of it, by any means. The Martyrs are to be envied because they have given more to God, not less, than most of us. They have given that proof of love greater than which no man can give, says our Blessed Lord. But do you suppose they won their crowns suddenly, without preparation, without effort? This is not the law of success or the road to glory either in this world or in the next.

> "The heights by great men reached and kept,
>   Were not attained by sudden flight;
> But they, while their companions slept,
>   Were toiling upward in the night."

There was plenty of weariness, and not always successful effort. Then came the final act of heroism, and as you say—there was an end of it.

"And are we like their companions who slept?" Far from it. Sleepers do not ask questions and cast about for ways and means of reaching their journey's end. The probability is that the lot of most of us will be the longer road of the confessors, who, as St. Paul says, "die daily." Any way, it behoves us to remember that none of the Saints, the Martyrs least of all, attained to final perseverance except by daily perseverance, daily fidelity to daily graces. Let me tell you a story of one who gained the grace of martyrdom in reward of an act of charity and self-denial when he was a lad at school.

Early one summer morning a troop of boys were off for a day's outing. Just as one party was about to start, an old priest appeared on the scene, asking for some one to serve his Mass. He was deaf and infirm, and said a very slow Mass. Most of the boys failed to hear his request, or "really were very sorry, but couldn't spare time just then." One heard. There was a moment's struggle, and then he went into the sacristy, put on his cassock, and cheerfully sacrificed an hour of his holiday. Many years later when as a missionary he was about to lay down his life for his Faith, it was revealed to him that the grace which enabled him joyfully to meet death for his Master's sake, was won in that Mass long ago, when in the college chapel he knelt by the old priest's side.

IV
Why Sin Is So Bad

A king of this world provides his soldiers with all they need to face the enemy—arms, kit, instruction, drill, medical aid in case of mishaps. He expects them to turn all these things to account as occasion requires, and, not only when they are face to face with the enemy, but always to remember their calling and keep themselves in training.

God expects the same of His soldiers. We have only to turn over the pages of our catechism to see how abundantly we are provided with means of saving our souls. The last two chapters are the summing up of the whole, and show us that our religion is not a thing to be kept for church and Sundays only, but is to be brought into the duties and ups and downs of our daily lives, that we may behave ourselves always as children of God and soldiers of Christ.

To know our catechism thoroughly from cover to cover is a great thing. But then comes the practice, and it would be a sad pity to content ourselves with knowing these last chapters and never doing what they teach us. Is it rash judgment to fear that many of us do this?

The names of these chapters are very instructive: "The Christian's Rule of Life;" "The Christian's Daily Exercise." A rule is a direction for our guidance which we are expected to observe, and daily exercise means some labour of mind or body which by constant habit has become easy, and as it were second nature to us. Let us see how we stand here.

The first question and answer of the Daily Exercise are:

"How should you begin the day?"

"I should begin the day by making the sign of the cross as soon as I wake in the morning and by saying some short prayer, such as, "O my God, I offer my heart and soul to Thee."

"I'm sure I never do that."

"And I grumble most days when it's time to get up."

Well, you see, there is some truth in what I was saying, and that the Daily Exercise, which habit should have made easy by this time, is not second nature to us yet. But is it not a pity to go on so to the end? We can hardly suppose the Bishops wrote these chapters for the sake of something to do. Yet if nobody pays more attention to them than some of us do, their Lordships might have saved themselves trouble. Shall we have some talks about these chapters and find out what they teach us, and how, put into practice, they would help us to lead noble and useful lives worthy of the Faith that is in us?

The noblest lives are those that are most like the Life our Lord led on earth for our example. He came to be our Model, and He says to each one of us: "Learn of Me."

"But we cannot go about preaching and doing miracles."

"No, I wish we could. Wouldn't it be splendid to be like St. Francis Xavier and raise the dead to life!"

We cannot imitate our Lord in everything, and such things as preaching and the working of miracles are not for all of us: they are helpful, not to him who does them but to others. It is His virtues that our Lord wants us to copy: "Learn of Me," He says, "because I am meek and humble of heart." Two things take in all His teaching. If we learn these two things well, we shall be all He wants us to be. The first is hatred of sin. We must hate sin above all other evils, so as to be resolved never to commit a wilful sin for the love or fear of anything whatsoever.

"I can't feel about sin as I know I ought. I mean I can't feel it is so dreadfully bad. I wish I could but I can't."

The wish is good and only needs prayer to bring you to a very true hatred of sin. It is one of the terrible evils of the present day to make light of sin. You will hear people say of things which you know are offences against God that they are mistakes, or bad form, or faults against society, or against our better selves. But that sin is an offence *against God*—this they do not think of or speak about.

An offence against God! If only we would think what these terrible words mean. We count an offence against one of ourselves to be great if the person offended is of great dignity. Now the greatness of God exceeds anything we can have any idea of in this life. The points of light in the midnight sky are thousands, some of them millions, of times bigger than our world. Yet in His sight they are mere specks.

"They don't look much bigger to us, do they?"

Because of our distance from them. But God is quite near to every one of them, upholding them and guiding them even while they rush with lightning speed through the heavens. There is no numbering of these vast worlds, yet He who created them could in one instant destroy them and the next instant create as many more, quite different, more beautiful, more grandly furnished. And He could go on so creating and so furnishing—for ever. What must His immensity, His power, His wisdom be!

If the vastest of these worlds is but a speck in His sight, what must we say of our little earth, and the men and women and children on it! And what must it be for creatures so small to rise up against a God so great!

Sin is terrible also because of its ingratitude. Though there is such a distance between the great God and His little creatures, He loves them dearly. He made them out of love that they might be happy with Him for ever, and He expects them to love Him in return. These creatures that He has made out of nothing are His, they belong to Him more than a book or a picture belongs to him who made it. And they have to do as He tells them.

"Of course, that's only fair."

And this is what He tells them. "Love Me in return for all I have done for you, for having created you, redeemed you, given you all you have and all I have ready for you in Heaven. Your hearts are very small and can hold only a little love, but give Me that little and I will be content. And show your love by doing as I tell you. Remember that your soul is Mine, more Mine than yours. It is yours because I have given it to you, but it is Mine still and I love it dearly. Do not displease Me by hurting it. Sin hurts it, that is why you must hate sin above all other evils. I tell you what you must not do, as a father tells his child not to play with fire.

"See here, My child, try to understand this. All the good and the happy things of the next world belong to Me. No one can be happy there except with Me. Those who are My friends have and enjoy all My good things because they are with Me. Those who did not want to be My friends when they had the chance, who would not come to the marriage feast when they were invited, have to go without all I had prepared for them there, without all that would make them happy, for there is nothing good or happy away from Me. If you do not love Me now, if by mortal sin you break away from My friendship and die unforgiven, I cannot have you with Me among My friends. You must go away and be miserable for ever. See now why I tell you to be afraid of sin."

So the great God speaks to me, His little creature. The wonder is that He should take the trouble to teach me, that He can care at all for anything so small, which can be of no use to Him or make Him any return worth speaking of. There is only one reason for it all—He loves me. You remember the "litle thing the quantitie of a hasel-nutt" that Mother Juliana saw; how she thought it might "sodenlie have fallen to naught for litleness," and how she was told, "it lasteth and ever shall, for God loveth it." She saw that because God made it and loveth it, He keepeth it, that is He takes care of it and will not let any one hurt it. And will not let it *hurt itself*. This is why He gives directions how it is to be treated. "Wit it well: Love is His meaning" in the Commandment He gives us.

And now see what sin does.

This tiny little creature of God, this pet child of His, created out of nothing and given all that it has now and the promise of Heaven by-and-by, lifts itself up against Him and says: "I will not do as You tell me; I will do as I like and break Your Commandments. To please myself I will use against You the very things You have given me, my eyes and my hands and my tongue, my talents and my time. I don't mind if I lose my place in Heaven and lose You and all You have got ready for me."

"But I don't mean to say all that when I commit sin, I don't really."

We cannot break the law without offending the lawgiver. God says to us by His Commandments: "Thou shalt not." And I say by act at least: "I will." This is hurting God as far as we little creatures can hurt Him.

"Even if we don't think of it?"

We must think, children. When your father says to you seriously: "You must do this," or "I forbid you to do that," we do not disobey him and then say carelessly: "I never thought of it." God expects us to think. If we would think sometimes of the punishment sin deserves, of its unfairness, of its ingratitude, we should see it is the most reasonable thing in the world to hate it above all other evils, so as to be resolved never to commit a wilful sin for the love or fear of anything whatsoever.

One mortal sin deserves the punishments of Hell which last for ever. For a *forgiven* mortal sin Adam and Eve had nine hundred years of punishment—sickness, death, difficulty in doing right, all the troubles of this life. And this punishment remains, and is borne by their children to this day. The punishment of sin shows its badness. Sin makes the infinitely good God so severe. It made the sufferings of our Lord in His Passion so terrible. We must ask God to give us light to know its badness and to hate it, lest we come to commit it and meet with the punishment it deserves.

"What does 'above all other evils' mean?"

All the things that can hurt us or cause us pain. The martyrs suffered frightful torments rather than offend God. Men, women, and children all the world over are at this very time suffering bravely the loss of friends and goods, or bearing patiently the unkindness of those they live with, rather than commit sin.

"You mean people who are persecuted for being Catholics; but we shall never have to bear things like that."

We shall all have to bear what is painful if we mean to avoid sin. See what your examination of conscience shows you every night and when you go to confession. All those sins and faults came from your choosing some pleasure God's Law forbade rather than being willing to bear the pain of denying yourself.

"Then the Catechism doesn't mean mortal sins only?"

It means all sin. We should be resolved to make every sacrifice rather than break God's Commandments even by venial sin, because all other evils that can happen to us are less than the evil of offending God.

"But what's the use of making a resolution we can't keep, for everybody does little sins?"

"Yes, or they wouldn't go to confession."

There is always use in aiming high, higher even than we expect to reach. The marksman does it when he points his rifle, not directly at the bull's eye he wants to hit, but above it, for he knows that, swiftly as the bullet travels, the weight must bear it down. Boys and girls do it when they try for honours. All have done it who have achieved anything great in this world. What would you think of a son who should say: "I don't mind how much I grieve my father so long as he doesn't turn me out of doors?"

"I should think he ought to be kicked out for saying it."

God is so good that we must not offend Him wilfully even in little things. "If only God were not so good," the holy Curé of Ars used to say, "but He is so good."

For the sake of our own safety, too, we must avoid venial sin. Holy Scripture says: "Catch us the little foxes that destroy the vines." It does not say, "Catch the lions and the bears," but "the foxes," "the little foxes." Mortal sin frightens us, but venial sins do not, yet like the little foxes they are very mischievous. Oh the harm that little things can do! Who could be afraid of a rabbit? Yet rabbits have proved so serious a pest in Australia that vigorous measures had to be taken for destroying them. Locusts are not much bigger than grasshoppers. Yet they can stop trains and bring famine and ruin on a whole country. And you have only to be in Venice one night to know what mosquitoes can do.

"But I want to know this—what does 'must' mean? The Catechism says we *must* be resolved. Are we obliged to feel like that about venial sin, because I'm afraid I don't."

We are strictly bound to be resolved to deny ourselves any pleasure, and to suffer any pain rather than offend

God by mortal sin. But if we love God and our own souls as we ought, we shall do more than this, and resolve to suffer anything rather than offend Him by *deliberate* venial sin. This is the kind of sin of which the Catechism speaks. Holy Scripture tells us that the just, that is good people, fall seven times a day, which means often, into little faults of weakness or surprise—hasty words, laziness, carelessness, and the like. They must be sorry for these faults, but what the Catechism says we should be resolved at all costs to avoid, are wilful, deliberate sins which prepare the way for mortal by strengthening evil in the soul.

Those whose resolve goes no further than to stop short of mortal sin, will not stop short of it. Such a disposition shows very little love of God and desire to please Him; and when a strong temptation comes, their resolution to avoid even grievous sin will break down, and they will fall.

"I can't feel that I would never commit a wilful sin for the love or fear of anything whatsoever."

Nowhere in the Catechism do we find that we must *feel* this or that. Neither God nor His Church requires feelings of us, because these are not in our power to have when we like. Often when we want them most they run furthest from us, like wayward children that will not be caught. It is our good-will that God looks at; "Peace to men of good-will," the Angels sang on the first Christmas night. It is a good-will that says: "I will keep out of mortal sin; but that is not enough. I will be willing to go against my likes and dislikes rather than commit wilful venial sin."

"What does the Catechism mean by 'the *love* or fear of anything whatsoever'? I see how we could commit sin by being afraid of torture or death, like the martyrs, or even of being laughed at, but I don't see how the love of anything could lead us into sin."

Many of the martyrs and many who are bearing their cross bravely after Christ, have more to suffer from love than from fear. There is the pain—sharper at times than fire or sword—of giving pain to those we love. How many do wrong rather than annoy a friend! Among those we love, our own *self* comes first, and whenever we do wrong it is out of a foolish love for this friend. Rather than displease the body, we break the Church's law of abstinence, some of us; lie in bed when we ought to be at Sunday Mass; exceed in the matter of eating or drinking or amusement. Oh, it is not hard to see how we have to resolve not to be led into sin by the love of things!

"I never thought of that before."

V

Temptation and How to Meet It

Have you ever thought of the meaning of the wonderful words with which St. Matthew begins his account of our Lord's temptation by the Evil One? "Then Jesus was led by the Spirit into the desert to be tempted by the devil." These words teach us two things which we must lay well to heart—that we cannot altogether escape temptation, and that we can make it very useful to us by meeting it as we ought.

Jesus, Son of God, very God of very God, Creator of that wicked One, having nothing in Him that could give rise to temptation, the All Holy who hates the very shadow of sin—He was tempted.

Is the servant greater than his Master? If the devil dared to tempt our Blessed Lord, can I wonder in the very least at temptation coming to me, so careless, perhaps, in God's service, so weakened by bad habits, so fond of whatever is nice, dainty, comfortable, amusing, whatever holds out the prospect of pleasure in any shape? Even without the help of the devil and the world, would there not be temptation enough from myself?

"I can't imagine why the devil hates us so. We haven't done him any harm."

"We are going to have his place in Heaven, and the places of the other bad angels, that's why."

Yes, he envies us the happiness that once was his. But he is enraged against us still more from the hatred he has to God, and since he can do nothing directly against God, he turns his fury against those who bear the image of God and are dear to Him. This is why God looks upon our battles as His own and takes our part against the devil.

There are three sources, the Catechism tells us, from which temptation comes,—the devil, the world, and the flesh.

"I am most afraid of the devil."

And yet he is not the most dangerous of the three. It is not the strongest creatures, you know, that are always the boldest.

"No; I was reading yesterday about a great black greyhound named Bruce, that was with some soldiers on the march. He wouldn't keep with the other dogs, but went ranging about on his own account. Well, one day the soldiers saw him come tearing towards them at full speed, never stopping till he had taken refuge among the horses. They were wondering what had frightened him, when a tiny lamb that had got lost and had taken the dog for its mother came running up. Bruce had often run after other animals but had never been run at before, and there he was crouching on the ground, frightened out of his life—by a lamb!"

"And wasn't it fun what happened the other day in Berlin, when they put a mouse into the lion's den in the Zoo! The lion was after him at once, and the little fellow scampered into a corner squeaking with fright. But just as the lion lifted his paw, the mouse changed his mind and sprang straight at the big brute's head. The lion was terrified and gave a great leap backwards, roaring with fright. Of course the mouse made off then and all the people clapped him."

Just the kind of example I wanted. We may be as small as mice, and as timid as lambs, yet we can overcome our great, strong enemy if we will. It is not strength he counts on

so much as snares. He is like that ugly monster, the anglerfish, which lies quite still at the bottom of the sea, waiting for its prey. Its huge mouth, full of sharp teeth, is wide open, the fringe that covers it waves to and fro, and, raised aloft on the top of its head, is the long spine tipped with a lump of soft, fleshy membrane looking like raw meat. Half hidden in the mud, it dangles its tempting bait before the eyes of the dozens of small fry passing by. What wonder that some stop through curiosity to look at the strange creature. Suddenly, there is a snap…the cruel teeth close…the fringe begins to wave again…the angler is ready for another victim!

"What would the devil's baits be, I wonder?"

Pleasures or comforts indulged in without restraint, dangerous reading, unwise friendships, a good match—as people say—but with a Protestant, a good position, but with the risk of losing one's faith. Anything naturally pleasant can become a danger if we get too fond of it. There is no harm in liking to be a favourite, to be thought good-looking, clever, good at games. Yet unless we are on our guard and practise self-restraint, these things may easily harm us and lead us into sin. We have to be careful. The lower animals may teach us a lesson here. They are marvellously on the alert to scent danger and avoid it.

The migrations of the cariboo, or Canadian reindeer, are so regular, that these creatures cross certain fords leading to the lake country at the same time every year, as at Fort Rae, where they cross without fail on All Saints Day. But their instinct makes them change their route in places where they have been frequently slaughtered, as the Indians, who depend on them for food, and lie in wait for them near their accustomed crossing places, know to their cost.

To know how to meet temptation is an art and has to be learned like everything else.

We have seen that we are not to be surprised at it. Neither must we be cast down nor frightened. No matter how strong the attack may be, God is with us and we need not fear. The first thing to do is to be prompt.

"What does that mean?"

Putting it away at once, as soon as we come to know it is there. A London fire brigade can "turn out" within thirty seconds of receiving the alarm. Americans think this slow, twenty seconds is their average time, and the men often turn out quicker even than that. Each horse is taught to hurry from his stall to the pole of the engine and put his head through the collar. The animals soon learn their lesson and pride themselves on their speed. And shall we, who are supposed to have sense, trifle with a bad thought, more dangerous, more destructive than any fire! We must not be twenty seconds—no, nor one—after conscience has sounded the alarm, but the instant we hear its warning note "turn out" like the firemen.

"Flee from sin as from the face of a serpent," Holy Scripture tells us (Ecclus. 21). And how is that? Instantly, without a moment's hesitation. No stopping to think: "Shall I stay and play with that deadly thing?" No looking back. Our Lord's answer to the tempter was short and sharp: "Thou shalt not." The answer of a young Catholic to one who pressed him to do something against his conscience was simply, "It's wrong, and I won't do it."

We sometimes look at a pedlar's wares through curiosity, without any intention of buying. It is not safe to do this with the devil's wares; something might tempt us!

We must be prompt, and we must be prudent; not frightened, not gloomy or upset. The Almighty God is on our side; why should we be afraid? The proverb says one man may lead a horse to water, but ten cannot make him drink. And no number of evil spirits can make me sin against my will. A favourite subject with the painters of olden days was the temptation of St. Antony. The Saint is represented in prayer, surrounded by his tormentors in all manner of horrible or fantastic forms. They try to terrify him by their hideous shapes and noises, or to distract him by their charms and antics. But the Saint prays on, his countenance showing signs of struggle indeed, but still more of unshaken determination. He knows that all the demons in hell cannot hurt him and spoil his prayer without his own consent, and that if the evil ones are near him, God and His holy Angels are nearer still.

There is nothing, then, in temptation to alarm or discourage us. God will never let us be tried beyond our strength, and we can never be hurt against our will. The devil is like a chained dog. He can bark and does bark at every one, but he can bite those only that put themselves within his reach. And as a mother whose little child has been frightened by a fierce dog takes it into her arms when it runs crying to her, and presses it to her breast, and soothes and pets it, so does God tenderly receive and protect those who call upon Him and run to Him for help.

With this help a tiny child is a match for all the devils in hell. Little David said to Goliath: "Thou comest to me with a sword and a spear and a shield: but I come to thee in the name of the Lord of hosts." And with his five stones from the brook, and his shepherd's sling, he felled the giant.

St. Ignatius of Loyola used to comfort himself in temptation with this thought: "As I shall not be rewarded for the good thoughts of the good Angels, so I shall not be punished for the evil thoughts of the evil angels." They are theirs, not ours. Even if they get them somehow into our heads, there is no harm done if only our will says "No." The devil can get things into our imagination, but our will is a strong fortress that can always hold out against him.

We are told that crocodiles seem to fascinate their prey. A traveller in Sumatra once saw a large crocodile looking up from the river in which he was swimming, to an overhanging tree, on which a number of small monkeys were sitting. The poor little creatures, though in perfect safety, were so beside themselves with fright, that instead of remaining quietly on their perch, and leaving their enemy to swim away when he was tired of looking at them, they let go their hold and fell into the water, where he was waiting for them. We can never fall into the devil's power without wanting to do so, but we can be so frightened as to neglect to help ourselves by means of prayer. This is letting go our hold of the branch that keeps us beyond his reach.

"I saw a picture this morning of Daniel sitting in the lions' den. They are going about sniffing in every corner, for they are awfully hungry, poor things; they have had nothing to eat for six days. Some are looking at him and lashing their tails in rage, but they can't touch him."

"They must have been a great nuisance all the same."

Undoubtedly. So was that barrel organ this afternoon when you were trying to study. You did not want to hear it, you tried to stop your ears. But the man went grinding on, and there was no remedy but patience. So it is at times with thoughts that come plaguing us; we cannot shut them out of our minds; if we drive them away, they come back again and again.

"What must we do then?"

The best thing, after a short prayer, is to turn our thoughts to something that will occupy and interest them. For there are two ways of meeting temptation—by fight or by flight.

If some one has vexed me, and the temptation comes to pay him back by refusing him some service, or by having nothing to do with him, I must not fly here, but fight against temptation and myself by going against the revengeful feeling, overlooking what has happened, and trying to behave as if nothing had passed between us.

There is a bit of work to be done in which I ought to take my share, and which through selfishness I am inclined to shirk. Here again I have to face the difficulty, and, praying for grace, which will always be given me, go to the place where duty calls me and do what God wants of me there. Both these temptations are met by *fighting*.

But there are others, as those against faith and purity, which we are to meet by *flight*, that is by turning our minds from them as well as we can. An act of the love of God and the thought of anything that will engage the attention will do this. See how much of the multiplication table you can say backwards in a breath. Find twenty places in England beginning with B; or say some verses of a hymn or poem. Turn to anything that will occupy your mind with something harmless. What do you do when there is a thunderstorm in the evening? Draw down the blinds, light up the room, and get out your book, music, chessboard—anything that will take off your thoughts from what is going on outside. Of course, as I said before, you will lift up your heart to God from time to time. He will never let temptation be above your strength, but He expects you to call on Him for help. You by yourself are no match for the devil, who is strong and cunning, but God and you together can conquer him easily. Learn a lesson from a baby.

A captain and his little boy were on deck. It was luncheon-time, and the child had a piece of bread and jam in his hand. Presently Mike, a large monkey belonging to one of the passengers, came by and snatched the tempting morsel from the boy, who thereupon set up a roar. The father came to the rescue, but too late, the bread and jam were gone. However, he caught up a bit of rope, and gave the thief a sound thrashing to teach him a lesson for the future. About a week later the little fellow was eating his cake at twelve o'clock, when Mike came up again and snatched it from him. The boy cried out for help as before. But this time no sooner did the thief hear the cry and see the father coming, than he handed back meekly the cake to its lawful owner and slunk away.

Temptation is like the Angelus bell: it is a call to prayer. Make an act of the love of God and then turn your mind to other things. An act of the love of God is better than an act of the virtue against which you are tempted. If you are driven to impatience by some one who, it seems to you, would try an Archangel, turn quietly to God and say: "My God, I love Thee, I love Thee, because Thou art so good!" This will soothe you and be more helpful than if you were to say: "My God, I will try to have patience with this provoking fellow."

A great preservative against temptation is occupation in plenty, both for head and hands. The devil must never find us idle. To idle people he goes as if by invitation. Busy folk have no time to listen to him. We must take rest and amusement, of course, but we need not be idle or lounge about doing nothing.

"Except at night, we can't do anything, then?"

To be sure we can; we have to get to sleep fast. And in the daytime our rest must be in changing what we do, never in doing nothing. The proverb tells us an idle brain is the devil's workshop; this is why we learn so many things as occupation for our leisure hours. Music or painting, botany or carpentry, carving, cricket, golf—better a thousand times a good healthy game than half-an-hour of idling, or five minutes of an unwholesome novel. There are plenty of ways in which we may employ ourselves pleasantly when we have no actual duty calling upon us, and it is well to have always some hobby to fall back upon—an interesting and improving book, a garden or pets to look after, anything that will occupy the head or the hands.

"There doesn't seem much chance for us with such a lot of dangers everywhere."

Not if we were alone, but God is never nearer to us than in time of danger and temptation. "Jesus was led by the Spirit," that is, by the Holy Spirit of God, "into the desert to be tempted." Led, therefore, for a wise purpose. Led into the battle that He might overcome. "He went forth conquering that He might conquer" (Apoc. vi). And conquer *for me*, to weaken my enemy, to leave me a crippled foe, to teach me how to act in temptation, how to fight and overcome. He was tempted that He might win grace for me in the time of temptation, and that I might take heart by seeing temptation is not sin. He was tempted, that He might be like me in all things, that He might know by experience this, the hardest of my trials. He felt the odiousness of the near presence of the tempter, the weariness of having to listen to him and send him away again and again.

"But He couldn't be in danger, and that is the worst part of it."

If He could not feel the struggle, the uncertainty, the fear we feel, let us thank Him for going as far as He could in His desire to be like us, for passing on to us the strength and the victory won for us by His own temptation.

"But suppose we do give in to temptation, you know people do sometimes?"

Then we must do what the little child does when it has fallen and hurt itself. It gets up at once and runs crying to its mother, and shows her the sore place that she may make it well. We must rise at once and turn to our Heavenly Father, whose arms are wide open waiting for us. At our first word of sorrow, "O my God, I am sorry for having offended Thee, because Thou art so good," He runs to meet us, He folds us in His arms, and forgives us.

"Even before we go to confession?"

Yes; an act of perfect contrition—that is, an act of sorrow for having offended the infinitely good God—is so pleasing to Him, that He forgives even mortal sin as soon as this act is made, though we are obliged to tell the sin and be sorry for it when we go to confession. Where, then, is there any cause for being disheartened at the faults we commit every day? Oh, if we knew the harm we do ourselves by discouragement, we should be more on our guard against it!

Our enemy does not go to work in the reckless way we do. He is cool and calculating. He thinks beforehand whether a temptation is likely to bring him gain or loss. "Shall I or shall I not tempt such a one," he says to himself. "It is likely enough she will fall, for she is as weak as a piece of wet paper. But the worst of her is that her falls do her so little harm. She is up again directly, and going on her way as if nothing had happened. An act of contrition, and she takes it for granted she is forgiven. I do my best to persuade her that she cannot really mean what she says, that she cannot be really sorry or she would have kept her resolution better. It is all no use. She says at once that she did not mean to grieve *"le bon Dieu,"* and if she has done so she is very sorry and will be more careful for the future. And she has the face to go on saying this time after time till I lose my patience and come away. It is too provoking to have to do with people who never know when they are beaten.

But with that other, things are very different. He is weak too, and a very little temptation is enough for him. He gives way, and forthwith turns upon himself with such surprise and spite that one would think he had never fallen before. It is all over with him, he says; no use trying any more. And down he sinks deeper and deeper into the sulks, which do him fifty times more harm than the fault itself. While he is in this state of upset, little troubles come and make things better for me. He is too cross and discouraged to meet them as he ought, and so there are angry words, more discouragement, and a whole harvest of faults before night.

"How clever the devil is!"

"And how silly some of us are!"

Yes, if we fall we must rise at once, humbled but not disheartened. Falls are like the rungs of a ladder, we can go up by them as well as down. St. Augustine says we may make our sins a ladder to heaven. If, like good children, we turn at once to our Heavenly Father and put it right with Him by a *mea culpa*, "My God, I am sorry," all will be well again. If we put off our act of sorrow till our examination of conscience at night, or till our confession a week later, there will be sadness, carelessness, and more falls, worse than the first. The devil is beaten again and again, but he is never discouraged. He is always ready to try again. Are we less wise than he is?

Let us do in behalf of our souls the exact contrary of what he does to harm them. Before we commit sin, when he comes with a temptation, he whispers: "It is only a venial sin, and you are going to confession on Saturday; it is just as easy to say you told an untruth seven times as six." But if we listen to him and give way, he turns round upon us and says: "There, you have done it, and after all your resolutions, and it was not only a lie but a calumny; there is no knowing what mischief you have done or where the harm will stop. It is no use your trying to be good. Don't try. Give it up and enjoy yourself. No, don't make an act of contrition, at least not yet. Wait till you can mean what you say. It would be shabby to go back to God now when you have behaved so badly to Him—wait."

"Do you know I have felt all that, just as if it was said to me, and it makes you feel awfully discouraged."

Then do the exact contrary of what the devil advises. When temptation comes, remember that he who tempts you now will accuse you by-and-by if you listen to him. The very things he wants you to choose instead of God he will hold up at the Judgement-seat against you. Will you give him his triumph?

"Is it good to think of Hell and things like that when the devil tempts us?"

Our Lord Himself bids us think of the punishment of sin that the fear as well as the love of God may keep us from offending Him. I may think of one of my own age who has committed a mortal sin and died unforgiven. Where is that soul now? When I think of that place, of the pain there, pain that never, never ends, is it hard to fear mortal sin above all other evils, so as to be resolved never to commit it for the love or fear of anything whatsoever? I am afraid to be in an open field during a thunderstorm lest I should attract the lightning and get killed. And shall I dare to have my soul in such a state that it draws down upon itself the terrible wrath of God!

The holy fear of God is a very great grace, and one we should often ask of Him. There are times when temptation is so strong that this fear is the only thing that will keep us from sin. "O my God!" cries out St. Ignatius, "if ever through my fault Thy love should grow cold in my heart, at least let the fear of Thy punishments keep me from falling into sin." Surely, if such a Saint needed the fear of God to preserve him from falling into sin, we are not safe without it!

"I'll tell you what I think is so strange. I understand about the devil tempting us, and our giving in, and all that. But when we sin God forgives us, and if we do it again He forgives us again, and as often as we do it He forgives us—that's what I can't understand. I couldn't do it. Perhaps I might once or twice, but I couldn't go on always."

We shall never understand the goodness and kindness of God because it is infinite, and because the generosity with which He treats us is so different from our way of treating one another. There is no measure to His mercy. No sin and no number of sins is too great to be forgiven. Once more, then, what excuse have we for discouragement?

We should arm ourselves against temptation by noticing where we fall oftenest and find it most difficult to conquer ourselves. Dangerous occasions we should avoid when we can, and when it is impossible to avoid them, we should ask our confessor what we ought to do.

A great help in resisting temptation is to know how to deny ourselves little things when we are not obliged to do so in order to keep from sin. Those who can sometimes refuse themselves little things at meals—the piece of tart they happen to fancy, sweets in Lent, the sight of something in the streets, such as these will find it much easier than others to say "No" to themselves when they must say "No" to avoid mortal sin.

The great remedy in all sorts of temptations is to be quite open with our confessor. He is our soul's doctor and will give us some advice that will do us good. It is foolish to think we can cure ourselves. When we are ill we go to the doctor. When we are tempted we should speak to our confessor.

"Does the devil ever stop tempting people and leave them in peace?"

Holy Scripture tells us that there is a time of war and a time of peace. The time of war is as long as we are in this world.

The next life will be a time of peace, therefore our Heavenly Home is called Jerusalem, the City of Peace. We must not, then, look for rest and security in this life any more than a labourer looks for rest before evening, or a soldier for security on the battlefield. Soldiers can only be hailed as victors when they have fought and overcome. "Let the boy win his spurs," said Edward III when told that his son was hardly pressed on the field of Creçy. "Be thou faithful unto death, and I will give thee the crown of life," our Lord says to us.

Holy Scripture tells us, too, that all things work together for the good of those who love God. Temptation is one of these things. It strengthens good habits just as a strong wind makes the young trees take deeper root. It does for our souls what the rough wave does for the rocks, purifying and enriching them. They stand in the midst of the raging sea, not swallowed up nor moved a hair's-breadth out of their place, but only kept white and glittering by the harmless spray and adorned by it with exquisite seaweed and lovely shells.

Temptation teaches us many lessons we could learn in no other way. It shows God's power and goodness in bringing good out of evil; that the devil can be made to serve the servants of God against his will; and that he can never harm them against their own. We are rough stones which have to be cut and polished before they can be made ready for the Temple in the Heavenly Jerusalem. The stones for Solomon's Temple were prepared at a distance that there might be no sound of hammer and chisel to disturb the City of Peace. So is it with us. Far away from the Holy City we have to be prepared with much labour and suffering, to ourselves and to others, for the glorious place we are to fill there one day. Meantime the cutting and polishing hurts. Of course, but there is no good in crying out. We must bear it and comfort ourselves by thinking more of the result presently than of the pain now.

In allowing us to be tempted, God gives us the opportunity all His servants must have of showing themselves loyal to Him. Is there anything disheartening in this? It is a proof of His love for us. "Because thou wert acceptable to God it was necessary that temptation should prove thee," said the Angel Raphael to Tobias. Of those who pass bravely through this trial Holy Scripture says: "The Lord hath proved them and found them worthy of Himself."

Temptation is a good sign, then. The devil does not tempt those who are securely in his clutches. We do not hunt tame animals that live peaceably with us, but those which try to escape from us. So does the devil.

Few of us, perhaps, think when we are tempted that we have a splendid opportunity of shortening our Purgatory. All pain rightly borne rubs off the rust of sin, and leaves less to be done by the cleansing fires by-and-by. To those who love God, temptation is keenest pain. Their comfort must be that it cleanses the soul instead of soiling it as the devil wants.

"I don't see how."

Fuller's earth takes the stain out of boards and carpets. We use furniture paste and muddy preparations of various kinds to polish our fireirons and chairs. Whilst it lies dull and heavy upon them, there is no sign of the work it is doing, but afterwards, when it is cleared away, how bright everything looks!

Then temptation humbles us, another service. We are apt to think a good deal of ourselves, not knowing how weak and mean we are. But when we find ourselves tempted to anger, revenge, jealousy, impatience, peevishness, greediness, and other bad things, we feel how poor and miserable we are of ourselves, and how much we stand in need of God's pity and help. Again, temptation is a strain upon us, and strain, unless we are upon our guard, makes us cross.

"I wonder how you know that?"

Dear child, we are all made out of the same clay, and are one and all of us tempted, you to-day, I to-morrow, you at ten o'clock, I at eleven.

Only one word more, for we should never have done were we to try to tell all the good that comes to us from this troublesome thing, temptation. It serves to remind us that this world is not our home, that we are travellers in a foreign land, pushing on to our Heavenly Country. Now it sometimes happens that travellers bound for a certain place let themselves be drawn aside if they meet with some pleasant meadow or path on their way. We do the like. As long as things go well with us we forget where we are, and live as if we were to stay here always. Temptation and trouble remind us that we are still on the road.

A priest visiting at a beautiful house in the country, was standing with his hosts at a low window and expressing with much enthusiasm his admiration of the scene before them. Sky, park, wood, and water—all was perfect.

"Don't like it too much," said little Barney, the son and heir, "'cos you're not going to stay here, you know!"

VI
"You Romans"

One of you said that the enemy he fears most is the devil. But we must not forget those two other enemies, the world and the flesh, against which the Catechism says we must fight all the days of our life.

"The world is the place we live in. I don't see how we can fight it."

"No, and if we could, it's much too nice, especially in summer."

Yet with all its beauty the world is not to last for ever. It is the battlefield of God's soldiers where their victory is to be won. It is the ladder on which we are to climb up to our eternal dwelling-place. When the last soldier has won his victory, when the last child of God is safe in his Home, the world will be destroyed, for its work will be done. Now just as Americans or Italians are so called from their native land, and are known everywhere by its stamp which they bear upon them, in their face and voice, and character and habits, so those who look upon this passing world as their home, who care for no other, and live as if they were to stay here for ever, are called by its name—"worldlings."

"Are they wicked people, then?"

The Catechism asks: "What do you mean by the world?" And it answers: "By the world I mean the false maxims of the world and the society of those who love the vanities, riches, and pleasures of this world better than God."

Let us see if we can make the idea of worldliness, or the spirit of the world, clear to ourselves.

In the strong-room of the Standards Office in London there is a fireproof iron chest which contains a bar of bronze. Into this bar, near each end, are sunk two golden studs, and across each stud fine lines are drawn. The distance between these marks is called the Imperial Standard Yard. All yard measures should be the same length as between these marks.[1]

"Suppose the bar was stolen or lost, what would they do?"

Several exact copies have been made and are securely kept in different places. There is consequently very little danger of all being lost or stolen at the same time.

"That's like the golden shields of Rome, isn't it?"

Lengths are not measured in yards in all countries. In France, for example, the standard length is what is called a metre. In Paris a bar of a similar kind to that kept at our Standards Office is carefully preserved. The distance between the two marks in the golden studs is the standard known as the metre. A standard, then, is a rule of measurement adopted by a country and binding on all who buy and sell in that country. They must take great care to conform the measures they use to it or they will get into trouble.

Now two vast kingdoms divide this earth between them—the Kingdom of Christ, and the kingdom of Satan, or as our Lord calls it, "the kingdom of this world." In these kingdoms utterly different standards are employed, and the subjects of each are expected to use that which is authorised by their own sovereign. And just as we might compare the yard and the metre, so may we compare the rules or standards of these kingdoms. We have only to set side by side samples of each, to

---
1 *The School World*, January 1899.

see the vast difference between them, and the difference there will be in the lives of those who employ the one or the other.

CHRIST'S STANDARD OR RULE	SATAN AND THE WORLD'S STANDARD OR RULE
"Blessed are the poor in spirit," who are content with what they have of the good things in life and do not envy those who have more.	"Blessed are they who have plenty of the riches, comforts, and pleasures of this world, and a long life in which to enjoy them all to the full.
"Blessed are the meek," who can bear in patience and in peace the difficulties and contradictions that come to them from others.	"Blessed are those who can stand up for themselves, whom no one dares to contradict, and who can make those smart that offend them.
"Blessed are they that mourn," that so bear the cross with Christ in this life as to deserve to share with Him His Kingdom in the next.	"Blessed are they that laugh, that get through life with as little pain as possible, that manage to have a good time always—excitement and pleasure in every shape."

"I think I begin to see what 'the world' means."

In the Epistle for the Mass of Christmas Day, at that Midnight Mass when we think of our blessed Lord coming to us poor, and suffering, and meek, St. Paul tells us to deny ourselves "worldly desires," that is the excessive love of riches and comforts—pleasant things to eat, pretty things to wear, entertainments and games—the enjoyable things that nature likes, and that the world loves and treasures up. Now I know you are going to ask at once if it is wrong to like these things. It is not wrong in moderation, and so I said "the excessive love" of them. The Catechism says we must not love the vanities, riches, and pleasures of this world "better than God."

"How can we tell if we love them better?"

If we will not give them up rather than offend God. Unless we deny ourselves these pleasant things sometimes, we shall find they will draw us into sin. For we shall get so fond of them that when conscience calls out, "Stop!" we shall pay no attention to it, and—there will be sin.

"Why, I think the world's worse than the devil, because it tempts us in a more sneaking kind of way."

You are right. We have to be on our guard against pleasant things because they are enticing, and moderation in the use of them is not always easy.

But it would be a great mistake to suppose that all the people we see enjoying themselves are worldlings, and that every rich man is condemned by Him who said, "Blessed are the poor in spirit. Woe to you that are rich!" This beautiful earth on which we live is full of interest and delight to such as have eyes to see and ears to hear, and there is a vast amount of innocent enjoyment everywhere, a great deal of secret charity done by the rich, plenty of good example for us to follow, as well as ill example to avoid. How much good we get will depend on our power of seeing how much real good there is in those about us. We are not to go among people with the idea that we are going to set them all right, and we must always bear in mind that it is unsafe and unfair to judge merely by what we see. At the same time, whilst we are careful not to judge others, we are bound to take care of ourselves, and we must not be led astray especially in matters of faith—that is what we have to believe, and in morals—what we have to do.

A vedette is a sentry stationed at an outpost to observe the movements of the enemy and so protect the camp. We are appointed to stand sentry over our own soul. Its safety depends on our vigilance, and there never were days in which we had to be more vigilant. Danger comes in all manner of ways, openly, secretly, unexpectedly, continually, and the greatest of all dangers, as we might expect, is to our Faith. It comes in a different form from that which threatened our forefathers in the days of persecution. Their goods, their liberty, their lives, were never secure. At any moment they might be betrayed, brought before unjust judges, and sentenced to imprisonment or death. Children were sometimes cruelly beaten to make them discover the hiding-place of some poor hunted priest sheltered beneath their roof.

"It's a good thing there are no persecutions for the Faith and English Martyrs now."

The dangers for which we have to prepare are of a different kind from those through which our forefathers had to pass. We do not fear the torture-chamber or the gallows, it is true. But our enemy is not asleep, he has only changed his plan of attack. We are wisely reminded that

> "Times are peaceful but times are ill;
> Need have we both of sword and shield;
> Faith is weakly and love is chill,
> And many are they that flinch or yield."

These are days in which the thought of God is put aside as far as possible. Men talk of great statesmen, great writers, great singers and actors. They stand in admiration before a glorious picture and learn all they can about the artist. But they see this beautiful world stretched out before them without ever lifting up their hearts in praise to Him who made it. Sunshine and starry night, wood and valley, and glittering sea and delicate flower—all speak to them of their Creator, but in vain. They search into the secrets of Nature; they discuss her laws; they make marvellous discoveries with regard to light, sound, electricity. The X-rays and the N-rays[1], the gramophone, the auxetophone[2], wireless telegraphy, the developments of motoring and ballooning, in turn take us by surprise in this age of wonders. But the God whose power and wisdom and beauty these marvels reveal, the God of Nature and the Framer of her laws—who speaks of Him? Hard questions are puzzled over—

---

1 A form of radiation discovered in 1903, later proven to be in error.
2 The auxetophone was the first phonograph to be amplified by electronic means, and was loud enough to be used in large halls or outdoors.

how health, comfort and pleasure can be enjoyed as fully, as long, and by as many as possible. But God is left out of it all. The newspapers for grown up people, the class-books for children, keep Him out of sight. He is to be banished altogether from the school. The crib, the crucifix, prayers, hymns—whatever tells of Him is to be forbidden. Children are to learn about oxygen, and hydrogen, and fossils, the ways of plants and of animals, the art of voice production; they must be clever in the gymnasium, and the football field, and the debating club. But the immortal spirit within them, its worth, its destiny, why it was sent into this world, what they must do to save it from eternal misery—this they are not to be taught.

"Oughtn't we to learn chemistry, then? It's the best lesson we have, especially the experiments."

"And mayn't we want to grow up tall and straight, and to be good at games?"

Our Lord was once asked a question, to which He gave the answer: "This you should have done and not have left the other undone." It is quite right to develop and strengthen our powers both of mind and body. But it is wrong to let the things of this world engross all our attention, or to give so much time to what is interesting and useful as to neglect "the one thing necessary." What would you say to the tutor of a little prince who should give all his time and care to training the prince's valet, neglecting his Royal Highness altogether?

"Do those men who won't let us learn the law of God want to do away with prisons and executions? Because it's very unfair to punish people for breaking it when you wouldn't let them learn what it was."

"And how can they let an oath be taken when people don't know what an oath is?"

"Yes, and then punish them for breaking it. Do they call that fair, I should like to know?"

You must put those questions to those who would banish religion from the school. They may be able to answer them more satisfactorily than I could do.

When you leave school you will hear many things that will startle you. You will be told that what is called "The Higher Criticism" has clearly shown that God could not have guided the writers of Holy Scripture. You will hear that History and Science have disproved many things that God has revealed and the Church teaches. Now you must not be surprised when such things are said, still less must you be shaken. God is the Author of the Bible and of our Religion, and of all true Science as well. He cannot contradict Himself. He knows the answer to every difficulty, but we do not. He sees how the bits of the puzzle fit together and are parts of one plan, not only no hindrance to the agreement of the whole, but necessary to it. We shall see this some day and wonder it was ever a puzzle. In the meantime we have to remember what every one of our lessons at school ought to have taught us, that because we do not see our way through a difficulty, it does not follow there is no way. A proposition in Euclid, a stiff bit of translation seems a hopeless muddle to me. But my bigger brother and sister in a higher class smile at my perplexity. They would laugh at me outright only they recollect that not so long ago these things were puzzles to them too. My teachers tell me to have patience, the light will come if I plod on, taking on trust what I am taught, because conscious of my own ignorance, without arguing or insisting on seeing everything for myself before I will believe, satisfied that there is an answer, and that all will work out right in the end. But could I expect them to keep their patience, were I to show myself such a little prig as to declare that Euclid is wrong and Caesar rubbish because I cannot see the sense of what they say, or that, because I have failed in an experiment, chemistry is all bosh?

Now we are all of us, even the cleverest man or woman that

ever lived, mere children when we come to the examination of things which belong to God and the soul. These things cannot be handled or analysed even by the most skilful chemist. We could make a guess here and there, which might be wrong or right. But to know anything certain about these things, God must come to the help of our ignorance and tell us Himself. What He tells is called Revelation. Whatever God reveals we are bound to believe, because God is the very Truth, who cannot deceive or be deceived. We know what God has revealed by hearing the Catholic Church, which Christ our Lord has commanded to teach all nations.

In these days when Science is bringing to light such wonderful secrets of Nature, some Catholics seem afraid lest the Bible, which is God's revealed word, and the teaching of the Church, should be found to be wrong. But this is impossible, as we have seen, because one truth cannot contradict another. It only seems to do so because we have not the clue to the puzzle. The man who stands on high ground in the midst of the maze at Hampton Court sees people wandering up and down, losing themselves hopelessly, furthest from the opening where they can get out, when they think themselves nearest to it. So do those deceive themselves and others who give out their discoveries as truer than God's truth. The Church is not afraid and her children need not fear. They can afford to wait and see. What is true in discovery will be found in the end to be all of a piece with what God has revealed and His Church taught. What is not true will be proved to be no true discovery at all, but one of those blunders which make a sensation for a little while and are then shown up and forgotten. So it has happened times without number. Of this we may be quite sure—men will never find the Wisdom of God tripping, or Him who calls Himself the "Faithful and True" deceiving those who have put their trust in Him.

Know your Catechism and understand it well, so well that in case of need you can use it as a skilful fencer uses his blade. Many a time have its simple words in the mouth of a little child brought light to the earnest inquirer after truth, or turned the arguments of the unbeliever against himself.

"Mother says we're not to dispute about our Religion till we're older and know what to say."

A very wise precaution. But I was hardly thinking of disputations. There are occasions in which a Catholic child is asked a simple question and ought to be able in the words of its Catechism to give a simple answer. Sometimes a child who is not a Catholic has used the little book to advantage.

"The Japs'll be as much puzzled as we are," said an intelligent-looking young tradesman, as he laid down his paper. "They're a clever lot and won't be humbugged. One set of missioners hardly have got a hearing before another'll come to upset all the first have done. They'll be told to stay at home and agree among themselves before they go out to teach others, that's my belief. But it'll be no worse muddle for them than it is for us, Annie," he added sadly. "Churches in plenty all round us, but who's to tell the Church of Christ among them all?"

"Don't you know such an easy thing as that?" cried Mamie, who was sitting on the floor at her father's feet playing with her dolls. "Why, it's in the Catechism. 'The Church of Christ has four marks by which we may know her: she is One—she is Holy—she is Catholic—she is Apostolic.'"

Father and mother looked at one another in silence. They knew their Bible well, and the phrase "out of the mouths of babes" rose to the mind of both. Mamie went to the convent school close by, but she was not wont to repeat for the benefit of her parents what she heard there. It was help from a strange quarter, but it was help for all that.

"Fetch me your Catechism, Mamie," said her father.

Long after their little one had been laid in her crib that night, husband and wife sat side by side turning and returning the pages of the much-begrimed little book. A week later they were waiting timidly in the priest's parlour to ask for instructions. Six weeks—and they were being received with Mamie into the One, Holy, Catholic, and Apostolic Church, their doubts and anxious questionings at rest for ever.

"Is that a true story?"

Quite true. I knew Mamie's father and mother, from whom I had it.

The wonderful people in the East who have suddenly taken rank as one of the foremost powers of the world, have learned much from Western nations. But in some things, as in the art of self-defence, called Ju-jitsu, they may well become the teachers of their masters. It is not by heavy blows that they disable their adversary. A slightly built and even puny man may venture to attack another possessing twice his muscular strength. Quickness, lightness, ingenuity in applying a knowledge of anatomy, are the secrets of Ju-jitsu, and give to those who have learned its lessons, such an advantage over others that a British arm capable of striking a blow that would fell an ox could, we are told, be seized and dislocated in an instant by a Japanese girl.

We must learn dexterity in the use of the spiritual weapons

put into our hands. Great learning is not always necessary or even useful when there is question of meeting attacks on our Faith. It is wonderful how much can be done by any young Catholic who has taken the pains to understand the Catechism. He may not always be able to disable his adversary, but he will succeed in defending himself, no mean achievement in days such as these.

Catholics now go freely to and fro. In the examination-room, at parties, in the tennis-court, Catholic children mix with non-Catholics. Everything looks friendly and they may ask: "What need for watchfulness in these days?" More, perhaps, than ever. It is just when things look quiet that the sentry doubles his vigilance. There may be no question now of your having to die for your faith, but it is pretty certain you will have to suffer for it.

"How?"

Many children nowadays are brought up without any religion at all. They know no more about God and their soul and the life to come than the little pagans out in Africa. But the strange thing is that whilst they know nothing, or next to nothing, of the doctrines of the Catholic Church, they are taught to think them very wicked or silly. And another thing is strange. Whilst little Anglicans, Quakers, Wesleyans, Jews, are left in peace to follow their own way of thinking, a Catholic child is often pursued and ridiculed for its Faith. Your companions may make fun of what the Church teaches and say it is foolish to believe what you cannot understand, but you are obliged to believe, they will say, and so they will laugh at you or pity you.

"Nobody likes to be laughed at. And it makes you feel rather ashamed of being a Catholic."

Ashamed of being a Catholic! Well, that is strange. But it must be my fault somehow, and the sooner I make reparation the better. Suppose we have a talk about what St. Paul says "we have in common, your faith and mine."

Ashamed of it—just think of that! Ashamed of being a member of the grand old Church that has produced martyrs by thousands—men, women, and children, who have died joyfully for the Faith that was in them! Heroes in every rank of life, kings and queens, statesmen and beggars, discoverers and inventors, masters in Science and Art, the greatest benefactors of their fellow-men the world has ever seen—is this an ancestry to be ashamed of!

Now had you told me you were dreadfully tempted to take a pride in your name of Catholic, I should have understood you. We sometimes have to remind those who come of a noble family that the name they bear comes to them without any deserving on their part. With far greater reason, one would think, we might have to warn our children against glorying overmuch in their name of Catholic. But to be ashamed of it!

"You don't understand a bit. Of course I'm not ashamed of being a Catholic exactly. But how would you like it when a Protestant begins to talk about '*you* Romans' and '*your* Church'?"

With a kind of pitying contempt, as if our Church were something very insignificant? I understand perfectly. But if he forgets, we mustn't, that we have to reckon not merely our numbers here, where we are scarcely one in twenty, but the multitudes of our fellow-Catholics throughout the world to-day, and through all the ages from the beginning. We are members of this great family—what wonder if our hearts beat high with joy and pride! An English Catholic is quite at home as he kneels to hear Mass in St. Peter's; so is a Frenchman in London, an American in Dublin, a Spaniard in New York. From pole to pole Catholics are one in faith and in worship, and in obedience to the successor of St. Peter, the Vicar of Christ on earth. Whatever our native land may be, our common Faith binds us all together in Catholic brotherhood. "A Catholic first, an Englishman afterwards," Cardinal Newman said.

As to the phrase, "you Romans," which seems to you so offensive, I take it as a compliment, do you know. It was to the Romans St. Paul wrote: "I give thanks to my God through Jesus Christ for you all because your faith is spoken of in the whole world....I long to see you that I may be comforted in you by that which is common to us both, your faith and mine" (Rom. i). Had I been one of "you Romans" in those days, I should have been rather set up, and I take it as no small honour that our noble ancestry should be acknowledged in this way by those who differ from us.

"But isn't it rather provoking when they tell you ' you *have* to believe this or that'?"

Some people speak of Faith as if it were a slavery. It is just the opposite—not a trial to be resigned to, but a power, a glorious faculty to rejoice in and be thankful for. How do you feel towards those who are cleverer than you are, who take in quite easily high and difficult things which your mind cannot reach at all—how do you feel? Do you despise them, laugh at them, pity them? Probably not. There may be feelings of envy perhaps, or at least of disappointment that you are so far inferior to them—but of contempt—most assuredly not. Neither can people who know what Faith is despise those who have it. They may envy them the far-reaching sight, the firm grasp it gives of those real things that our eyes cannot see, nor our ears hear, nor our hands touch, but they can no more pity them for this power than you can pity those who find the solving of your mathematical difficulties such easy work.

Oh yes, for those who know what Faith is—and it is surely not worth our while to trouble about the views of any others—

this glorious gift is a subject for admiration and congratulation. "Blessed art thou that hast believed," said St. Elizabeth to our Lady, who had the loftiest and most illumined intelligence of any merely human creature. Our Lord knew everything in Heaven and on earth. Nothing really surprised Him. Yet there were a few things on this earth of ours that called forth His admiration—the simple beauty of the wayside lilies, and the magnificence of faith. "O woman, great is thy faith!" When Jesus heard, He marvelled, saying: "I have not found so great faith in Israel." But to Thomas, who was not contented to believe but wanted to see, He said: "Blessed are they who have not seen but have believed."

"I'm sure I should have been like Thomas. I wish I could see better why it is so blessed to believe."

Look at it in this way. You know that your one great business, by the side of which no other deserves the name, is to save your soul. Now the narrow path you have to travel, the broad road that you must shun, the places to which these ways lead, cannot be seen with the eyes of the body. Yet they are more real than the sun in the heavens at noonday, and you must come to understand and feel their reality if you are to reach your journey's end in safety.

See, then, what God does. As He gives you your bodily eyes to guide you through the things of this world, so He has given you a spiritual sight to see eternal things. You may hear people say that we have the light of reason to go by and that this is enough. People who speak thus have not even that light or they would not talk such nonsense. We have this light indeed, but it is not meant to show us all we must know and do to get to Heaven. The light of reason is like the moonlight, good as far as it goes, enabling us to see our way in the night-time, but not powerful enough to do delicate work by. For this we need the more trustworthy light of the sun.

A lady whose picture was nearly finished worked at it for a couple of hours one evening. She went to bed pleased with her work; it looked all right—by moonlight. But oh! poor thing, her disappointment and horror when morning came and she saw it in the light of day. The light of reason is meant to guide us in the work of this life, and a noble light it is. But it is the light for this life, not for the next. It cannot do everything. Its chief and noblest work is to show us the necessity of taking as our guide for the things beyond its reach the brighter light God has provided for us.

It shows us, lying in the crib at Christmastime, the little Babe come into this world to suffer and to die for us. It shows us flowing on Good Friday the Precious Blood that has redeemed us and given us back our right to Heaven. It shows us on Easter Day Jesus risen from the dead and promising us a glorious resurrection like His own if we are His true followers till death. It is our Faith that leads us to the confessional to have our sins forgiven, and to the altar rails to strengthen our souls with the Body and Blood of Christ. It is our Faith that bids us pray in time of need, and that comes to our help when temptation is strong by lifting the veil that hides the other world from us, making us see the fearful sights and hear the dismal sounds of the eternal prison-house of Hell. Above all it is by Faith that we look up to the Home waiting for us when this short life is done, to the many mansions of our Father's House, and all the joys getting ready for us there. It is Faith that makes Heaven such a reality to us even now. We go in and out among the Saints as freely as into our father or mother's room, and tell them what we want, and expect attention and loving help. St. Antony must be always ready to find what we have lost, St. Joseph to replenish our purse when it gets low, our Lady to be our Perpetual Succour in every need.

But it is when the end comes, when we lie down trustfully to die, with the crucifix in our hands and the dear beads clasped fast, with

> "All Sacraments and Church-blessed things
> Engirding us around,
> A priest beside us, and the hope
> Of consecrated ground,"[1]

it is then that we know what our Faith has done for us. With the names of Jesus, Mary, and Joseph on our lips, and their blessed presence, unseen but felt, protecting and encouraging us; with the strengthening words of Mother Church in our ears—her Last Blessing the last sound reaching us from earth, we fall asleep in her arms, and are lifted into the waiting arms of the God who made us.

This is what God has done for us, this is what He gave us in the Faith of our Baptism.

> "O Gift of gifts, O grace of Faith,
> My God, how can it be,
> That Thou who hast discerning love
> Shouldst give that Gift to me!"[2]

---

1 Faber.
2 Faber.

VII

"I Am a Child of the Church"

It is hard not to be proud at times. Dreadful things, we know, happen to the proud. We were very little indeed when we heard the sad fate of Humpty Dumpty, and were told that Pride always has a fall. But for all that, it is hard not to be proud sometimes and to feel we have a right to be proud. Shall I tell you why? Not certainly on account of our family, though like the King we could trace our descent from Egbert, for we are told:—

> "Though your ancestors you show
> Proudly standing in a row,
> Death won't mind your pedigree,
> Pride of name is vanity."

Nor yet on account of our personal appearance, whatever that may be:—

> "Though you be as morning fair,
> Decked in beauty past compare,
> In your grave what will you be?
> Beauty's merest vanity."

Still less for what are called the goods of this world, for

> "Though your jewels may be seen
> Thick as daisies on the green,
> Canst thou take but one with thee,
> All such toys are vanity."[1]

---

[1] *Vanitas Vanitatum* (Mission Hymns).

Why then?

Because of a gift beside which all these things look paltry and miserable indeed.

"I know what it is."

Yes, we all know. I was wrong to say that family and beauty and wealth are not to be prized exceedingly. To belong to our Lord's family, the family of all the Saints from the beginning, to count among our ancestors Apostles and Martyrs, Confessors and Virgins—the noblest and the best of every land and of all times—is not this something to be proud of? And I may do this, for I am a Catholic.

There is a beauty which in the sight of God and the Holy Angels is something more attractive than the fairest things in this world of beauty. It is the soul of the little child as it comes from the waters of baptism with the Faith planted in it. God sees and the Angels see what that seed will blossom into if only it is cared for. That beauty is in my soul, for I am a Catholic—and I may be proud of it.

And there is a jewel, the pearl of great price, which thousands have given all they have to buy. It is the Faith of the One Church—and this is mine, for I am a Catholic.

Oh yes, it is hard not to be proud of one thing—our Faith! To think that the Faith once delivered to the Saints (Jude 3), the Faith that has been the light of the world ever since poor Adam and Eve were turned out of Paradise into the darkness outside, that was given like a torch to guide men through those weary four thousand years before our Lord came, that was handed down in the Jewish Church, passed from prophet to prophet, taken by our Lord from the Synagogue which had betrayed its trust and put into the hands of His Church; that has guided Apostles and Martyrs and Confessors and Virgins—all Saints into the Kingdom of God; that has come down undimmed through nineteen hundred years, is now given *to me*—is it not hard to take no pride in this? The Faith of Peter and John, of Lawrence and Agnes, of Ambrose and Jerome, of Augustine and Paulinus, of Edward the Confessor and Louis of France, the Faith of Benedict and Francis of Assisi and Dominic, of Ignatius and Francis of Sales, and Vincent of Paul, the Faith of Teresa and of the Curé of Ars—this is mine too. It was their Faith that made them what they were and has brought them where they are. The same Faith, please God, will bring me into their company one day.

The Saints gloried in their Faith. Yes, they who despised the passing greatness and pleasures of this world were proud of one thing: "I am a child of the Church," said St. Teresa. And when the thought of Death and Judgement came to frighten even her great and courageous soul, she strengthened herself with the same thought: "After all, I am a child of the Church."

A bright-faced, eager child of twelve was in the examination-hall waiting for her Preliminary Scripture Paper. The Delegate coming to her remarked: "I suppose you are not a Catholic?" She sprang to her feet and exclaimed with a blush of pride: "I suppose I am."

The Middle Ages are called by hard names—"Dark," "Iron," and plenty more. No doubt they deserved some of them. But they were "The Ages of Faith." Deep down in the hearts of lawless barons and ruthless tyrants and cruel oppressors of the poor and the weak, was the Faith that survived when other virtues were dead, and that brought back repentance and saved the soul at last.

"It was very fine for cruel men to get into Heaven just at the end like that, when they couldn't be bad any more, and when it didn't matter to them if they did free their slaves and try to make up for what they had done."

This is what those say who scoff at a deathbed repentance, as if it were cowardly for a man to pull himself up at the brink of a precipice. Let us rather thank God that such a repentance is possible. We must never trust to it; this would be most unsafe. But we may well think with tears of gratitude of the many, many souls rushing to their ruin to whom God has been merciful in His "great mercy," as David says.

Nor must we think such late repentance did no good to those who had been wronged and to many besides, and that it served only to encourage men in lives of wickedness by leading them to put off conversion till they came to die. You yourself have remembered one work of lasting good that such deathbeds often brought. Faith, that terrified them by the thought of going into eternity with unrepented sin upon their souls, taught them also what true repentance requires. And so restitution, in every direction where there had been wrong done, was the first thing thought of. Would it not be a blessed thing in these days, for themselves and for those whom they have wronged, if those who ridicule the fear that drove men to repent at the last, were to imitate them in this respect when they come to die!

Oh yes, children, Faith is the friend of us all, and our friend always, when she warns and threatens, when she encourages and supports. We shall see this on the Day when the secrets of all hearts will be made known.

VIII

Is Seeing Believing?

"I heard a man talking to father the other day, and saying it was unreasonable to believe what we cannot understand."

It is not believers, but those who refuse to believe, who are unreasonable. They will not believe the miracles by which Jesus Christ proved that He was God because *they* did not see them; because *they* cannot understand how these wonders were wrought. And so with the other dogmas of Christianity. They will not believe them because they think they have the right to disbelieve whatever they cannot understand.

"But doesn't common sense show them that they are believing every day things they haven't seen themselves? Why do they read the newspapers if they don't believe what's in them?"

"No, they didn't see all the things the papers talk about, I expect."

"And do they understand all the new inventions?"

The Catechism says children are generally supposed to come to the use of reason about the age of seven years. But it must be borne in mind that we are not bound to come then, or even to come at all. St. Teresa used to say she would give up hopes of a woman who had not arrived there at forty. But there are women, and men too, who to all appearance never get so far though they may be seventy or eighty. They talk as if God were one of themselves, to whom they can behave as to an equal. His thoughts must never be beyond their thoughts. His words and acts and reasons must be perfectly intelligible to them if they are to be expected to believe them, or to approve of them. They are surrounded by mysteries from the sky above their heads to the blade of grass at their feet. In light and sound and electricity there are marvels which baffle all their efforts to comprehend. Yet what they are told *on the word of God* they refuse to believe if they cannot understand it.

"Why, if they could understand they wouldn't be able to believe."

Exactly. Much of the world's wisdom is stored up in proverbs. As a rule they contain a vast amount of condensed truth. But now and then they contain what is not truth. "Seeing is believing," we say—which is just what it is *not*.

There have been men in the world's history, and young men, who have declared themselves ready to answer any question within the whole range of human knowledge, from the heavens above, to the earth beneath and to the waters under the earth. But he would be a bold man who would venture to-day to think he has fathomed even one of Nature's countless stores, that do but broaden out and let us down into further depths the more we try to explore them.

Men are beginning to feel how very little the wisest of us knows. They tell us that the marvellous discoveries of Science made of late years are but the fringe of what lies beyond, and that what is at present out of our reach will quite change the face of Society if the world last a few centuries more. How is it, then, that some of them can be so foolish—we will not just now call it wicked—to treat the God of all these wonders as they do? They deny His existence. They say all the marvels that come to light in the X-rays, in electricity, in radium, are not the work of any one, but are the outcome of mere chance. They will not allow that any of these things, themselves least of all, have a Maker, for that would mean they have duties towards this Maker and that they must do as He tells them. So the world and all in it, and the starry skies, and the orderly round of day and night and seasons, come about—by chance.

Matter, they say, is the cause of all that exists—stones, plants, animals, our bodies and minds and feelings and will, all came from matter. But when we ask them what matter is, they say they know nothing about it, neither what it is, nor where it came from; it is all "unthinkable." The only thing they know about it is that it was not created.

If we ask them where living matter came from, they own that they know absolutely nothing about that either, except that it was not created. Some of them say everything is alive, even a stone; others that life came of itself or by chance; others again that it may have been brought to our world by a beetle alighting here on a meteoric stone shot off from some other planet.

There is nothing, they tell us, beyond the things we can see and feel, and hear, and smell and taste. There is no such thing as a soul within us, or conscience, or right and wrong. All these things are the inventions of silly people, and only make us uncomfortable if we believe them. We can no more help what we do than the tiger of the jungle can help springing on the native that he kills and eats.

When we die, all of us dies; there is nothing beyond this life—how can there be? Why should men be rewarded or punished if right and wrong are only names, and what we do we cannot help? There is no Heaven, they say, nor Hell. As this life, then, is the only one, let us enjoy it while it lasts, let us have a good time, "let us crown ourselves with roses before they be withered, let no meadow escape our riot" (Wisd. ii).

Some of those men say the only thing we have to do in this world is to think of ourselves and our own enjoyment, and that we should not mind how much others suffer if only we can secure pleasure for ourselves. Others say this is quite wrong; we ought not to care at all about our own welfare, or wish for any good to happen to us, but think only of others, and try to get them all the comfort and pleasure we can—in this world. As to any other world, it is not worth a thought.

"It is like the old heretics, isn't it?—in trying to put down one false doctrine, they fell into another."

Let us thank God that we have His Church to teach us what we must believe and what we must do. She tells us that we are to love both ourselves and others with a rightful love which will make us seek first, both for ourselves and for them, the happiness of the life to come. In one of her beautiful prayers she bids us ask "that we may so use the good things of this world as not to forfeit those of the next," and that "amid all the changes of this life our hearts may be fixed on that place where true joys remain."

We are not forbidden, you see, to enjoy the good and beautiful things God has provided for us here. Whilst we are young we enjoy these things very keenly, so we have to remember that the immoderate and selfish use of them would do us harm and that we must be on our guard.

"Shall we ever see any of these foolish people, do you think, when we grow up?"

It is quite possible that long before you grow up you may meet—not men and women only, but boys and girls, who will laugh at you and think you very silly for believing what the Church teaches. A boy of twelve may tell you that he believes in nothing—he is an atheist like his father.

"Then I should tell him what comes in the Bible—'The fool says in his heart there is no God.' "

It is not wise to say what can only make people angry, and unless you have studied a great deal it is better not to begin to argue. Do not ask them questions, and if they ask you any, say you believe firmly all the Church teaches, and that you know a priest who will be glad to explain Her teaching to them if they really want to know it.

Another danger for which you must be prepared is reading. Many, perhaps most of the books we read, are non-Catholic, some of them may even be anti-Catholic. Now all this has its effect upon us. Men do not get better able to bear a bad climate, we are told, by living in it—quite the contrary. The atmosphere all around us in these days is not calculated to make us better Catholics, and—

"I don't know what you mean by the atmosphere."

I mean that as we are surrounded by the atmosphere and draw it in at every breath, so the ideas of those around us gradually become our own unless we are upon our guard. We hear a great deal that is useful and clever, and much that is harmful; we must take care to prevent the effects of this upon our thoughts and conduct. Subjects which you have been accustomed to speak of reverently and to think of great importance, you will hear treated lightly. The miracles in the Old Testament and in the Life of our Lord, His Resurrection from the dead, yes, even the Divinity of Jesus Christ, you may hear discussed as if we were free to believe these things or not just as we like. Unless you are prepared for this beforehand, it will come to you like a shock, and you may think: "Is there no certainty, then; is there no truth in all I have been taught, in all I have believed till now?"

"Is it wrong to ask *why* we have to believe what is in the Catechism?"

A Catholic must never ask a doubting "Why?" because what he believes he believes on the word of God. But it is so far from being wrong to study our religion and to see why we believe what the Church teaches, that it is a serious duty for us to do so, especially in these days, that we may be able, as we grow up, to defend our Faith against attacks. "Be ready always to satisfy every one that asketh you a reason of that hope which is in you"(1 Peter iii), St. Peter wrote to the first Christians.

"But that's just it! What are we to do when we don't know the reasons?"

Notice what St. Peter says. He does not bid these converts see the reasons—that is, understand the mysteries of their Faith; that would be an impossibility. But they are to be satisfied as to the reasonableness of their hope, and of the Faith from which hope springs; so satisfied that they can put the reason of it clearly before others. We do not believe the truths which the Church proposes to our belief because we understand them, or can prove them, but simply because God tells us these things, and He is the very Truth and cannot deceive. This is the reason.

To believe a thing because I can see how it is true, and can prove the truth of it, is not even human faith. How much I have to take on trust even in human things! In my History, Geography, Chemistry—in everything I learn, I have to take the word of my teacher for what I have not found out for myself. Why, then, can it be hard to believe, on the word of God, truths that are not against my reason—this they can never be—but above it, simply because He tells me it is so? "My God, I do not see how these things can be, but I believe them on Thy word and because Thy infallible Church so teaches;" this is an act of Divine Faith—does God ask too much when He asks for this?

"No, of course, if we are quite sure He tells us the things. If He could tell us Himself, everybody would believe then, wouldn't they?"

It does not follow. But we have to remember this always when there is question of God's dealings with us, that He is the Infinite God, our Creator and Master, and we are only His tiny creatures, less a great deal in His sight than the smallest insect is in ours. Is it becoming, then, that we should lay down conditions, or give out what we think would be His best way of treating us?

Tell me, do you refuse to take a message from your father because it comes through your mother whom he has charged to deliver it?

"Of course not, but all the same we should love to have heard Him speak to us, His very Own Self, I mean."

You are right, child, and that desire of your heart is the craving of every heart He has created for Himself. He is our Father, we long to hear His Voice. And He has satisfied us. From being far away in the Heavens, He has come down into this world. He has become a man like one of us, and, with a human voice that men could hear, and persuasive tones that went to their hearts, He has spoken to men and taught them what they must do to please Him and to deserve His rewards. To prove to them His right as the Word of God to teach them, He worked wonderful miracles in their sight, crowning all with the most stupendous miracle the world has ever seen, the raising Himself to life from the dead.

"We are quite sure all this happened, aren't we?"

Unless we go dead against our reason. All history bears witness to the appearance in this world, nineteen hundred years ago, of a very extraordinary Man who said He was the Son of God. His Coming is the most important event in the annals of the human race. We speak of all occurrences as having taken place before or after Jesus Christ. Thousands heard the truths He preached; thousands felt the effect of His miracles, His enemies as well as His friends. "For neither was any of these things done in a corner," as St. Paul said boldly before his judges (Acts xxvi). Men could see that He fulfilled all the prophecies which foretold Him. They knew that the fulfilment of His own greatest prophecy that He would rise from the dead, was first proclaimed by His bitterest enemies. They knew that at His death the sun hid its light, the earth rocked to and fro, the graves opened, the dead rose.

"I'm sure there was no excuse for the people that lived then, but *we* did not see these things."

And pray what is there so very special and excellent about *our* eyes and *our* ears that they should be the only trustworthy witnesses? Surely the testimony of others might be accepted if we were sure they were sent by God to teach us!

"Oh, yes, of course! But does not St. Peter say that we are to be ready to satisfy every one that asks us for reasons?"

Not quite. It is one thing to be able to tell why you believe, and another to be able to give the reasons or proofs of the truths you believe. Why do you believe anything at all in the Catechism?"

"Because the Church teaches it."

Very good; in other words, because God speaks to you through His chosen Messenger. You trust a message that comes through the telephone, not precisely because it comes through the telephone, but because of your friend at the other end, whose voice reaches you through this trustworthy channel.

"Well, then, if we believe the Church is infallible, we need not bother to study our religion."

I would not word it quite like that. You are perfectly right in saying that a firm faith in the Infallibility of the Church is sufficient to safeguard our Faith on all points of our belief. We may not be able to answer all objections—St. Peter did not mean those to whom he was writing to do this, and certainly not the boys and girls amongst them. But we can always say: "I believe what the Church teaches, because Christ has commanded me to hear her and she cannot teach me wrong."

On the other hand, it ought not to be a "bother" to study our religion and steady our faith, by seeing the grounds of our belief, and especially of that belief in the infallibility of the Church on which, as you rightly say, all the rest depends.

"What are the grounds?"

Let us see. We know that our Blessed Lord went about preaching and teaching during the three years of His Public Life, and that He carefully trained twelve men whom He kept constantly with Him, explaining to them apart what He taught to the crowds. He called these twelve, Apostles, or "messengers sent," because they were to pass on themselves, and after their death by their successors, the truths He came to teach. He gave them power to forgive sins, to consecrate at Mass as He had done at the Last Supper, to offer His unbloody Sacrifice in all places and to the end of time.

He made them teachers and rulers of that body of His which He called the Church. One of them, Peter, He made His Vicar. He gave him the keys of the kingdom of Heaven (Matt. xvi.), and supreme jurisdiction over the whole Church, committing to him the charge of the whole flock (John xxi). He prayed that his faith might never fail, and commanded him to confirm his brethren (Luke xxii).

Before ascending into Heaven, Our Lord gave His Apostles the solemn charge to teach to the whole world what they had learned of Him. "Go into the whole world and preach the Gospel to every creature"(Mark xvi), "teaching them to observe all things whatsoever I have commanded you"(Matt. xxviii).

Those to whom they were sent were to hear them as they would have heard Christ Himself, for "he that heareth you heareth Me, and he that despiseth you despiseth Me" (Luke x). And of one that will not hear, He says: "If he will not hear the Church, let him be to thee as the heathen and publican"(Matt. xviii). And again, "He that believeth not shall be condemned"(Mark xvi).

Now, could our Lord, who is just and good, give us this positive command to hear His Church and enforce our obedience with such terrible threats, without promising us that she shall never teach us what is wrong?

"I don't think He could."

"I'm sure He couldn't."

Therefore He promised to be with His Church to the end of the world (Matt. xxviii), and that the Spirit of truth should teach her all truth (John xvi). And He said to Peter: "Thou art Peter"(that is, a rock), "and upon this rock I will build My Church, and the gates of hell" (or the powers of hell) "shall not prevail against it"(Matt. xvi).

But some Protestants say it wasn't the Catholic Church He meant when He said it should never go wrong.

What other Church is built on the Rock? What other even pretends to be a Divine Teacher and infallible? And what other can show the four marks by which the Church of Christ must be known? Therefore we know with certainty what Jesus Christ has taught, by the teaching of His One, Holy, Catholic, and Apostolic Church which He has commanded us to hear, and which for our sakes He has made infallible.

No matter, then, what objections may be brought against this or that article of our Faith, no matter what difficulties may come into our own minds, we may rest with undisturbed trust on the word of the Church. There are difficulties even to such a mind as Cardinal Newman's. But what of that? What does he himself say about them? "Ten thousand difficulties do not make one doubt. Since I became a Catholic I have never had a doubt." If the Church teaches a doctrine, it is God's truth, therefore we believe it. If the Church has not spoken on any point, or we do not know what her teaching is, we are always safe in saying—"I believe what the Church teaches or may teach about it."

IX
"Mother Says So"

You must not, then, be surprised or troubled at anything you may hear. The difficulties brought up nowadays are nothing new. Every age has had its own. Those of our time are not like those of the last century, nor will they be like those of the next. Remember this, and there will be no shock to your faith when you first come across people who differ from you in religious matters. Turn at once to God and say to Him in your heart: "My God, I believe all that Thy Church teaches, because Thou hast said it and Thy word is true." Do not listen to what they have to say, and do not begin to argue with them or try to convert them; you are not ready for that yet.

If boys and girls are not on their guard and rashly run into danger, what happens to them is this:—At first they think and speak as children of the Church should do. They never dream of questioning the wisdom of her laws and the truth of what she teaches, and if asked why they believe this or that, or act in such or such a way, they are content with the answer of the little child: "Mother says so." When they hear others speaking irreverently of the Church, they are at first shocked. But little by little they grow accustomed to such talk, and by-and-by when some law of the Church checks them, when they want to eat meat on a Friday or to marry a Protestant, they ask peevishly: "Why does the Church make these laws?"

"That's like Luther, who called himself the Pope's obedient son until his book was condemned, and then he turned round upon the Pope and called him Antichrist."

If they give way often to these feelings of vexation, they begin to grow careless, prayer is neglected, and one by one the practices of religion go, till at last they give up their Faith altogether.

But is what they throw away lost? No, it is far too precious for that. God takes the Faith they have despised, and gives it to another, and with the Faith, the crown to which it leads. Catholics fall away, and Protestants get the light of Faith no one knows how, just as Matthias got the place that Judas lost. What an exchange is being made day by day all around us—Catholics giving up their birthright for the sake of some wretched temporal gain; converts parting with friends, the means of livelihood for themselves and those they love—all they hold dear in this life—in order to secure that pearl of price, the one true Faith with which they can purchase the Kingdom of Heaven.

Therefore our Lord says to us one and all in these days of danger: "Hold fast that which thou hast, that no one take thy crown."

"How can we keep our Faith safe?"

"By doing for our soul at least as much as we do for the body. How carefully we guard our eyes. Up go the hands if anything comes near them. Even babies are furnished with glasses nowadays. The sight of school children must be carefully tested and provided for. The light must fall from such a quarter, the desks slope at such an angle. No precautions are too great when there is question of safeguarding this most precious of the senses.

With much greater reason must we protect that eye of the soul—Faith. Nothing that could endanger it must be allowed near. Quick as instinct we must interpose to shield it from harm. Of all precious things it is the most precious; once lost, only a miracle of grace can restore it. Books, companions—all must be given up if we find they are hurting our Faith.

"It's awfully hard sometimes to give up a book just when it gets to the most interesting part and you want to know how all the people end."

How was it, then, that you gave up reading that beautifully bound edition of "Ivanhoe" which you got on your birthday?

"Because the print was so small it made my eyes ache, and father said he would not have me poring over it any more, for if I lost my sight not all the money in the world would buy it back."

And did you think that very hard?

"I did not like giving up the book, of course, but I saw father was right."

Trust your Heavenly Father, and run no risks when your Faith is concerned. Of all the good things He has given you, the true Faith is the chief.

"Oh, but there's Heaven, not quite yet, but promised!"

"And our Lady."

"And Grace."

"And the Blessed Sacrament."

And pray, without Faith how would you get to Heaven? And what would you know about grace, and our Lady, and our dear Lord's Gift to us of Himself! There is not a need of the body, nor a trouble of the soul, but Faith comes to the rescue, providing a remedy or soothing the pain. If you have offended God, it tells you how to get forgiven. If you are afraid of past sins, it bids you believe and trust in His infinite mercy. If you have lost a father, a mother, a friend, it raises your eyes to Heaven where those we loved and reverenced here are gone before us and are waiting for us. If you are anxious, fretful, tempted,

Faith comes to your help, leading you to pray, promising you grace and strength, comfort and victory, and an eternal reward for passing pain.

"I don't see how Faith can help the body; supposing I've toothache, or can't get my money, like that poor dressmaker we saw this morning."

A strong Faith in the Providence of God helps even here; indeed it is the only thing that does help. For it teaches me and makes me know and feel that God is a loving Father who lets pain and distress come to us because of the good these things bring, a subject we will talk about another day. But He is always by and watching. He will never let trial go further than is good for us or be stronger than we can bear. And if we believe in His fatherly care of us, and ask His help in any difficulty whatever, He will most certainly come to our assistance, not always as soon as we should wish, but the very minute He sees it will be best for us. Dear children, there are pains of mind and body so grievous, that without Faith men fall into despair. But with Faith, these pains are borne so nobly, so bravely, that even the unbeliever cannot withhold his admiration. Go among the poor in Ireland at a time of distress, when the potato crop has failed and the father looks round upon his tribe of little ones and trembles for the coming winter: "It'll be a heavy time, glory be to God!" he says quite naturally. Think of the Faith and trust in those words!

What makes the difference between this man and another who breaks out into angry rebellious words when trouble comes? Faith.

Faith, then, is our greatest treasure, and the devil, who knows this, tries to rob us of it, because if we lose this, all is lost. If by mortal sin we lose Charity or the love of God, we can get it back by a good confession. If we lose Hope, thinking it is no use trying to save our soul, we can recover our trust in

God by prayer, and by remembering what Faith teaches us, that He is always ready to forgive and help us. But if we lose Faith itself, what can bring us back to God and save us? Therefore we must dread above all other evils the loss or even the weakening of our Faith.

You are sure, sooner or later, to come across the religious questions and dangers of the day; some children meet them very early, so it is important you should be prepared. What do we do when chickenpox or measles are in the neighbourhood?

"Mother puts Condy's Fluid[1] all about."

"And Eucalyptus."

"And if it's very bad we go away to the seaside."

See what precautions to prevent harm to the body. We must be at least as prudent to keep harm from the soul. Unbelief and doubt, the spirit of criticism, independence, and revolt against authority, is found even in children in these days. It is round us on every side; we must provide against it. A great safeguard in this danger is to foresee it; not to be surprised when one hears or reads what is against the teaching of the Church; not to say with a start: "Oh dear, then the Catechism is all wrong!" but to think quietly: "This is just what I was told to expect."

Our Lord charged His Apostles and those who through their word were to believe in Him, to be on their guard against dangers to their Faith: "Take heed," He said, "that no man seduce you." He warned them against the decay of Faith which will increase as time goes on and the end draws near. Such numbers will fall away in the last great struggle of the Church,

---

1 Condy's fluid was a disinfectant marketed by London chemist Henry Bollmann Condy in the late 1800s/early 1900s. It was supposed to help treat and prevent many illnesses, including Scarlet Fever, and could be taken internally or used to disinfect and thereby prevent contagion. It was composed largely of Potassium Permanganate, a compound often used today in water treatment plants.

that He said: "The Son of Man when He cometh, shall He find, think you, faith upon earth?"

"I hope we shall not be living then."

Let us cling to Him who has loved us and died for us, and prayed for us one by one, as for Peter, that our Faith fail not. In the midst of the doubts and changing opinions of men, let us hold fast to this blessed Faith, remembering our Lord's words: "Every one that shall confess Me before men, I will also confess him before My Father who is in Heaven. But he that shall be ashamed of Me and of My words, the Son of Man also will be ashamed of him, when He shall come in the glory of His Father with the holy Angels."

"How can you help being ashamed when you are?"

"Oh what a question!—who could ever be ashamed of our Lord?"

Evidently some of His followers would be, or our Lord would not have thought a warning necessary. It is a useful question and one worth answering, for we have to consider, not what we ought to be, but what in our weakness we are. We have thought of many remedies already, but very often all that is wanted is a bit of pluck.

A young Catholic on going into residence at Oxford hung his crucifix over his bed. Some days later an undergraduate, paying him a visit, noticed it, and was beginning some speech about "holy Romans" when he was promptly pulled up by the master of the place.

"Look here," he said, "this is my room, and if you are coming here to make fun of my Religion, I will ask you to get out at once and not trouble yourself or me for the future."

"And did he?"

No. Taken aback by the manliness of the other, the visitor faltered out an apology. Nor was this all. His adventure got abroad, with the result that the Catholic got no more taunting for his Faith. On the contrary, the young men who came in contact with him respected him, and when he left Oxford there were not a few in whose souls good seed had been sown which we may hope bore fruit later.

Pluck will do something, but the chief remedy is prayer. For the right word here is not "shame" but "fear." Like St. Peter in the servants' hall, we are afraid of being laughed at or persecuted in some way for being Catholics. Take away the fear, and the shame goes.

"But how—that's just it?"

By often thanking God for the glorious gift of Faith and by praying for strength to take bravely whatever disagreeables or real suffering our name of Catholic may bring upon us. It was prayer brought strength to the martyrs to confess their Faith before tyrants. And it is giving strength every day to hundreds of faithful men, women, and children all the world over. Because he is a Catholic, a man loses his position in a college; an Irish girl seeking a situation is told she "need not apply"; the workhouse child is bidden by his companions to go off to his priest. It is by the strength got by prayer that all these are able to hold their own and bear up against what is so hard to flesh and blood.

"I pray, and I am ashamed all the same. When I was at Canterbury last summer, I didn't like having to go to our little church when my cousins were off to the Cathedral. And I don't like being laughed at."

It is not a question of liking. Our Lord does not ask us to like what hurts. He Himself feared mockery much more than we can fear it. This pain of being laughed at He bore, when they dressed Him up as a fool and took Him through the streets on purpose that all the rough people and the rude boys might make fun of Him. He was always trying to bear the same things we have to bear that we may be comforted by suffering in His company. And because He knows the extreme repugnance we have to anything in the shape of ridicule, He would be mocked again and again in His bitter Passion, and mocked in His pain, a thing He does not ask us to bear; at Herod's court by the wicked king and his soldiers; in the guardroom of Pilate by other soldiers who crowned Him with thorns, put a reed sceptre in His hand, and then made fun of Him, bowing before Him and pretending to cheer.

Oh, truly our Blessed Lord knows what it is to be laughed at, and He can feel for the child who has to bear pain of this kind for Him! The pain is soon over—and then! "If we suffer with Him," says St. Peter, "we shall rejoice with Him." The great Apostle remembers that when a servant girl once said to him, "Thou also wast with Jesus of Nazareth," and another said contemptuously to the standers by, "This is one of them," he was ashamed of his Master's service. But he remembers too with joy that he made up for his fall. After receiving the Holy Ghost he became so strong, that he was even glad to suffer reproach for the Name of Jesus, and he suffered with joy a cruel death for his Master's sake.

"I have been confirmed; why don't I feel like him?"

Never mind the feeling—try to *be* like him. The Holy Ghost did not take away the suffering that came of crucifixion and shame, but He gave the strength that made even such hard things welcome for the sake of Jesus. And He will strengthen you too. Tell me, did you turn back at Canterbury, and, leaving the poor little Catholic church with its humble worshippers, go to the grand cathedral?

"Of course I didn't. I'll tell you what I did. I thought how at the Last Day Canterbury will be all burnt up, the Cathedral and the little church too, and how it won't matter then where I went on Sunday so long as I kept my Faith."

It was the Holy Spirit who put that thought into your mind. He gives us in Confirmation, not only a sacramental grace, but a title to the actual graces we shall need in time of trial to show ourselves true soldiers of Jesus Christ. Here was one of those graces. It bore you safely through your trouble, and in the Last Day you will have your place and portion with those who have suffered something for our Blessed Lord's sake. "This is one of them," your Good Angel will say joyfully as he presents you to the Angel who is to "mark the servants of our God upon their foreheads," and place them on the right hand of the Judge.

"I always think of the Last Day when I'm tempted to do wrong. It helps me more than anything."

Many of us do the same. But just look at the clock! And we were to have given up early. Be off every one of you, or we shall be late for the tennis match after all!

X

Does it Matter?

"Well, it went off well, didn't it, and we weren't late. What are we going to have this morning?" You said yesterday and said truly, that we none of us like to be laughed at for our religion. Is it, perhaps, because we feel we are being robbed of our rights? For the laugh, you know, ought to be on our side. Safe in the Bark of Peter, that for nearly two thousand years "has braved the battle and the breeze," we might surely look down with a smile on the poor little craft that, one after another, our great ship sees rise and sink around her. Some make her their butt, and think to prove themselves "destroyers." Others do her the compliment of copying her institutions, her observances, and her very garb. She passes calmly through them all. She sees them breast and even ride the waves with her—for a moment, but only to fall behind when their short-lived strength is spent, and be lost to sight in the distance; while she holds on her way, purified by the storms that seemed to threaten her with destruction. Now and then a man falls overboard; at times officers and crew bring disgrace upon her. But nothing turns her out of her course, or hinders her from bearing her precious freight safe into port. Is such a ship a thing to be ashamed of? Ought we not rather to beware lest by over-glorying in the name of Catholic, we forget that it is by God's mercy alone that we are riding on securely towards the haven whilst so many are battling with the waves, or exchanging one little bark for another which promises to be more seaworthy than its fellow?

"I think I see almost all those things about the ship, but not quite all, you went too fast. Those who left the ship were Arius, and Luther, and Calvin, and a lot of others like them."

There is one thing about the ship which bears out what we were noticing the other day about metaphors and similes. They help us to get at truths which we cannot easily grasp without such aid. But they only take us a certain distance. We must not pursue them too far, but leave them when they have done their work, as we get out at a station when the train has taken us as far as it can on our journey. We should be very wrong, as the youngest of you knows, to take it for granted that all who sail in Peter's Bark reach the shore for which she is bound, so here our figure fails us.

"Oh, but it doesn't. You mean it's no use being Catholics if we die in mortal sin. Well, a ship doesn't take her dead members into port either, but throws them overboard. So I think it's quite like after all. As long as we keep living members of the crew, we shall get to shore all right."

Bravo! You saw ahead of me there. I must take care how I backbite your favourite similes which have such sharp brains to defend them. I suppose I must not expect you, though, to go on to show us what we must do to keep living members?

"That's harder, but I'll try. It's rather fun, you know, giving you instructions, instead of you us."

"I want to know something else about the ship. Are all the people lost who are not in Peter's Bark? Is it quite like the Ark, I mean?"

None are ever lost except through their own fault. Our Lord has founded His Church to bring all men to salvation. But all are not aware of their duty to submit to her. So long as they have no suspicion that She is the true Church which Christ has commanded all to hear, they are not in fault for remaining outside her communion. But if they have any idea that She may be the one true Church, they are strictly bound to pray for guidance and to inquire; and, once convinced of her claims to their obedience, to put themselves under instruction and be enrolled among her children.

"But if they are Protestants because they don't know any better, they can get to Heaven, can't they, and so it doesn't matter so very very much whether they are Protestants or Catholics?"

That we must never say, for it would be quite false. It is a great misfortune to be outside the true Church, even when this is not one's own fault. The means of salvation which She provides are infinitely greater than those which are to be found elsewhere. Think what it is to know for certain the truth about One God in Three Persons; about the Incarnation, Death, and Resurrection of our Saviour; the work He came to do in this world; our Redemption by Him, and the means by which that Redemption is applied to our souls; what we must do to escape everlasting misery in the world to come and secure for ourselves eternal happiness. Think what it is to have in the Church a living voice which cannot tell us wrong; to have in her Sacraments ever-flowing fountains of grace; to know exactly what we must do to get forgiveness of our sins; to be able whenever we will to strengthen our souls by the real presence within them of their God and Redeemer.

Take one point alone. Forgiveness of grievous sin can be obtained in one of two ways, (1) by an act of attrition—that is, sorrow for sin because it has lost heaven and deserved hell—together with the priest's absolution in the Sacrament of Penance; or (2) by an act of perfect contrition—that is, sorrow proceeding purely from the love of God. By this sorrow the sin is forgiven immediately, even before confession, though there is a strict obligation of mentioning it in the next confession.

Now, for a Protestant, who cannot have recourse to the sacrament of Penance, attrition does not suffice; there must be perfect contrition for the sin to be forgiven.

All around us men are saying that it does not matter what we *believe* so long as we *do* what is right. How amazing such a statement would have appeared to the first Christians. We are told of them that they persevered in the doctrine of the Apostles—persevered in spite of persecution, and fire, and the sword. And rightly, for had not one of these teachers said to them: "Though an angel from heaven preach a gospel to you beside that which we have preached to you, let him be anathema," that is, accursed.

But why this steadfast clinging to what they had been taught if it matters little what we believe? Why did the Apostles who were sent into the world as sheep among wolves, become as lions when they found any one trying to change the least tittle of the Faith delivered to them? Because their Master had founded one Church, and only one. To her His promises were made; with her His Spirit was to remain to the end of the world, to lead her into all truth. She was appointed to teach all nations, and all were commanded to hear her. The Apostles were to be her first teachers, and among them Peter was to be chief and to confirm the rest, that the Church might be one.

And because she was to last to the end of time, and to the end there would be questions and disputes, Peter was to live on in his successors—to *teach*. Men were not to make up a religion for themselves, or to puzzle one out from that Book which just because it is the Word of God is hard to understand. They were not to spend their lives disputing as to its meaning, but in doing as it bids them. And that bidding they were to learn from the Church into whose keeping the Holy Bible is given. Our Lord, who is tender and wise, has provided an easy way to Heaven for the simple and the little children who are not able to puzzle out difficult questions; for the toilers and the poor who have to work for their daily bread. He does not say to them, "Read the Bible, and make out a religion from it as well as you can," but, "Hear the Church."

All around us is disagreement and confusion. People waste their time in disputing about the way to salvation instead of walking in it. Hundreds of religious bodies claim to be the true Church. But let men look out for that one which goes up to the Apostles, whose pastors come down in an unbroken line from Peter to Pius. She was waiting for us when we came into the world, to receive us into the number of her children, to teach, and guide, and train us for the Heavenly City to which we are travelling.

Many, however, trust to getting there without a guide, or with a guide of their own choosing. This is foolish. The way is long and difficult, with enemies and pitfalls on every side. Their guides cannot agree, and say plainly they may be mistaken and may mislead the travellers who trust in them. Thus these poor people move on in uncertainty and fear. Doctrines that they hold to-day to be necessary they drop to-morrow, for there is no *authority* to which they submit, and although they may think or hope that their beliefs do not matter much so long as they try to do what is right, they have moments of terrible anxiety when the thought presses upon them: "What if I am on the wrong road! If I find at the end that I have been misled, there is no coming back to try again. Oh, if I only knew for certain where to find the truth!"

How different is the lot of those who were either born Catholics, or through God's mercy have found their way to the truth. They are like little children walking safely home by their mother's side, their hand in hers. They have no anxiety as to the way, for she knows it, and has led their brothers and sisters before them. Whatever they need for the journey, she provides. All they have to do is to hear her voice and do as she tells them. These are the children of the Catholic Church.

It matters, then, very much what men believe, and we can never be too thankful that we hold the true Faith of the One, Holy, Catholic, and Apostolic Church. You were going to tell us, when we went off into this long digression, what we must do to keep living members of the Church.

Suppose I give you a start. Falling into grievous sin, and falling away from the Faith, come from giving way to temptation. Hence our Lord says to us: "Watch and pray that you enter not into temptation." Now, what is it to watch?

"It means ever so many things."

"I know; let me say. You know that picture in the nursery over the fireplace?"

"Suspense," by Landseer?

"I don't know its name, nor who did it. But I know all about the dog. He's by the hall door at night, and he thinks he hears a sound under the crack. But he's not quite sure, so he keeps quite still till he knows. And his great feet are wide apart,

and his ears are cocked, and his eyes are looking sideways at the crack; and we've often said we shouldn't like to be the robber outside if there is one."

How can we be like that faithful watch-dog?

"We must keep our master's house safe—that's our soul. And we mustn't be asleep on the doormat, but awake, ready to pounce on thieves who want to come in."

In what shape do the thieves come?

"You told us before. They might be bad books or bad companions. And they would rob us of the grace of God if we let them. So we mustn't let them get in, and when we feel by our conscience that we're in danger, we must shut the book up and not go with the companion any more."

I see you know what it is to be on guard. But there is another thing to be done if we want to keep our Faith strong and vigorous. We must exercise it. Think of the constant practice needed by pianists and violinists to keep the skill they have acquired.

"Yes, and it's the same with our scales before the examination day."

If, then, we want our Faith to be strong enough to bear us up in the time of need, we must exercise it. How?

"I should think by saying your prayers properly."

"And keeping the Commandments."

"And going to Confession and Communion at the right times."

Exactly—leading, in short, a good Catholic life. This will strengthen our Faith by exercise and by the new graces God will give us. We must not watch only, but practise and pray. One who does this, and does it, not for a few weeks or months, but perseveringly year after year, grows so strong in Faith, that, far from being ashamed of it, he glories in it and has a most earnest desire to draw to it the minds and hearts of others. His Faith has become a part of himself; he rules his life by it; it is his strength in time of trouble and in the day of temptation. He may hear it scoffed at as being behind the times; he may find the truths of his Catechism denied, and the laws and observances of the Church ridiculed; but his mind and heart remain firm and untroubled. Temptation and example that overthrow others leave him unharmed, because he feels as well as knows that his faith is from God. He knows that the opinions of men and the science of this world will pass away and be forgotten like a dream; that the things which we now believe by Faith, the real and lasting things, will then be seen, and heard, and felt; and that those who have guided their life by these truths, whom Faith, like the star in the East, has brought safe to the feet of Jesus, will then with the holy Magi rejoice with exceeding great joy.

"Do you know what I wonder sometimes? If God loves us so much, why doesn't He make things so plain that people *couldn't* go wrong—I mean couldn't help seeing which was the right religion, and hadn't all these puzzles?"

I might answer by saying that "Why?" is a dangerous word when we come to God's dealings with us. The first temptation began with "Why?"

"Why hath God commanded you that you should not eat of every tree of Paradise?"

It succeeded then, it is succeeding every day by making God seem hard, as if He begrudged us what would make us happy. Satan never asks: "Why does God love you so much? Why has He done so much for you?" No, he puts into our minds only discontented "Whys?" and if we are foolish enough to take his answers, we shall lose our happy trust in our Heavenly Father and wander down a path that will lead us very far from Him.

I might answer your question, then, by saying simply that "Why?" is a dangerous word which we must not use. But I would rather give you another answer which, because it is the true one, will or ought to satisfy us.

God does this or that—*because He is God*. He is absolutely free to do as He wills in all things. If we do not see this clearly, it is because our ideas of God are very low and muddled. He is Lord of us and of all things, and can dispose of all just as He wills. He can do nothing but what is perfect in every way, and therefore, though we cannot understand all He does, we know that just because He does it, it is the best thing that could be. This is what King David meant when he said those grand, beautiful words, worthy of his loyal heart: "Thou art just, O Lord, and Thy judgment is right"(Ps. cviii), "The judgments of the Lord are true, justified in themselves"(Ps. xviii). They do not need the approval of our little minds to make them just; they are God's doing, that is enough.

Nothing gives God more glory, nothing does us more good, than to feel as David felt about this. Nothing will keep us safer and happier, because close to God, nothing will make us love and trust Him more, and deserve a greater reward hereafter. To see and be glad to see God's right to do as He wills in all things, is to be like the Angels and Saints already and to be getting ready fast for our place amongst them.

But it is not enough to believe and own that God has a right to do whatever He wills because He is Lord and Master of all things; we must also believe firmly that because He is our Father, He does all for the good of His children.

And so there will be no peevish "Whys?" when we see things we do not understand or when things happen that hurt. We shall say with the High-priest Heli[1]: "It is the Lord, let

---

[1] More commonly known today as Eli. *Heli* is the rendering of this name in Latin, and as the Catholic Douay-Rheims bible sought to faithfully

Him do what is good in His sight"(1 Kings iii). I shall see His reasons some day; meantime I can trust my Father—and wait.

"But when we see bad people getting on and good people all in trouble, we can't help wondering why, can we?"

When the enemy puts "Why?" into our minds, we can answer:

"Because God allows it—*that's why.*"

People ask sometimes how it is disasters overtake God's faithful servants who are working for His glory or are the happiness of their home. A mother who seems to us necessary to her little children, is carried off by fever. A priest out in Africa crossing a river with his precious baggage—chalice, vestments, whatever he needs for the Holy Sacrifice—gets upset and loses all. Why do these things happen? This is God's secret. Surely He may have His secrets. Even we, little as we are, have ours. We guard them jealously, tell them to whom we like, and keep them from whom we like. The great God does the same. Have we anything more to say?

Sometimes a father says to the "Whys?" of his little child: "You would not understand, my boy, if I were to tell you. When you get bigger you shall know all about it." So our Heavenly Father says to His children. We must trust like children now. Some day it will be all quite clear.

We shall see how beautifully right everything has been, and be—oh! so glad that we trusted our Heavenly Father in all the puzzles of this life.

"Wit it well: Love is his meaning" in all He does—and we shall see it some day.

---

preserve as much as possible of the Vulgate from which it was translated, the traditional Latin names were used rather than their anglicized versions.

XI
About Friends

The Catechism tells us that by the "World" is meant "the society of those who love the vanities, riches, and pleasures of this world better than God." This brings us to a very important subject—we shall not find many more important—the choice of our companions and friends.

What our friends are, we shall sooner or later be. We must not, then, be in too great a hurry to make friends, nor be guided in our choice of them by frivolous reasons, such as money, a good position in society, good looks or attractive manners. Do not let your admiration of a good tennis player, or even of one who has come out top in an examination, so run away with you, that you forthwith determine to make a friend of her. Nor suppose that because some one seems to have taken a fancy to you, you are obliged to respond instantly and vehemently. Look for something more solid than all this in one whom you are thinking of taking as a friend. Do not be content to know that you like a girl, but ask yourself *why*?

"I make friends with people who like the things I do."

Very good, friends should have tastes in common, but this should not be your only reason for liking them. Do not like people merely for selfish reasons, for your own convenience, pleasure, or profit. If you cannot love another for her own sake, for what you see and admire in her, you have no right to call her friend.

From the words of Holy Scripture we learn both the value of a true friend and the care we should take in our choice of friends:—

"Be in peace with many, but let one of a thousand be thy counsellor. If thou wouldst get a friend, try him before thou takest him, and do not credit him easily. For there is a friend for his own occasion, and he will not abide in the day of thy trouble. And there is a friend, a companion of the table, and he will not abide in the day of distress. A friend, if he continue steadfast, shall be to thee as thyself. A faithful friend is a strong defence, and he that hath found him hath found a treasure. Nothing can be compared to a faithful friend, and no weight of gold or silver is able to countervail the goodness of his fidelity. He that feareth God shall likewise have good friendship, because according to him shall his friend be"(Ecclus. vi). "Forsake not an old friend, for the new will not be like to him"(Ecclus. ix). "Keep fidelity with a friend in his poverty. In the time of his trouble continue faithful to him"(Ecclus. xxii).

The word of God tells us, too, whom we should not take for a friend: "A friend is known in adversity....For an hour a wicked man will abide with thee; but if thou begin to decline he will not endure it"(Ecclus. xii). "If thou have anything, he will live with thee. If he have need of thee, he will deceive thee, and smiling upon thee will put thee in hope, he will speak thee fair and will say: 'What wantest thou?' And at last he will laugh at thee, and when he seeth thee he will forsake thee, and shake his head at thee....Believe not his many words, for by much talk he will sift thee, and smiling will examine thee concerning thy secrets"(Ecclus. xiii).

No one, however dear, must lead us to do what is against our conscience: "If thy friend whom thou lovest as thy own soul, would persuade thee secretly" (to do what is wrong), "consent not to him, hear him not"(Deut. xiii).

From Jonathan's friendship for David, we see what a true friend should be. "The soul of Jonathan was knit to the soul of David, and Jonathan loved him as his own soul"(1 Kings xviii). He warned him of danger, stood up for him when he was in disgrace, was ready to suffer for him, rejoiced in his prosperity, wept with him when he was in trouble. "And Jonathan stripped himself of the coat with which he was clothed, and gave it to David, and the rest of his garments, even to his sword, and to his bow, and to his girdle"(*Ibid.*). "Whatever thy soul shall say to me, I will do for thee"(1 Kings xix.), he said to him. "Thou shalt reign over Israel, and I shall be next to thee"(1 Kings xxiii).

What wonder that when this true friend was killed in battle, David in anguish of heart cried out: "I grieve for thee, my brother Jonathan, exceeding beautiful and amiable. As the mother loveth her only son, so did I love thee"(2 Kings i).

It is plain we cannot expect to have many friends if they are to be such as the Scripture paints them, and that most of those whom we call friends are little more than acquaintances. My friend is my other self. By reason of the union between us of mind and heart, his influence will go a long way in the formation of my character. Provided, then, he be worthy of the name, there is nothing of this earth, the Scripture tells me, to equal his worth.

Think what it is to have at hand one who will counsel us wisely in times of difficulty and perplexity, whose sympathy will uphold us in the day of trouble, whose approval or disapproval does not adapt itself to our likes or dislikes, but stands on the right side always as an encouragement or a check. In the company of a good and wise friend we are lifted above our littlenesses and meannesses; what is best in us comes out; noble, unselfish aims are put before us; we are encouraged to think less of the amusement we can get out of persons and things than of the service we can render to others, of spending our time usefully as well as pleasantly, of cultivating our gifts, and fitting ourselves to do useful work in the future.

And is it not a grand thing to have found one who does not flatter us; who will tell us the truth about ourselves, and bravely give us a word of warning and, if need be, blame; who can draw us out of our natural selfishness and teach us what it is to be devoted; one whose welfare we prefer to our own convenience; for whom we are ready to labour, to suffer, to practise self-control? For, remember, friendship has its duties and its trials as well as its joys and its privileges. Call no one your friend from whom you will not accept a word of advice or warning; with whom you are quick to take offence; for whom you are not ready to put yourself to inconvenience or trouble. Without unselfishness, without generosity, without much patience and forbearance—for your friend, like you, will have his faults and his bad days—without readiness, nay eagerness, to give sympathy, and time, and toil, help in any needed shape, true friendship is an impossibility.

"How can we tell if people would be good or bad to have for friends?"

"Try him before thou takest him," the Scriptures tell us. Take time to observe people, see if you can admire and esteem them, if you can value them, not for what they have, but for what they are. Ask yourself if you would wish to be like them. If you find their conversation silly, frivolous, ill-natured, and full of criticism, perpetually running upon dress, amusements, pleasure, "having a good time;" if they flatter you, or try to lead you to do what is against your conscience; if they want you to keep secret their liking for you, and to promise not to tell your father or mother what they say or do; if, in short, instead of helping you to do what is right, they laugh at those who are determined to serve God in earnest, and who are afraid of sin, your own conscience will tell you whether their companionship will bring you good or harm. Be wise in time, and turn away resolutely from such friendships.

Mind, you will not find out all at once people of this sort. They will wait a bit before saying or doing what they know will shock you. But if they see you have no strong principles and are like a weathercock, blown this way or that by a breath of ridicule, that you are pleased with a little flattery, and more afraid of offending them than of displeasing God, they will soon show themselves in their true colours. Either by soft words, or by laughing at your fears, they will get you at last to think and speak and act as they do. You will have gone a long, long way out of your road to Heaven, and who knows whether you will have even the desire to return to it!

"But we are not obliged to imitate the people we like?"

Place two mirrors opposite one another and see how they reflect whatever is found in each, whether beautiful or otherwise. So is it with friends. Consciously or unconsciously, they copy one another. Their views, tastes, words, example, exercise a powerful influence over one another, and help to mould each other's character, and thus—

"What is character?"

The tendency our will has acquired to act in a certain way under certain circumstances. By acting often in a particular manner we form a habit of so doing. Our habits make and reveal our character.

"And what do you mean by 'principles'? You spoke just now of people having no principles."

To answer your question fully would take more time than we can give to-day. Habits form our character, and habits come from repeated acts. What lead us to act in this or that way, are those convictions which are called "principles" or beginnings, because they are the sources from which our thoughts, words, and actions flow. To have no principles is to have no sound and steady convictions to rule our conduct. But we will have a talk about this another day.

One word more before we leave this subject of friendship. If you are happy enough to find one whose friendship lifts you up, inspires you with generous desires, brings out what is best in you, encourages you to useful effort in any direction, and to perseverance in well doing, be glad, and very thankful to God, for He Himself tells you, you have "found a treasure."

I said just now that it is difficult to find a true friend. But perhaps it is not so hard after all—for us Catholics.

"You are thinking of one's confessor, I expect."

Yes; whatever is most valuable in friendship—counsel that is wise, disinterested, fearless; instruction and warning; encouragement and support; the power to help that wide experience gives—all strengthened and supernaturalised by the grace of a Sacrament—this is within the reach of most of us.

To profit by it as we should, there must be on our side faith and confidence, simplicity and sincerity. We must be honest in the account we give of ourselves and of our concerns, seeking only to know God's will in our difficulties, and determined to go away and try to do it. We must not talk for talking's sake, nor try to make the best of ourselves, nor throw all the blame of our faults on others.

And, children, as we grow up, let us beware of unsupernaturalising the help offered us in the Sacrament of Penance. There are some who seem to think more of the long talk they are going to have after confession than of the forgiveness of their sins. In season and out of season, they are never weary of talking about themselves, and directors and direction. They continually bring conversation round to this subject, and turn a Sacrament—the Sacrament *of Penance*, into a bit of pleasurable excitement.

Those who gain most profit from this Sacrament are not those who talk much about it. Such talk is more harmful than you would suppose. The advice we received in confession is meant for ourselves amid our own surroundings. It is not intended to be passed on and to be a prescription for others whose circumstances are different from ours. Therefore to quote what has been said to us, as if it were meant to be a rule for all, may be not only mischievous to our hearers, but a real injustice to our confessor. And he has no redress, if, in consequence of our imprudence, harm is done. Should it come to his knowledge he cannot explain, his lips are sealed. Oh, can we not learn a lesson from the care the Church takes to preserve the secrecy of the confessional! Her priests are bound at the cost of life itself to keep our secret. Can we not, for their sakes if not for our own, make a little effort to restrain our tattling tongues?

One would think that advice on this point should not be necessary.

"My secret to myself, my secret to myself," says the prophet (Isaias xxiv). And surely if we have a secret we should wish to keep to ourselves, it will be the history of our soul, its struggles, efforts, temptations, its inner life with God. The Ark of the Covenant was enclosed within the Holy of Holies and hidden by a veil from the eyes of all. The tabernacles in our churches, relics, sometimes even pictures, are kept veiled. And is our soul, where God dwells as in His temple, so little sacred to us, that we unveil it for the curious gaze of every passer-by? Doors are left open where there is nothing of value within. Let us guard the gates of our sanctuary by a wise reserve.

And let us respect in others what we guard for ourselves. The sanctuaries of God are on every side of us, wherever there is a soul in the state of grace. We must treat them reverently, not prying into them curiously, not asking indiscreet questions. Talk about confessors and direction, the length of time So-and-So remains in the confessional, the frequency or infrequency of her communions—this is no business of ours, and no topic for conversation. We should neither start it ourselves nor take part in it if it is made the subject of gossip.

But see those wandering eyes there. We have been talking over the heads of some who should have been sent out to play. The difference of age among you is a disadvantage. We must try to keep our older talks for times when the younger ones are not here.

XII

About Books

"I was going to show you an awfully jolly book one of my cousins gave me yesterday, but mother does not like me to have it. She says she will keep it till I'm older. I wonder why."

She has a good reason, depend upon it. Our books are like our companions; we have to be careful in our choice of them, and our parents are better judges than we are. As it happens, we are going to have a talk about books to-day, so you have done well to start it.

I suppose I may take for granted that you are clear at least upon two points—that we are not free to read whatever comes in our way, and that all we see in print is not necessarily true. We can no more read everything that comes to hand, than we can go into a chemist's shop and drink whatever we find there. Before putting anything to our lips, we take care to find out from one whom we can trust what will do us good and what would hurt us. So must we do with the food and medicine of the mind.

Books, like medicine, will keep us in health, restore our strength if it is run down, give us what the doctors call "tone." But there is something else they *may* do. They may take strength from us instead of giving it; instead of infusing vigour, the desire for healthy exercise and labour, they may act upon us like those poisonous drugs which lull their victims to sleep, rob them of all energy, of all that is good and noble in them, and bring them at last to a state of absolute selfishness, in which they drag on miserable and degraded lives, useless and worse than useless to themselves and to others.

"Father won't let us buy the red and yellow books at stations, not even to read in the train when we've nothing else to do."

"And he won't let us read newspapers either, except bits that he picks out sometimes. He says there are things going on in the country that everybody ought to know, but he won't let us look them out for ourselves; he says he can find them quicker. Sometimes we read them to him, and he talks to us about them."

"Our cousins bought some of the yellow books from a railway stall because they said they didn't want to waste time on the road, but father said it was silly to do oneself harm for the sake of doing something."

"How can we know whether we may read a book?"

Get father or mother, or some friend you can trust, to tell you whether it is worth reading.

"But why does it matter so much what we read? We shan't go and do bad things because we have read about them."

It is to be hoped not. Yet what we read, whether good or bad, is bound to have its effect upon us. Why did your father stop you the other day when you were cutting that wood with your new knife?

"He said I should dull the edge and spoil it for finer work."

Which is just what you will do with your mind if you employ it on objects unworthy of it. Anything coarse, vulgar, unsound, would rob it of its delicacy, its fineness of perception, dull its sense of what is true and noble and beautiful, confuse its notions of right and wrong, and in the end ruin it.

"Do we know it does us harm, know of ourselves, I mean?"

At our baptism there was put into our soul a bright light, which instruction, and more and more of the grace of God, has increased. By this light we see, to some extent, the dangers that come in our way. Even without the warning word of others, we may feel instinctively that a book we have taken up is not doing us any good. We don't care for father or mother to see us reading it. We should not like to have to read it aloud. Its teaching is different from our Lord's and from the Catechism's. The people that we should have thought were wicked, it would have us admire. They do quite as a matter of course and without blame what we have been taught is against the Commandments. Yet they are made interesting and attractive. What is wrong does not seem so bad somehow—we are puzzled.

"Are pirate stories bad, then—because they're the best of all?"

No, you may keep your pirate stories. It is not of such books I was thinking. I see the elder ones among you know what I mean, and it is to them I say—When you close a book ask yourself what it has done for you. The answer of your own heart will decide whether it is a good book—not for so-and-so who has read it and assures you it did her no harm but—*for you*; whether, therefore, you may finish it with a safe conscience, or whether you must resolutely give it up.

"It is awfully hard to give up a book sometimes, even when one feels what you have said."

We must learn to do hard things. You stopped carving your initials on your paper cutter for fear of spoiling your new blade. And will you hesitate about closing a book that would spoil the delicacy and beauty of your mind? Let us learn once for all that hard things will have to be done all our life through if we are to keep our soul for life everlasting, as our Lord says. Once beyond this time of risk and trial, we shall be set free from the law of self-restraint. Then "nothing shall cross thee, nothing shall stand in thy way, but all thy heart's desire shall be there together present, and shall satisfy it to the full," à Kempis tells us. No need of caution, no prohibition—Paradise, and no forbidden fruit.

"Are novels bad things?"

Not in themselves. On the contrary the best novels, besides the advantage of providing us with pleasant recreation, may do real good by strengthening right principles, forming the taste, putting before us noble characters and ideals, widening our views, our interests, and our sympathies. Ruskin says: "Good novels well read have serious use, being studies of human nature in the elements of it. But they are hardly ever read with earnestness enough to permit them to fulfil their function."[1] For those whose brains work hard, a certain amount of light reading is almost a necessity for resting the head and making it ready for work again.

For this, mind, is the true usefulness of novels. They must be our relaxation, not our occupation. Of all good things that have been abused, novel-reading is among the chief. A girl who has no habit of self-control will in a very short time become the slave of her book, or rather of her own selfishness. No call of duty, or friendship, or charity has any effect upon her. Work of every kind is cut down, to secure more time for what has become her absorbing occupation, the business instead of the recreation of life. The exciting scenes that fill her imagination make the humdrum duties of home life, first distasteful, and at length intolerable. She escapes from them at all hours to get back to her book. If she becomes the mistress of a family, things are worse still: husband, children, servants—all are neglected. No need to say that prayer, examination of conscience, the Sacraments, were laid aside long ago. Our

---

1 "Sesame and Lilies."

Lord would reproach too persistently in prayer and Holy Communion; conscience cry too loudly in self-examination. Confession would require a change for the better, which she has no intention of making. "After all," she says to herself, "it can't be very wrong, there is no mortal sin."

"And there isn't, is there?"

It would not be easy to say how much sin there is in an utterly useless and selfish life. When we think of the waste of time and grace, of the neglect of prayer and of serious duties and responsibilities, and this going on for years, it is hard to see how grave sin can be avoided. We can only live our lives once. Holy Scripture tells us that in a little while the life that is lent us will be called for again (Wisd. xv), and we shall have to give a strict account of what we have done with it.

> "Knowing ourselves, our world, our task so great,
> Our time so brief, 'tis clear if we refuse
> The means so limited, the tools so rude
> To execute our purpose, life will fleet
> And we shall fade, and leave our task undone."[1]

"What does 'task' mean? There are no more tasks when we leave school."

We will have a talk about that some day. Just now I want to say a word or two more about our reading and its importance.

Wise people tell us that our character can be told from our companions and our books; not of course from the books we are bound to use, but from those we turn to when choice is left us. Such books help to form our character, both by their subject-matter and by the way in which they are read. Let us take an example.

Two boys at school have the same hobby, they are both voracious readers. When a play-day comes, and others are up and doing, scampering all over the place and sitting down

---
[1] Browning, "Paracelsus."

only for meals, these book-worms lie stretched under a tree in a quiet nook, absorbed in other and very different scenes from those around them. Can we gather any information, I wonder, by peeping over their shoulders, so as to learn something of their characters and their tastes?

"We know already—they like reading."

Exactly, but there are readers and readers. One of our friends here chooses from the library the lightest, flimsiest tales he can find, never anything that takes the least effort to follow—schoolboy scrapes, slave-hunting, a prisoner's escape, an execution. He skips anything he finds about character, any historical background, any descriptions of scenery, anything in short that gives his mind more to do than wander lazily from one exciting scene to another. A solid block of print he shuns as a matter of course; the short paragraphs, the inverted commas, this is all he looks for and enjoys.

"But it's a holiday—mayn't he read what he likes?"

Certainly, I never meant he was doing wrong. All I said was—Shall we try to find out something about him, and see if he is reading in such a way as to help his mind to grow and strengthen by the exercise of its faculties? This can only be done by labour—pleasant labour it may be, but there must be effort of some kind if good is to be done. An immensity of good may be done in a pleasant way and on a play-day, as the lad stretched on the grass beside him seems to be finding out.

"I hope he has got a tale book too—he'll be stupid if he hasn't."

He has, and it happens to be a prisoner's escape, like the other's. But he is reading it differently from his neighbour. Not content with running through the dialogue between the Countess of Nithsdale and the gaoler when she presents herself at the prison on the eventful night, he is going carefully through the whole account. He has the Jacobite rebellion of 1715 in the period of History he is taking at the coming examination, and is interested to find his story takes him over the same ground as his text-book yesterday. He notices points in which the narratives differ, and determines to look up in another book some further particulars of the Earl of Derwentwater and see if he really did suffer for his faith and die a martyr.

He has read all he can find about his period and is getting quite interested in it. He is learning to think too. He notices how accounts differ. He compares statements and views, and is beginning to see that before taking for granted the correctness of what is said, he must consider his author. Macaulay he does not altogether trust for facts, and he reads with caution a Protestant historian on the Spanish Inquisition and the Massacre of St. Bartholomew. He stops at the end of a powerfully or beautifully written passage and re-reads it. He notices beauties his companion over there never sees. I do not mean to say that he is always hard at work when he is reading, but I do mean that the thought of self-improvement does not leave him on a play-day, and that it enters even into the reading of a tale. He is developing not only a servant greater, but that power of taking pains which is said to be akin to genius. It will keep him out of an amount of mischief later, and will have much to do with whatever work in the future he may take up.

"But how can a taste for History be any good except for examinations?"

That is the least part of its goodness. A taste for the study of History or of Languages, of Mathematics or of Physical Science, of Painting or of Music, is of use to us in many ways. Such tastes bring us into communion with the great minds of all ages, and this companionship raises and inspires us. They form our views upon noble models, cultivate a love for the refined and beautiful, make us admire what is best in literature and in art. They exercise, and by this means strengthen, the faculties of our mind; they steady us, compel us to take pains and to overcome difficulties; train us to habits of accuracy and industry, of patience and perseverance. And—which is no small advantage—they take us out of ourselves, and our little frets and worries, and provide us with interesting and profitable occupation for our leisure hours. One such taste will open out to us many other spheres of useful knowledge. History, for example, not only records what happened in times gone by, but shows us why it happened. We feel that God is behind that moving scene; that the men and women have not everything in their own hands; that, controlling all the governments of this world, is a Divine Government guiding all things; "that in the long run it is well with the good and ill with the wicked."[1] In this way History serves us both for encouragement and for warning. "History," says Carlyle, "is the letter of instruction which the old generations write and transmit to the new." Biography, which is history on a smaller scale, teaches us the same lessons. Amongst its heroes we find the Saints of God, and the good that comes to us from the study of their lives, who shall tell!

"You said just now that the last boy would see beauties the other wouldn't. How can you help not seeing when you don't see?"

We can learn to see. Is there no one here who can tell us how?

"I think I can. I was in the National Gallery the other day with mother. You know how fond she is of sketching. Well, she stopped at a picture of a pool on a moor, just a bit of brown water with heather round it, and some clouds. It wasn't bigger than a racket without the handle, but there she stood. I got impatient, 'Mother, do come on,' I said. And then

---

1 Froude.

she called me to her side and made me see what she saw—the shadows from the banks in the brown peaty water, the glow in the western sky, the feeling of peace everywhere, even in the smoke from the cottage and the home-coming of the cows. Of course I can't explain it all as she did, but I got quite interested. We didn't finish the Gallery, and when I went again, I hunted up the landscapes and tried to find things out by myself."

Very good, that is just what I meant by learning to see. And what is true of a picture is equally true of a poem, or of first-class music. With a little help from a friend, an eager mind may teach itself to see what may make all the difference to it in after life.

"What are the best books for play-days if you like to read?"

I should say, read such as interest you most. "In brief, Sir, study what you most affect," is Shakespeare's advice. We have each of us our tastes. Some like Biography, others Travel, others again Natural History; whilst for some there is nothing so interesting as the delineation of character, or the descriptions of scenery which they find in a good novel, or a picture of times, people, manners and customs different from our own. Take what you like, provided it be good and worthy of your time and attention. You will find such reading refreshes your mind, and makes it readier for work afterwards than if you had skimmed a hundred pages of a sensational story.

One last word. Reading as recreation should be taken like all recreation under certain conditions and with moderation. Such reading is an excellent test of our power of self-control. It requires no little moral courage to deny ourselves a book which in spite of warning we are curious to read, a book much talked about, perhaps, that girls younger than ourselves have read, that every one reads, we are told.

Again, it is no slight exercise of self-control to determine the amount of time we may give to light reading and to close our book when the time is up. The effort to follow an author when the sense is obscure, the patience to read and re-read a noble passage till it has sunk into mind and heart and become part of ourselves—all this is excellent self-discipline.

"Can we tell from the name of the author whether a book is good or bad?"

Not always. Some books of certain authors may be harmless, whilst others it would be unwise to read. Ask some one who has read a book you want to read, some one you can trust, if you can read it with safety.

Reading, then, as recreation—and to many it is the most enjoyable of recreations—affords ample opportunity for the exercise of self-restraint. If we are wise, we shall improve these opportunities and try to acquire early such tastes and method in our intercourse with books as will stand us in good stead in after-life.

It may be well, perhaps, to say here, that we are not necessarily debarred from reading a book because we foresee that here and there a passage may suggest what might be dangerous. Provided we read—not for the gratification of unwholesome curiosity, but from a good motive, for the useful information we shall find, for the beauty of style, or even for the innocent amusement a book affords—having always a general resolve to turn quietly from anything harmful without letting our mind dwell upon it, we may read it without difficulty. Unless this were a sound principle to act upon, we could never open a book or an album with safety.

"But might not some girls say: 'In that case I am free to read any book, for I can always resolve to turn away from anything dangerous'?"

The rule does not apply to books that are dangerous to faith or morals—that is, to what we must believe and what we must do to keep the Commandments of God. Such books we are bound to avoid, and it is the duty of those in charge of us to warn us against them. This done, the responsibility of what we do rests with ourselves. If we neglect advice, we can do so, for our will is free. But we have the solemn warning of the Holy Ghost Himself, "He that loveth danger shall perish in it"(Ecclus. iii); and in our mother Eve a sad example of the misery one act of curiosity may entail. Never read books that make you mistrust the Church, her teaching, or her practices. It should be quite unnecessary, I hope, to add, that medical books, and the indiscriminate reading of Encyclopedias and newspapers, no girl should allow herself.

Among your favourite books will be numbered, I hope, the Holy Scriptures, especially the Gospels, the Lives of the Saints, and of those noble followers of Christ and the Saints, the men and women of our own times who have sanctified themselves in the same station and by the same duties that have fallen to our lot, who have battled with our difficulties and temptations, used well our opportunities, and led beautiful, unselfish lives of blessing to all around them.

Such books are plentiful in our day, and it would be a sad pity to miss the encouragement they give us. Remember that our mind is like the plate of the camera. The objects we put before it, whether noble or paltry, will be imprinted on it. What kind of impressions do we want engraven there?

XIII
A Traitor

"The talks are getting very dry. I didn't understand a bit about the books yesterday."

"No, we never have anything nice now."

You are right. It is really too bad of the big ones to ask the questions they do and spoil the talks. There must be a change this very day. What would you like, now, for our talk this evening?

"It couldn't be about a sea-serpent or a magician, could it?"

"Or a ghost?"

Would a traitor do as well? That I think we could manage, and we will begin with the priest-hunters, who always interest us.

For more than two hundred years, as you know, our Catholic forefathers in this country could say, with St. Paul, "We die daily." The prisons "were so crammed with Catholics that there was scarcely room for the thieves." And the prisons themselves, apart altogether from the torture chambers, were so horrible, that the frequent deaths from the sufferings endured there excited no surprise. Year after year these sufferings went on—fines and imprisonment, torture and death, the penal laws increasing in number and severity as time went on. It was death to become a Catholic, death to harbour a priest, death to confess to him. Those who would not go to the queen's church in the reign of Elizabeth were punished with ruinous fines, and, if they could not pay these, were imprisoned and had their ears bored with red hot irons. Even those who lived in great houses spent their days amid fears and dangers.

But the nights must have been the worst. Think of lying awake, trembling at every sound, for the precious life of a priest was sheltered beneath the roof, and at any moment the hunters for that life might break into the house and search it from garret to cellar.

Of all the perils that surrounded them, what did they fear most? Not their declared enemies without, but a traitor within the house, a servant who for a miserable reward might betray his master and bring ruin on the household.

"What a pity the masters did not find the traitors out in time and put them in prison!"

"If I found a traitor, I'd chain him in a prison underground and give him nothing but bread and water for the rest of his life."

I am not so sure about that, but we shall see.

"Then are there any traitors now? I should love to see one—chained up, you know."

It is just possible you may have your desire before we have done. In the meantime let us try to get on the traitor's track.

The Catechism tells us that the last of the three enemies we have to fight against all the days of our life is "the flesh," that is, "our own corrupt inclinations and passions, which are the most dangerous of all our enemies."

"Isn't it rather hard, don't you think, to have to fight against our very own selves?"

Not rather, but very hard indeed, and this shows it was not part of God's plan in the beginning. He did not mean anything to be hard for us. It is sin that, by spoiling His plan, has brought

in all this pain and trouble. In Paradise nothing was difficult because all was in order. The body was subject to the spirit, never hurt it, never hindered it, never wanted what was not good for it, or more than was good for it; was never idle, selfish, going wildly after pleasure, even forbidden pleasure, simply for pleasure's sake. The body obeyed reason and conscience, and these obeyed the law of God. Whilst this subjection lasted, all went well and happily.

Then came the serpent with his temptation, different for each; and our first parents fell, Eve through curiosity—she wanted to see what would happen if she ate the apple, if they would really become gods as the serpent promised—Adam through his love for Eve. He could not bear to refuse her anything, and ate the apple to please her.

At once all the order of that peaceful garden was disturbed. Adam and Eve, the creatures of God, had rebelled against Him, and in punishment, everything rebelled against them. The earth they had seen covered with flowers and fruit, that they had cultivated and cared for by way of pleasant recreation only, became stubborn, and, except by hard labour, grew nothing but thorns.

But all this was nothing to the rebellion within. Anger, revenge, the mad desire of pleasure, any pleasure, all pleasures, rose up in their hearts and clamoured for gratification. The rest of their lives was a struggle with these unruly passions; and this lifelong conflict with self they left behind them as a miserable legacy to their children.

We find it waiting for us one and all when we come into the world. As soon as we can be made to understand anything, we have to be taught how to say "No" to ourselves. When we come to the use of reason, our passions, which have grown with our growth, begin to give more trouble, as those who have charge of us in the nursery and the schoolroom could tell us. Confirmation comes, making us soldiers of Christ, and soon we are in the thick of the fight. The years from ten to twenty are for the greater number of us the most dangerous time of life. The passions are strongest then, and unless by God's grace we are stronger still, they will overcome and ruin us. The words of the Catechism are unmistakably plain: "Our natural inclinations are prone to evil from our very childhood, and, if not corrected by self-denial, will infallibly carry us to hell."

"I thought only mortal sin could bring us to hell."

True; but any one of the passions if not held in check—anger, covetousness, vanity, gluttony, idleness, the excessive love of comfort—will drag us into mortal sin. We must be on the alert; we must find out where our special danger lies, and protect ourselves specially there.

"How can we find it out?"

In most of us there is one passion which dominates or lords it over the others, and for this reason is called the predominant passion. It is on this the devil mainly relies for our ruin. "If I am to get that soul," he says, "my chance is there." He is very quicksighted, he has studied us carefully, he knows us well. He could tell us to a nicety what our ruling passion is. But we can discover it for ourselves.

"How?"

By finding out in our examinations of conscience, not only what we have done, but why we did it. If we discover that many of our faults spring from the same root, we have a clue to our predominant passion.

"But what do you mean by 'passion'? I thought it was getting into tempers."

We use the word in that sense, but it has a much wider meaning. The passions, properly speaking, are tendencies or inclinations which draw us towards certain things and away from others,—towards anything that holds out to us a prospect of pleasure, away from what would bring us pain. Pride and vanity make us like praise and flattery, whatever will raise us in the opinion of others and in our own; sloth and gluttony incline us to all that gratifies our taste or our love of comfort. Anger, revenge, and envy are the rising up of our nature against something that has thwarted or vexed us.

"Then the passions are bad things?"

If by "passions" you mean simply the likes and dislikes God gave us in the beginning, it is clear these are not bad in themselves. They were meant to be helps, not hindrances, And this they may be even now. Love, hatred, fear, desire, all help us on our way to Heaven. The Saints had, most of them, strong passions, but they kept them in check as a skilful rider controls his steed and makes it go his way and not its own. St. Francis Xavier was naturally ambitious. He wanted to do great things. And he did great things—few men have done greater. The desires which, left to themselves, would have spoilt all that was noble in him, and made his life a thoroughly selfish one, he turned to the glory of God and the good of his neighbour, and thus his natural temperament, aided by grace, helped on his own salvation and the salvation of the thousands who, under God, will owe their eternal happiness to him.

The passions, then, may help us very much, and as long as they are under the control of reason they do help us. It is when they escape from the control of reason that they become bad and lead us into sin. And, unhappily, they are constantly trying to escape. Since Adam's fall they are like restive horses that rear and try to throw their riders, and want to rush here and there just as they like.

The predominant passion of us all is selfishness in one form or another.

"It seems so natural to love one's self that I can't think how people can help it and how it can be wrong. And yet I know, of course, that selfishness is hateful as well as bad."

There is a proper love of self which is reasonable and right. We are bound to love our soul above everything in this world, to keep it from harm, to get it ready for Heaven. We are bound to take a proper and moderate care of the body as to health, food, work, rest, and the like. And we are bound to desire for soul and body the eternal happiness prepared for them.

But this rightful love of self is apt to get out of order, and so we have pride, vanity, ambition, springing from an excessive self-esteem; sloth, gluttony, impurity, which come of an excessive love of the body. Anger is the indignation we feel against everything that contradicts our likes or dislikes; Covetousness, the craving for pleasure, that makes us desire the goods of others; Envy, the repining at another's success because we wanted this for ourselves.

Most of us, if we examine our hearts honestly, will find that one or other of these is our predominant passion. The greater number of our faults spring from it. Without it we could go freely on our way to Heaven. We must resist it, then, bravely and perseveringly, not thinking we can conquer it in a week, not discouraged if we fall again and again. Every blow weakens it and deserves an eternal reward. If on our deathbed we are still fighting it, our Lord, when we meet Him at Judgement, will say to us: "Well done!"

Some, who have much at heart the conquest of their predominant passion, go to work in a very systematic way. They keep a little book in which, like good merchants, they enter their daily losses and gains. They compare day with day, week with week, month with month, thanking God when things have gone well with them, humbling themselves without discouragement when the record is disappointing.

"I call that business like!"

The reason why the third enemy of our souls is more dangerous than the other two, is because it is so near and dear to us. The devil and the world are outsiders, but the flesh is part of ourselves,—far harder to tackle therefore than the others:—

> "All others are outside myself;
> I lock my door and bar them out,
> The turmoil, tedium, gad-about.
>
> I lock my door upon myself,
> And bar them out; but who shall wall
> Self from myself, most loathed of all?"[1]

"Why, you said just now we love ourselves, and now you say we loathe them!"

Get a little older, and you will understand how in this case we can both love and loathe. Self is a companion whom we flatter and pet, though we know it is always getting us into trouble. But there are times when we feel it is a traitor, when, <u>afraid and weary</u> of it, we cry out:

[1] Christina Rossetti.

> "If I could set aside myself,
> And start with lightened heart upon
> The road by all men overgone!"[1]

"Is the devil quite real—a real person, I mean?"

As much a person as our next-door neighbour. Though we cannot see him, he is constantly near us, watching us, whispering to us now and then, waiting to see if we will do as he tells us. He is very clever and cunning, and he hates us so much that he will never be satisfied unless he can see us utterly and hopelessly miserable. But in spite of his strength and malice he can do us no harm, except by forming a league with the traitor Self, who keeps the keys of our fortress.

You remember the story of Tarpeia—how she coveted the golden bracelets of the Sabine soldiers, and promised to betray the fortress to them on condition of receiving what they wore on their arms. So do our enemies from without gain entrance into our soul, let in through the eyes, ears, and other gates by a traitor, for the sake of some miserable gain.

"The story is not quite like. She didn't get anything for her treachery, because they crushed her to death with their shields as they went in. But we do get some pleasure, don't we, if we let in the enemy—I mean just for a little while?"

Undoubtedly, or there would be no force in temptation. It is the fidelity which renounces the pleasure there would be in yielding to the tempter, that God rewards. But, after all, the gratification we find in satisfying our passions is very short and leaves behind a lasting sting. "It is by resisting our passions, not by giving way to them," à Kempis tells us, "that we find happiness and peace."

The earlier we begin the conflict with self, the better it is for us. You could have easily killed the baby lion that the keeper put into your arms the other day. But wait a few years

---
1 *Ibidem.*

till it gets strong, and it would not be hard to tell whether you or the lion would do the killing then.

"I couldn't have killed it, I really couldn't. It looked so sweet with its round yellow eyes, and its velvety paws, I wanted to put it down and play with it."

Just what we say to the bit of friendly advice: "Get rid of that habit of staying in bed in the morning after you are called; of taking wine whenever you can get it; of speaking in a saucy way to those above you. The habit is stronger than last year, it is growing dangerous, get rid of it." And we, poor silly things, say: "I can't overcome it, I really can't. Some day I will, but there isn't much harm in it now, you know." And so, whilst we are playing with it and fondling it, the lion cub grows.

It is the beginnings of harm that we must watch and check; "after-remedies come too late," à Kempis says. "If we would use a little violence in the beginning," he says again, "we might afterwards do all things with peace and joy." We must watch over our thoughts, our imagination, our inclinations, our will. If we find we are inclined to indulge the body overmuch in the matter of food, drink, sleep, comforts, or amusements, we must go against these inclinations and deny ourselves in these things, remembering what we said just now, that the sooner we enter the fight, the easier, quicker, and more thorough will be the victory.

And the happier we shall be. Is not a free man happier than a slave? Do we not prize our liberty above all things? Then we must guard it jealously or we shall be robbed of it. Dear children, there are boys and girls who are slaves already to a tyrant passion. It has got the better of them, they feel helpless in its clutches. They would like to shake it off, but it is too strong for them, they say, and so they sink down discouraged and give up the struggle.

"What ought they to do if they feel like that?"

Remember that nothing is too strong for the grace of God, which they can get by prayer and the Sacraments. If their will is weak, these will strengthen it; if they want advice or help in any shape, there is their confessor at hand. They must never give up the struggle, not if they break their resolution twenty times a day. God is on their side, loving them, pitying them, calling them back to Him, never tired of them however often they fall, never giving them up.

"But it's very hard, isn't it, to be always trying and never being any better?"

That would be hard certainly, but it is not the truth. We are always better for trying even when we fail. Effort is always gain before God, though before others and before ourselves even, it often counts for nothing. So we must take courage and begin in earnest the fight with our lower nature. "If you want peace, prepare for war," says the proverb. There is no other way of getting it. We must rouse ourselves, show some pluck, rise above the fear of difficulty that keeps us from being what we might be, what God wants us to be.

> "God harden me against myself,
> This coward with pathetic voice
> Who craves for ease, and rest, and joys:
>
> Myself, arch-traitor to myself;
> My hollowest friend, my deadliest foe,
> My clog whatever road I go.
>
> Yet one there is can curb myself,
> Can roll the strangling load from me,
> Break off the yoke and set me free." [1]

"Is that all? You promised we should see a traitor before we had done."

And surely you are satisfied. "What greater traitor could you wish to see than the body, which, instead of helping the

---
[1] Christina Rossetti.

soul, its master, is always ready to betray him to his enemies?

"But I meant a real, live traitor, a proper one, you know."

The one we have discovered is real enough, and very much alive; not proper, there I agree with you, nothing could be more improper than for the servant to turn round upon his master and fight him. Yes, surely, you have found the traitor you were seeking. Here he is, ready to your hand, to be thrust down into "the underground dungeon and kept upon bread and water all the days of his life," as you threatened.

"I didn't know he was going to be me!"

No, and so you spoke out honestly and told us what a traitor deserves. If he does not get all his deserts, at least give him a taste of them now and then, and keep an eye upon him always.

Is there any one else who thinks the traitor has not been found?

"I have been thinking that the soul and body are like Samson and Dalila. He knew she would betray him to his enemies, yet he kept on loving and trusting her all the same."

XII

"Work Your Work Before the Time."[1]

We were saying yesterday that we have to go against ourselves and our unruly passions or we shall be quite spoilt, not only of no use in this world but in the way.

We have a work to do in life, and we must fit ourselves for it. Again and again, both in the Old and New Testaments, we are reminded of this—that heaven is held out to us *as a reward to be won*, not as a rich legacy that will come to us of itself without exertion on our part and whether we deserve it or not. "Work your work before the time, and God will give you your reward in His time"(Ecclus. li). "God hath tried them, and found them worthy of Himself"(Wisd. iii). "Trade till I come," says our Lord (Luke xix.); "The labourer is worthy of his hire"(Luke x). In the parable of the Labourers He shows them coming for their pay in the evening. He shows us too, in another parable, the unprofitable servant severely punished, not for making a bad use of the talent entrusted to him, but for making no use of it at all.

Many leave school, where they have learnt no end of things, without having learnt this lesson. It never seems to have come home to them that work, real labour of mind or

---

[1] Ecclus. li.

body, is a duty laid on all, high and low, rich and poor, clever or dull, the rudest and the most refined.

English law deals in a very simple, straightforward fashion with those who fail to understand this, and refuse to work for the support of their family. In 1905 a man was charged with doing nothing whatever for the maintenance of his wife and three little children. He had worked for three days and a half since his return from South Africa four years before. He lay in his bed each day till noon or later, singing in a drowsy voice:

> "Here lies the body of poor old Bill,
> Who never worked and never will."

His sentence was six months' hard labour, which sentence he received, the public were told, "with some surprise."

The chief thing we have to learn at school is how to work, how to turn to account the gifts God has given us, that we may be able to employ them later on the task in life awaiting us.

Catholics no longer live a life apart from their fellow-countrymen. The old gloomy house within iron gates, where Cardinal Newman, as a boy, was told Catholics lived, is a thing of the past. We have come out of the seclusion of penal times in which our forefathers passed their days, "the world forgetting, by the world forgot."

But Emancipation, if it has freed us from persecution and restored us to our rights, has brought us new duties. There is question now, not only of preserving our Faith, but of living a life of Faith openly before our countrymen and countrywomen, drawing them to respect it, to admire it, and, please God, to love and embrace it. Our concern now should be, not what we *must* but what we *may* do in the service of God and of the Church.

To educate, as the word implies, is to "lead out" the powers that lie within us, to develop them by exercise, and—which is quite as important—to teach us how to control them, so that they may be serviceable, not harmful to us. Its object, if it is worthy of its name, is to make the best of every boy and girl, by training the heart and the conscience as well as the mind and the body; forming their character as well as cultivating their gifts, and this, not for the children's welfare only, or to turn out good citizens useful to their fellow-men, but first and foremost for the service of God and for that work in life which He is going to entrust to each.

Now, who do you suppose has the chief part in the work of our education?

"Well, it depends; I should say our nurses and our mothers when we're quite small, and then of course our masters when we go to school or college."

"And the sergeant for drill."

All these have their share, but I asked who has the chief part, without whose help all these labour in vain?

"I expect you mean ourselves."

I do. Unless we go heart and soul with our instructors, our education will be more or less of a failure. Nothing satisfactory can come of halfhearted work.

"You don't know our sergeant or you wouldn't talk like that. I shouldn't like to be the fellow who would try to give him half-hearted work."

"No, nor some of the other masters either."

Go heartily with all who have to help you, in what, mind, is your own work, the cultivating of your gifts, the making the best and most of yourself. There are boys, and girls too, who will throw themselves with goodwill, nay, with enthusiasm, into one department of their training—say their drill or their sports. They won't grudge sixteen shillings for a bat; they will sit up at night and rise early in the morning to study for an examination. But they have no time or interest to give to the care of their soul, to its training, to preparation for the examination it has to pass. Is not this a great mistake? If the aim of education is to cultivate the habit of finding interest in serious subjects, surely the most important subject of all—our Religion—ought not to be an exception.

To develop ourselves on one side only is to be like the *Welwitschia mirabilis*.

"The what?"

The *Welwitschia mirabilis*, an African tree which attains the age of a hundred years and more, yet never grows higher than a few inches above the ground, and never gets more than its first two leaves. The trunk increases in circumference yearly, till it may be eighteen feet in girth. It stands like a round table, growing year by year but never rising. We must not be like the *Welwitschia mirabilis*.

What we neglect to cultivate, we lose at last. You wished the other day you could transport your cousins' garden here and look after it for them.

"Yes, it's completely spoilt since they went to school."

Any one been meddling with it?

"No, it's just because no one goes near it that it's in such a state—roses eaten up by grubs, carnations lying all over the ground, beds crammed with weeds; the whole place so disgracefully neglected that it might never have had any pains taken over it—and it used to be so lovely!"

There are a few roses still, I believe, the *Malmaison* and *Gloire de Dijon*?

"Yes, but worth nothing, they've gone into quite common kinds."

See how soon beautiful things degenerate if left to themselves. We shall be like that garden if we let ourselves run to waste. If we neglect the proper care of the body, disease will set in; if we fritter away the time given us to improve our mind, we shall grow up ignorant and useless. Worst of all, if we leave our soul uncared for, if we simply let ourselves go—no effort, no restraint in any direction—there will be sin, and, sooner or later, mortal sin. Think what a shame it would be if, with all the advantages you have now, you were to leave school with your mind as uncultivated and your character as unformed as when you went.

"Couldn't we make up the time afterwards?"

No more than you could sow your seeds in the autumn and expect a plentiful crop. It is too late, the time for sowing is past. Your mind has lost its freshness, its power to take interest, to seek out its food and grow upon it.

> "Youth once gone is gone:
> Deeds, let escape, are never to be done."[1]

The ponies that live down in the coal-mines become blind; an arm or a leg never exercised would get rigid and useless. Men in solitary confinement go mad because their mind has nothing to work upon. And the powers of our mind and

---
[1] Browning, *Sordello*.

heart, if not cultivated whilst we are young by healthy exercise, become enfeebled and ruined.

"I always wonder why the servant who hid his talent was punished so much, because after all he didn't do any harm with it or lose it. He kept it safe and gave it back when it was wanted."

You forget this—that he *was* a servant, the talent was not his own. It was entrusted to him to trade with in his lord's service. His master had a right to receive it back increased by his industry, as in the case of the other servants. Because he had neglected to do this, he was justly punished. Our gifts, whether of mind or body, are not given merely that we may enjoy them selfishly. A strict account of the use we have made of them will be demanded of us, and we must every one of us labour, yes, really labour to improve what has been confided to us. If we think that because we have received small gifts only, because we are not brilliantly clever, we may fold our hands and do nothing, we shall be punished like this servant who was called not "slothful" merely, but "wicked."

And notice this—what he had refused to use properly, was taken away from him and given to a servant who was already rich, because our Lord and Master is so pleased with those who put to advantage the talents bestowed on them, that He rewards them with new favours.

We are bound, then, to cultivate for the service of God what He has given us. He will know how to make use of it when the time comes. Try to improve any talent you may have. Do not think the duty of improving yourself ends with school life. So far is this from being the case, that your life at school will have done much for you if it has aroused the desire to carry on afterwards the line of study there begun.

Be sure of this—that God wants some special work of you, a work for others as well as for yourself; the reward He has ready for you hereafter depends upon your doing this work for Him. Therefore He has given you certain gifts which He has not given in precisely the same way to any one else, because no other is to have the privilege of doing Him this particular service. "Work *your* work," He says to each one of us. But the gifts you will want for your work are not put into your mind and heart full grown and ready for use. They are seeds which you have to cultivate carefully so that they may be ready when God's time has come. When that time will be, you know no more than you know what the work itself is to be. God leaves you in this uncertainty that you may hunt up and bring forward *all* He has given you, that you may look into yourself and notice what your capabilities and tastes are, for a reasonable taste often points to that work in the future which is to be given into our hands.

None of us, then, are free to go through life without a purpose, or to let the possibilities within us be wasted for want of development. Just think how ridiculous it would be to leave undeveloped the photographs you took last week.

"But how can we have a purpose when we don't know what we ought to do, nor what we're good for?"

A sensible question. We cannot know at the outset of life what our life's task is to be. But we know there is a vocation for every one of us.

"But I'm going to be an admiral, not a priest!"

"And I'm not going to be a nun!"

A vocation is not merely for priests and those who take the vows of Religion. Vocation means "call," and there is such a call for each one of us. Work for the service of God which is to win us our crown in Heaven, means any good done for His sake, and there is plenty waiting to be done on every side.

We labour in the dark, more or less, cultivating the gifts, which He has fitted in an admirable way to the service He has in store for us. Suddenly, when we least think of it perhaps, our work is laid before us. Opportunities open out; our long preparation produces its fruit; we take up earnestly what God has put in our way, and, carrying it on resolutely and perseveringly, find in this work, not only the means to a reward hereafter, but a source of peace and contentment, a very real happiness even here.

Don't waste time dreaming of what you might be and do if only you were in a different place and different circumstances from those in which God has placed you. But take up the work that lies ready to your hand, and do it brightly and courageously for His sake. Until your great choice of a state of life is made, and you know the place and way in which God wants you to serve Him, make the most of what you do know. The best way to learn His Will for us in the future is to do It faithfully where It is made known to us in the present.

"How can we choose a state when God has chosen it for us already; mustn't we do His Will when we know it?"

There are some things as to which God lays His Will upon us by way of precept and under pain of sin, which means that we cannot go against His Will in that matter without sin. In the Ten Commandments He imposes His Will in this way, as a Law.

But often it is not His Will to bind us under sin. He would like us to do this or that; it would be good for us and bring us most securely on our way to Heaven. And so He invites us and promises us the grace we need. But His Will here is a counsel only. If we are wise we shall follow it. But we may choose, He leaves us free.

"Does God want us all to choose the best life, like priests and nuns?"

Certainly not. What is best in itself is not always the best for us. The life of a priest or a nun would be no help to many on their way to Heaven, and God does not call them to it. For many there is no choice in this matter; ill health, the duty of caring for parents who depend upon them, family troubles, and many other circumstances, may show plainly that God's Will for them is where His Providence has placed them, and that it would be folly to seek for it elsewhere. Everywhere there is work for Him to be done—in a crack regiment, among the little ones in the nursery, in the rush of a London season, beside a deathbed, with an invalid mother in a country home. Showy work even in God's service is not necessarily the noblest or the best. The most heroic is often found in very humble life where humdrum duties and daily trials are gone through cheerfully and perseveringly for God's sake. What we have to do is to find out His work *for us*. This we discover, as I said before, by prayer and by noticing our capabilities and our circumstances as well as our inclinations and our desires.

The marriage state is holy, and our Lord has made a special Sacrament for those who enter upon it. He honoured the marriage of Cana with His Presence, and worked His first miracle there out of kindness to the bridegroom and the bride.

So much, both for ourselves and for others, both for our happiness here as well as hereafter, depends on a right choice when the time for choice comes, that boys and girls should pray earnestly for guidance: "Lord, what wilt Thou have me to do?"(Acts ix). "Teach me to do Thy Will, for Thou art my God"(Ps. cxlii). "Make the way known to me wherein I should walk, for I have lifted up my soul to Thee"(*Ibid*.). If they will pray like this, they may be sure that God will take the care of their future upon Himself and "order all things sweetly" for them.

"Do all boys and girls pray to know what they ought to do?"

That is not for me to say. But if we may judge by the mistakes that are made later by so many, the hasty steps taken without reflection, without inquiry or advice, we should fear that God's Will and His loving designs for them are too often forgotten, and that the gratification of their own desires is all they think about.

It is very unchildlike as well as very foolish not to take their Heavenly Father into their confidence in this matter on which their happiness both for time and eternity may depend. He does not send us into this world to find our way back to Him as well as we can, by any road. But He has prepared a path for us, provided with all the helps we shall need to profit by the opportunities, the joys, and the trials of life. He earnestly desires to see us enter safely on this path, and we may be sure there is no prayer to which He listens more willingly than to the cry of His child to find its road: "Make the way known to me wherein I should walk; teach me to do Thy Will, for Thou art my God." Nor is there any matter in which our Lady of Good Counsel shows herself more interested and more motherly than this. Let us ask her, then, to take it into her keeping:—

> "Be of all my friends the best and dearest,
> Be my Counsellor, sincere and true,
> Let thy voice sound ever first and clearest,
> Mother, tell me—what am I to do?"

But just look at the clock! Your questions take a great deal of answering, and we must put off till to-morrow what I was going to say when you turned me out of my course.

XV

Joan

We have missed a day; I forgot the school treat was coming, and that we should be away all the afternoon.

"Hadn't we a glorious time! I do wish school treats would come every day."

"I don't; I hate them; they're stupid."

"Why, I'm sure there was plenty to do. What with keeping the children supplied with cake and strawberries, and amusing them after tea, we hadn't a minute; and they did enjoy themselves."

"Well, I didn't. I began to tell them about the ghost of Maddern Hall and they wouldn't listen, and wanted me to play at Hopscotch with them."

"And did you?"

"Of course not—a vulgar street game like that!"

"And what happened?"

"I don't know; I didn't stop to see; it was hot, and I got into the shade and read a book I took with me."

"I'll tell you what happened. Joan came along and they asked her. And she said she didn't know the game, but she'd try. So she did. But she hopped all wrong. And you know how fat she is. And they did laugh. But she didn't mind. And then some of the babies got hold of Father Pat, and dragged him to the squares and made him try, and stood and watched him. And he tucked up his cassock and gave three great hops, all wrong. You should have heard them laugh. And then they made him be a grizzly bear and run after them. Oh, it *was* fun; I do wish it could come every day!"

"Didn't Joan look hot and tired? But she stayed to the very end, and helped to dress the babies when they went home at last. Their pockets were stuffed full of bits of cake, and some had strawberries squashed up in a bit of paper to take home to "Dadda" or "Mummy."

"I wonder why Joan is always in such request at school treats?"

"Because she's always so happy and makes other people happy, I suppose. She's always like that, you know, not only at treats but always. She is going to take the little ones to the seaside next week all by herself, and you can think what a bother it must be to be with them all day."

"Well, I do call that cool!"

"Oh, I beg pardon most humbly, 'the present company excepted,' I should have said, but you are not one of the quite little ones now. I don't know what they do without Joan when she is away; the whole house goes to rack and ruin I expect. She is her mother's right hand, and there is always some bother with the servants when she is not there; but they will do anything for her, she's so nice to them. And so she is to people who call—to stupid people even, and it makes them stay ever so long; it must be awful for her, but she doesn't seem to mind."

"And you know how she enjoys the theatre or a dance. Well, she gave up her chance of going to see 'Peter Pan' because her father, who is almost blind now, likes her to read his newspaper to him at night—all about the Stock Exchange and stupid things like that."

"I don't wonder at her being kind to her poor father, but she's kind even to people she doesn't know. Mother says that at a dance she'll find out the shy girls and the oldish people, and talk to them and make it pleasant for them. You know some girls seem afraid to open their lips and look quite scared if you speak to them. Well, she finds out what they like to talk about, and they do talk to her and get quite lively and enjoy themselves. It's a gift, mother says."

Yes, but you must not mistake mother's meaning. When she says it is a gift, she does not mean that it has come of itself without the trouble of cultivating it, like the flowers in Paradise. No one can be habitually kind to others—to father and mother, little brothers and sisters, servants, neighbours, strangers—and be a welcome presence everywhere, above all in her own home, without a great deal of self-forgetting charity. So we must not think that because we do not feel Joan's "gift" in ourselves, we are therefore excused from the duty of showing kindness to those among whom we live. It will never do to find out some day that we too had this "gift," and that it was meant to bring joy into the lives of many, but because we were too selfish to cultivate it, it has died down and borne no fruit.

Dear, bright, unselfish Joan! Let us learn from her to put our likes and dislikes into our pockets when we want to be of use to others. At school treats we will think, not what would amuse *us*, not what *ought* to amuse those poor children, but what *does* amuse *them*. They are cooped up in their narrow courts and stuffy homes all the year round, and when July brings their one grand holiday, they must be left free to enjoy it in their own way by using their legs and their lungs to the utmost. Let them go scampering and shouting all over the place. Step down from your dignity and let them have a laugh, even at your expense. Help them to amuse themselves after their own fashion, unless of course they want to do it by breaking their necks. Forget yourselves; remember it is doing a great work for God to make a little child happy, and that our Lord has promised to take as done to Himself whatever we do for these dear little ones of His.

"He wasn't speaking of school treats."

"He said 'Whatever you do,' therefore school feasts are included.

It is this spirit of cheerful self-denial that has called forth our Holy Father's admiration for the Catholics of Germany.[1]

"The blessing of God," he says, "is visibly extended over the action of the German Catholics, as a reward for their deep and constant spirit of sacrifice, and of their Christian spirit of abnegation."

"Doesn't he admire it in English Catholics too?"

That I have not heard. But if we want him to do so, we must afford him the opportunity, and give evidence of the noble spirit we would have him admire. We must look to ourselves and see if there is any foundation for a charge that has been brought against us.

We are told by those who see a good deal of English girls, Catholics and non-Catholics, when they have left school, that whilst in every town and village the non-Catholics are actively taking part in the good works afoot for bringing help and comfort into the homes of the poor, the Catholic girl seems to think that, beyond working now and again for a bazaar, she has nothing to do for any one outside her home circle, and may harmlessly spend all her time and energies on hockey, golf, hunting, or even fencing. Abroad it is not so. French

---

[1] This appears to be a reference to the *Kulturkampf*—that is, the systematic repression of Catholicism by the Prussian Protestant majority following the unification of Germany in 1870. Despite increasingly draconian measures, the Catholics remained defiant, and by the 1890s the aggression had substantially calmed.

Catholic girls are, as a rule, much more active in charitable work among the poor, by taking a Catechism class, by visiting, needlework, &c.

Now this is a serious charge. Can it be that our Catholic girls fail to realise that when they leave school they go out into the world to do *a work* there, and that only by work is a reward to be earned? Many of course do realise it, and go out with eager eyes and hearts to seek for their life's task—

"I can devote myself; I have a life to give."[1]

This is the cry of their souls. They hear with envy of what girls are doing elsewhere; of Irish girls who even at school have formed themselves into a guild under the direction of one of the nuns, with some "old girls" and married ladies as the managing committee for advice; who have their needlework guild, for which each girl makes one garment a month; their "milk association" to supply new milk to the destitute poor that have young children or invalids; their monthly meetings to make known cases of distress and distribute clothes according to the needs ascertained from *personal* knowledge. For some of the older girls are allowed to visit the poor in their own homes in order to discover the most deserving objects for charity.

The girls also endeavour to promote neat and well-kept cottages among the poor by offering small prizes to those who come up to the requisitions for cleanliness and order laid down by the visitors. These prizes, given at Easter, prove very attractive to the poor people, and astonishing changes have been brought about in a few months in homes which were formerly pictures of squalor and destitution.

This girls' guild has interested me so much, that I cannot resist giving you an account of the prize-giving in the words of one of the energetic young workers:—

---

1 Browning, *Paracelsus*.

"When Easter came, the greatest excitement prevailed, which was equally shared between competitors and visitors. We all wrote our reports in the 'big book,' and at a meeting of the sodality these were read out and compared.…So thorough and widespread was the reform, that out of forty houses only five or six were considered undeserving of rewards. The prizes consisted of useful household articles, such as cups and saucers, spoons, plates, teapots, kettles, jugs, also pictures, table-cloths, quilts. We all started, laden with gifts, looking more like a troop of travelling gipsies than anything else. The joy with which we were received in each little home could not have been greater had we been the bearers of fortunes to each, instead of such simple rewards. What was more satisfactory was that the inmates themselves, in most cases, had turned over a new leaf. They began to realise that they too were God's creatures, and that they should respect themselves as such— the result was clean faces and a tidy appearance, and in many cases more frequent attendance at Mass."

"For many weeks before Christmas," one of the members writes, "all our spare moments were employed in making clothes for the poor, but it was only the privileged 'visitors' who were allowed to remain in after school hours to do extra work. How we enjoyed those evenings in, all sitting round the table chatting merrily and working the machine in turns— some cutting, some tacking, some silent. Then when the day came for distributing the clothes, what times we had, and how we enjoyed seeing the delight of the little children over their new frocks!

"When May came it was suggested that the guild should erect little May altars, in each of the houses of our poor, and we spared no pains. Before the month began we made little lace curtains and altar cloths, &c., for thirty altars of Mary, and on 'May Eve' we had a 'bran pie,' out of which each of us drew a statue; each of us had a favourite amongst the poor and wished to secure for her the prettiest statue of our Blessed Mother. It was delightful to see the warm reception our poor people gave us, and you could scarcely imagine the change which the promise of 'May altars' had worked in many of the houses. Instead of the dirt and rubbish which before disfigured them, they looked bright and cheerful, the walls white-washed, and in some places decorated with coloured paper and silver stars. The little ones ran off to gather flowers, and soon returned laden with primroses and violets; one poor woman had a statue of her own, bought by her son, which she had safely treasured for almost twenty-five years. To another poor old widow, almost bed-ridden, the May altar was a source of delight and consolation. We erected it over her bed, and she says now when she is awake at night, she is not in the least lonely."

Another member of the guild writes: "We had a Mass celebrated for all our poor who had died during the year." The guild has also supplied a *Basket* for their parish priest, containing all the requisites for carrying the last Sacraments to the dying. And they have a *St. Anthony's Box* which has brought bread to many a starving family.

But who shall tell the gain to the workers themselves! Let us hear the experience of one.

"The first day we went to visit the poor, we learned many things we never knew before. We could not believe that such rude poverty, often starvation, really existed amongst these poor people almost close to our doors, and whom we passed every day in our careless glee. Their patience and resignation, their unfailing trust in Providence, and many other beautiful virtues made a great impression on us."[1]

---

1 A. Wilson, "Catholic Social Work," *The Crucible*, March 1906.

"I wish we could do things like that, but we shouldn't be let."

"I should love to make the 'May altar' and the 'bran pie.'"

"And to carry the kettles and jugs and spoons and plates to the cottages."

I am sure you would, but you must bear in mind that the work of the guild is not all pleasant by any means. Though the members paint the bright side of the picture only in the extracts I have given you, there is another side which we must not forget. Once the novelty is over, it is not always enjoyable to turn out of one's comfortable home to visit the little homes of the poor, to give up a game of golf or hockey because one's petticoat or frock is not ready for the monthly meeting; to put by some part of one's pocket money for the prizes; or for many weeks before Christmas to remain in after school hours to do extra work. Mind, I do not say it is not pleasant, but that it is not always pleasant. So that if the pleasure to oneself in giving, the joy of being received gratefully in each little house, the delight of making a bran pie, were the only or the chief motive of the workers in their charitable labour, they would soon tire and give it up.

The intention, by which the value of such work is to be judged, is tested by the way in which a girl meets the disappointments it is sure to bring here and there. If she is disgusted and angry because the appearance of a little home is not improved at once on her representation, or because the "May altars" are not dressed to suit her taste, or because the gratitude of her poor, so gushingly expressed at first, dies down somewhat after a time, and her help and presents, which really cost something, you know, come to be taken as a matter of course; if she is huffed because the elder ladies of the committee do not take her advice, or the parish priest under whose supervision the girls act does not approve her schemes straight away; if, in short, because she cannot have everything her own way, she becomes disgusted with the whole business, neglects her engagements, and shows herself unreliable and difficult to work with, she may have plenty of "go" in her and the best of brains and hands, but she has not got that without which no undertaking for others can be carried on with patience and perseverance—the power to forget oneself in the service of God, and plod on steadily, not because we like what we are about and find it as interesting as it was at first, but because it is something we can do for His Glory and for the souls He loves.

Those who can labour for this motive, who can cheerfully persevere in face of difficulties, and sacrifice for God's interests, not only money, time, ease, and pleasure—but *Self*—these are the people by whom great works are carried through.

Such must surely be the motive that animates these brave young members of the girls' guild, for we find that when their school-days are past, they look forward to taking their place on the committee as managers and thus continuing their service on a larger scale.

Let us wish them success, and learn a lesson from them. If we cannot take up all their good works, there is sure to be something we can do, and every little helps.

"I asked Father Pat to take me with him last week when he went to see the poor man in the condemned cell, and he said: 'Run away and make the Stations for him instead.'"

And did you?

"No, because I hadn't time, I had my rabbits to feed."

What was it you said to mother yesterday when she told you you might help her to tear up old linen for bandages?

"Oh, I said I didn't care for that, but I would have gone with her to the hospital in a minute."

Never mind "caring" for this or that act of charity. Do it for something better than your own amusement—because you can help one who is in trouble, because you can serve our Lord in His poor suffering members, because He will take all you do for them as done to Himself.

"But you don't mean it is *quite* the same as if we made bandages for our Lord?"

I only know what He says Himself: "I was hungry and you gave Me to eat, thirsty and you gave Me to drink, naked and you covered Me, sick and in prison and you came to Me."

"Well, I never thought of that before."

"Look here, I was horrid at that school feast, but I'll see what I can do next time."

XVI

Home and Homemakers

"The little ones have tired themselves out with their day at the Zoo, and are gone to bed. Couldn't we have that talk that was to come off some time when they were not here?"

By all means. We go over their heads a good deal, I fear, but they are very good and patient with us.

What I should like to say after yesterday's talk is this—if we wish to do good work later when big opportunities may come to us, we must make a beginning, and seize upon small occasions now. Tear up linen for bandages, run errands, make yourself useful where you can, gain little victories over yourself, all this is capital training for the future. It is like nursing. When there is war abroad and a call for nurses comes, only the trained are sent out. It is too late to qualify oneself when the need appears in the papers. Those who want to go must be ready with their certificates, which show them to have gone through a long course of training and to be experts in the arts of unquestioning obedience and self-conquest. We, too, must train ourselves in good time if we want to be of use later on.

"Lots of nurses that we knew went out to South Africa, without being certificated."

Yes, and these inefficient helpers were called at Mafeking the "plague of ladies." I was speaking only of the competent nurses sent out from Whitehall.

If we want to do really useful work later, we must go in for training now. It is disconcerting to be told that Protestants are found to be more self-sacrificing and persevering in what they undertake than Catholics; that Catholic girls seem to look upon their charities, and even upon their home duties, as all very well when nothing more important or interesting comes in their way. But of course these occupations must not be allowed to interfere with their pleasure. Because their work was taken up voluntarily, they seem to think they may dispense themselves when they please from the duties it imposes. Without any thought of the consequences to others, they will sit down and write a note of excuse: "I shall be going to the theatre to-night and be too tired to attend to-morrow." These notes come so often, we are told, that the services of Protestants are preferred.

"I call that most unfair. Look at Joan and that guild in Ireland. Those Irish girls do not take up work and leave it just as it suits them. And if Joan does not do much outside her own home, it is because she is at every one's beck there from morning till night, and surely her first duty is to her own people!"

Certainly. I agree with you perfectly. But, after all, Joan and the Irish guild do not make up the sum total of the girls turned out by the Catholic schools of the United Kingdom. Mind, I am not admitting the truth of the charge, but should there be the slenderest foundation for it, we should look well to ourselves and seek out the cause and the remedy.

The main danger on leaving school is worldliness. Many Catholic girls seem to live for nothing but excitement and pleasure. Unless they have a lawn-tennis party or a dance in prospect, they are out of sorts, wearied and bored at everything. They must see and hear whatever is going. If there is a hippodrome or a military tournament, they must see it; a famous singer or player, they must hear him.

"And where's the harm?—there is nothing wrong in a circus or a concert."

No, not in *a* circus or *a* concert, not in moderation therefore. But when pleasure becomes the occupation of life, it is wrong. For then worldliness sets in. God is left out of that life; the soul is neglected and starved, and sooner or later it will die.

"Yes, girls are so soft, always thinking of dressing up and enjoying themselves. I'll tell you some worldly ones. There are those—"

Never mind them. What we want are home thrusts, not attacks on our neighbours. It is not by any means our girls only who have to examine themselves here. "The growing spirit of selfishness," we are told, "is a real menace to the country, and it will break out in all sorts of ways unless our young men are taught to realise its ugliness and to fortify themselves against it. What is wanted is that they should stir up in themselves a real desire to make the best of their lives, to build up their characters, to enlarge their knowledge and their sympathies, to work together shoulder to shoulder in order to remedy the social evils of the day."

"You always come back to selfishness."

Because it is this that spoils us all. If we would wage war against it, gaining a little advantage every day, we should find our lives expanding in every direction. New interests and new desires would wake up within us and take us out of ourselves, new powers of mind and heart develop, and a new happiness shed its brightness over our own life and the lives of many thus brought into contact with ours.

"I have heard people say there is so much misery in the world that anything done to relieve it is but a drop in the ocean."

And is that a reason for doing nothing? If those who content themselves with lamenting the evil in the world would show some practical sympathy, by contributing even one little drop towards its alleviation, in the shape of money, clothes, time, offers of service—how much they would find might be done!

"Where could one begin?"

In that sphere where God Himself has placed you—your own home. There is our first field for exercising ourselves in the virtues of patience, forbearance, helpful and indulgent kindness, in the habits of self-control and self-sacrifice which must enter later into any work for those outside.

Do all you can to contribute to the brightness and happiness of home. Pass over unnoticed little slights and annoyances; "*Laissez tomber, laissez passer,*"[1] as Père de Pontlevoy used to say.

When a girl leaves school and has had some weeks, perhaps, of rest and holiday, she should take up some serious occupation and regular duties—that is, she should have at a fixed time in the morning some regular employment for which she is responsible. You know some girls who are expected to give their mornings to self-improvement in one shape or another.

"Yes, their mother lets it be understood that they are not free, as a rule, to go out sightseeing in the morning—not as a rule, you know, but she is always glad that they should enjoy themselves in the afternoon."

"And they do, I promise you, ever so much more than those who have the whole day to do what they like with."

It would be well if at least one hour a day could be devoted to some intellectual pursuit, whether morning or evening, as circumstances require. Unless the habit of study is kept up when we leave school, all relish and capacity for mental effort is gradually lost. It is not a bad thing to go in for stiff music or drawing examinations, for instance.

---

1 "Forget about it, let it pass"

"Some people don't approve of examinations; they think they make girls conceited."

We have good authority for saying that toil, real, hard toil, is a preservative against conceit.

"But what is the good of it all? Your music is only wanted now and then, and your drawing never."

If preparation for such examinations were merely a means of employing our leisure hours innocently, and of giving pleasure to others later, it would be well worth the time and labour. But there is much more than this. The cultivation of a rational taste opens the door to knowledge in many directions, and gathers together stores which will be sure to be serviceable in the future. God will make use of all, none of it will be wasted.

"Mother says she will not give up the housekeeping to us when we leave school. She likes to keep it as long as she can."

Then you will have the advantage of seeing and learning a good deal before these duties devolve upon you. But I am sure there are some things she will be glad to make over to you. Set yourselves to get a practical knowledge of these. A girl who can cook a dinner, make a dress, entertain company, has opportunities in her hands which give her a great advantage over those who are helpless in these respects.

The great thing is to be thorough in all you do, and reliable. "Whatsoever thy hand is able to do, do it earnestly," Solomon says (Ecclus. ix). Some girls are profuse in their offers of help, but they must do things after their own fashion, and so long as there is no great tax upon their time and their convenience. But if their methods are not appreciated and at times call forth remonstrance, they give themselves airs, answer saucily, cause disturbance, and the matter ends by the tired mother taking back into her own hands the duties she had been persuaded to relinquish, and remedying as best she may the mistakes of the young amateur.

It is in the home, as Wordsworth tells us, "that we find our happiness, or not at all."

And the makers of home happiness are the wives and the mothers, the daughters and the sisters there. If these are not what they should be, the house may be as stately as you like, but it will not be a "home." But where they realise their responsibilities and are unselfish and devoted, there, however poor and lowly the household may be, is home and happiness.

The peace and gladness of a home depends on the order there. Parents are to be reverenced as well as loved. "Honour thy father and thy mother," is a Commandment of God, and one, it is to be feared, much neglected in these days. Children forget that they have to show themselves respectful and obedient as well as affectionate. Their predecessors in the English homes of pre-Reformation days, could teach them many a useful lesson in this matter. They were taught to say with respect, "Yea, father," "No, mother;" in their morning prayers to ask that the coming day might be spent

> "To Thy honour and joy of our parentes,
> Learning to lyve well and kepe Thy commandmentes."

They were warned never to be wanting in due reverence and courteous behaviour to their parents: "What man he is your father, you ought to make courtesye to hym all though you should mete hym twenty tymes a daye."

> "When that thy parents come in syght doe to them reverence.
> Aske them blessing if they have been long out of presence."

You will all remember how the Blessed Sir Thomas More, even when Lord Chancellor, was wont, before sitting in his own court, to go to the place where his father, Sir John More, was presiding as judge, and there on his knees crave his parent's blessing on the work of the day.

The beautiful custom of the Evening Blessing which still survives in some countries, in Belgium for instance, where grown-up boys will kneel for their father's blessing before going to bed at night, was common in English homes in the days when all England was Catholic. How one would like to see the practice revived amongst us!

Speaking of the Fourth Commandment, an old writer says:

> "Teche your children to axe blessing every night, kneeling before their parents under this form: 'Father, I beseech you of blessing for charity,' or thus, 'Mother, I beseech you of charity give me your blessing.' Then let the Father and Mother holde up both ther handes and joining them both togyder look up reverently and devoutly unto heaven and say thus: 'Our Lord God bless you children,' and therewith make a cross with the right hand over the child, saying, *In nomine*," &c.
>
> "And if any child be stiff hearted, stubborn and froward and will not thus axe a blessing, if it be within age, let it be surely whysked with a good rod and be compelled thereunto by force. And if the person be of forther age and past such correction and yet will be obstinate, let them have such sharp and grievous punishment as conveniently may be devised, as to sit at dinner alone and by themselves at a stool in the middle of the hall, with only brown bread and water, and every person in order to rebuke them as they would rebuke a thief and traitor. I would not advise ne counsel any parents to keep such a child in their house without great affliccyon and punishment."[1]

A parent was frequently warned in those days "not to spoil his son," by neglecting a "gentle whysking," when it was deserved.

Let me read you a few sentences, which will explain this duty of reverence to parents better than I can do.

"God did not deem it necessary to give a command to parents to love their children, but He did command that

---

1 "Christian Family Life in pre-Reformation Days." Abbot Gasquet.

children should honour and love father and mother. Children should never forget that the greatest sufferings of parents come too often from their own children, not merely when they seriously offend them, but also when they treat them in a cold, contemptuous way. Parents are more sensitive to a look from a child than a child is to a blow from a parent. This comes, in part at least, from the children having no memory and the mother a very keen one, of all the anxieties, perils, and trials which she had to endure for her children when they were young. Children who have come to a certain age have a right to give their opinion in free matters, and even remonstrate if they think a parent too severe, exacting, or unreasonable, provided they do so in a respectful manner. But in any disputed question between members of a family the child should, of course, yield to the parent, not the parent to the child."[1]

"What are children to do if they can't honour their parents, if their father and mother are cruel to them or bad as they are sometimes?"

Let us see what our author says about that.

"If, on account of serious faults or unfair treatment, children cannot have for their parents that love and respect which they would desire, and that they even have for them a feeling of dislike, they must still observe the Fourth Commandment and treat them with respect. This is not easy and it can be done only through grace and from a supernatural motive. But children so placed should console themselves by the thought that if they overcome natural feeling and act against it in order to observe the Commandment, they will have far greater merit, than if they were influenced by natural love. There may be merit, but not much, in doing a thing which costs little or nothing, or which we like to do. That which is hard to flesh and blood, when done for God, is the best?"

---

[1] "Woman." Fr. Walsh, S.J.

There are children who think it smart to be pert to their parents. They have no spirit of reverence, no respect for age or authority. It shows "spirit," they think, to toss their heads and proclaim their right to do as they like, say what they like, go where they like, for no other reason than because they like.

Our Holy Father Pius X says:

"There is a poison in the air which infects men with contempt of authority and those vested with it, and which is making great ravages among young persons."

Boys and girls who are well brought up are pained to see parents treated like this, and do not admire their children. Still less are they inclined to envy them, for they do not find in such households where the word of father and mother goes for nothing, the peace and contentment of their own homes. Visitors, instead of applauding the forward ways of such children with strangers, and their disrespectful behaviour to their parents, are disgusted. So that if a reputation for cleverness and spirit is what these children have in view, they are woefully out in their calculations.

But what is worse, is the harm to their own souls that comes of this disregard of God's strict command to honour parents, a commandment our dear Lord enforced by His own example when He was on earth. He had so much at heart this reverence to parents, that it is the only thing He would have recorded of His early years.

"He went down with them and came to Nazareth and was subject to them....And Jesus advanced in wisdom and age and grace with God and men"(Luke ii).

He gave three hours to the work of our redemption; three years to His work of preaching, training His Apostles, and founding His Church. But thirty years to teaching the children who were to be His followers, teaching them by His own example, the honour and reverence to parents which He so strictly requires of them.

What a wonderful thing obedience was in Him! For think who they were to whom He was subject —His own creatures, in one respect as nothing in His sight. Of the Three in that cottage home, He, the Child of the family, was the highest and holiest. Yet He was treated as a child, not consulted as to arrangements, not asked what He would like. His hours for work and play, for meals and sleep were fixed by His Mother. Her words to Him in the Temple, when at the age of twelve His Father's business required that He should act for once without her knowledge and permission, show her surprise at what was quite unusual with Him: "Son, why hast Thou done so to us, behold Thy father and I have sought thee sorrowing."

He asked their leave to go here and there: He spoke to them with reverence as well as affection, because they were the representatives of His Heavenly Father, and as such had real authority over Him. He consulted their wishes, was thoughtful and considerate for them, spared them anxiety and pain whenever He could; and after this one instance of staying behind in Jerusalem to be about His Father's business, was all His life at Nazareth—subject to them; subject therefore, long after the time when boys and girls believe themselves freed from the law of obedience.

"When are they free?"

As they grow up, the duty of obedience ceases to bind to the same extent, or as it was enforced a century ago, when people were treated as children till they were nearly thirty. But the duty of honouring parents never ceases. Not even when young men and women leave their parents' roof and go out into life and form homes of their own, can the Divine Commandment be set aside.

What, then, are we to think of those who at twelve or fifteen fancy themselves completely grown up, want to judge and manage for themselves, and too often resent all control!

"Parents," says one of our bishops, "ought to know whither their child goes, who are its companions and friends, and how the hours of recreation are spent. They ought to teach their children to be gentle and kind to each other. Brothers and sisters should dwell together in peace, their relations with one another should be marked by respectfulness, affability, and good temper. Dr. Grant used to say: "Teach children to be polite to brothers and sisters as though they were strangers.'"¹

An author I was reading this morning shows how much the happiness of parents depends on their children's behaviour to them. Shall I read what he says?

"If you like, and it's not too long."

"Nor about 'gentle whyskings.'"

You do not approve of that, I see. Yet the benefits of "whysking," whether gentle or the reverse, are not confined to the pre-Reformation child. A man of note tells us that at the age of twelve he announced to his father that he was no longer a believer in God. "Whereupon," he says, "my father gave me a sound thrashing, with the result that I have believed in God ever since."

But now for my author:

"One would like to get the ear of children and suggest to them how much their parents' life, which means peace, hope, and joy, depends on their conduct, in speech and deed, in manner and bearing. If young people could only put themselves in their parents' place, wonderful things would follow. Some idler who will not work from motives of fear, or ambition, might be spurred by love, if only to save his mother from reproach. Some thoughtless, selfish girl might deny herself whims and pleasures to bring satisfaction to the hearts of her people. Some young man might bear himself with a little more humility, and even condescend to give occasional information about his movements, if he had any idea of his father's feelings on certain occasions. Parents are kept at a distance, are denied proper confidence, have their wishes, tastes—if you please foibles—disregarded, look in vain for signs of affection and gratitude, have their just pride in their children wounded, not because the children are bad or cruel,

---
1 Bishop Gordon.

but only because it does not occur to them that, although they consider themselves independent of the old folks, the old folks are continually, willingly, pathetically dependent on them for what is more than living, or rather for what is the heart of all living—for love."[1]

Oh children, see what you can do and bear for those who have done and borne so much for you. Spare yourselves the pain of realising when it is too late what you might and ought to have been to them. A day will come when you will have to leave your home with all its familiar surroundings and sacred associations. "As the day draws near—a day no one can ever forget when he passes out of the old homestead for the first time—there is a tumult in the heart. The unspeakable privilege of a good home—the daily oversight, the spoken advice, the kindly offices, the sense of protection, the warmth of love—suddenly arise before the memory, and are appreciated to the full, just as they are about to be lost. The vague dangers of the new life, its strange faces, unaccustomed duties, lonely circumstances, unexpected temptations, possible hostilities, powerfully affect the imagination and darken the future. The lad does his best to show a smiling face, for the sake of those whom he is leaving, and he recognises that this outgoing is inevitable, but there would be something wrong with him if his heart did not sink and his eyes were not dashed with tears at the turn of the road."[2]

And there is another day sadder still, when those two who made the home are taken from us, and we know that we shall see their faces no more. How many look back then upon the past with regret, not to say remorse. There may be nothing very definite, perhaps, with which to reproach oneself, but,

---

1 "The Potter's Wheel." J. Watson.
2 *ibid.*

somehow, the most devoted and affectionate heart finds matter for self-rebuke then. It is not only what we did, but what we have left undone. We might have been so different! Words, looks, manner, the tone of voice, the neglect of little services, the heedlessness that was slow to see what pained, that was too sure of its road to put up with remonstrance or advice—all this rushes upon the mind and makes one long for one hour in which to plead with them that if we were thoughtless, wilful even in the past, the fault was on the surface only; that our hearts were right, and that deep down in them was what they were too careless, or perhaps too proud to show—their sense of the priceless blessing of a good home, of a father's and a mother's love.

XVII
Coming Out

"Why did you say yesterday that it is the mothers and wives and sisters and daughters who make the home? There are fathers and husbands and sons and brothers as well."

"And home's a noisy place, and I'm sure it's the boys that make the noise—mostly at least!"

As to the last statement I should not like to give an opinion. But noise is not the main thing in our minds when we think of home. There is plenty of it certainly, musical and otherwise—shrill voices and laughter, whistling even and singing, and the sound of nimble feet coming and going. All this no doubt is part of our idea of home, but not the chief part surely. What else is there?

"Oh, it's all so jolly, don't you know—no lessons and no rules—at least only home rules, and you can do what you like, and everybody's nice, and we are all together, and there's always some fun going—oh, it's glorious to be at home!"

"And there's a great deal more than that. Preliminaries and Juniors have no idea what real work is, and so they can't enjoy rest as we do when we come home. It's such a blessing to be able to sit down in peace and have some good reads without being driven about from one thing to another. And then we've father in the evenings and mother all day."

It is a shame to speak of analysing when we are talking of home and holidays, but were we to take our idea of home to pieces, we should find, I think, that it is to the womenfolk that the credit of being homemakers is mainly due.

The sense of freedom which you allow to be compatible with home rules, the atmosphere of cheerfulness and kindness, the contentment that comes of peace and order, and above all, the happy companionship of father and mother, and brothers and sisters—do not these things depend mainly on the wife and mother, the sisters and daughters of the household? Let these be selfish or indolent, disorderly or cross-grained, and where is home then?

"Could you not say the same if the men and boys were all those things? They can be quite as disagreeable and aggravating as women when they like, and disturb the peace even more."

No doubt; but the question was, not who can best destroy, but who can best make the happiness of home. By the nature of things the home is woman's domain; there she rules, and on the character of her rule depends the happiness of the household. It belongs to the mother and the wife, yes, and to the daughters and sisters, to make home cheerful for the father and brothers when they come in tired from work. They have a right to all that makes home attractive—cleanliness and order, and that attention to external beauty which adds so much to its refinement and power for good.

With the exception of the very poor, whose time and energy are absorbed by the earning of the daily bread and absolutely necessary cares, all can expend some small amount of money and interest on the adornment of their home. Flowers carefully tended in a cottage window argue well, it is said, for the state of things inside. Now, ordinary flowers and a few pictures are within the reach of most of us, and the difference their presence or absence makes, we must all of us have felt. You remember how it was by attention to such details that our friends of the Irish guild improved in so short a time the condition of the little houses around them.

But the chief attractiveness of home is found in its inmates, and it is not too much to say that it rests with the daughters and sisters quite as much as with the mother to make it all it ought to be.

A girl's real "coming out" is when—school life over—she takes her place in home life and becomes, let us hope, an important factor in its happiness.

She *comes out* then and there, not before or elsewhere. Up to that time—I am speaking of girls who have been for some years at a boarding school—she has been known to her own people in holiday time only, when more or less amusement and excitement, a great deal of unselfishness on the part of those about her, and on her own, a general sense of satisfaction at the efforts of all to give her pleasure, have hidden to a great extent her real character except from a few close observers.

It is when she settles down into the home circle as one expected to give rather than to take; when humdrum, trivial duties have succeeded to excitement and pleasure; when the little frets and rubs that occasionally ruffle the surface of even the most peaceful home, affect her as well as others; when her plans are crossed by father or mother; and brothers and sisters begin to treat her as made of ordinary clay; when, instead of the props to duty that have hitherto supported her, she has to rely on the promptings of her own conscience—then it is that a girl *comes out*.

It is a trying time; unless she is prepared for it, and has herself well in hand, she will be surprised to find *how* trying. It may be so chiefly in one of two ways, and either is a test of the stuff she is made of and of the training, particularly the self-training, school life has given. Let us look at the first of these ways.

Pleasure enters largely into the life of many girls for four or five years after they leave school. There is no harm in this. Youth comes only once, and some time may be given to innocent pleasure and society. But harm comes in, and great harm, when these things are made the business and end of life, when a round of exciting pleasure is the ideal life a girl sets before her. And there is danger of this being done.

The tendency nowadays is to bring as much pleasure into life as possible and to get rid of everything that interferes with self-indulgent ease. The alarming truths of the next life—Judgement, Hell, an eternity of happiness or misery—all this must be kept out of mind, or, better still—denied. Death cannot be denied, but it must never be thought about, still less mentioned. When it comes at last, it is either to lead straight to glory, as a matter of course, or to be a peaceful sleep with no awakening. Meantime let life here be as enjoyable as ingenuity with the help of science can make it—labour as light and as little as possible, convenience and comfort in food, dress, furniture, as much as can be secured.

You, in your well-ordered Christian home, know little as yet of the state of things outside, of the precautions taken to prevent the appearance and disqualifications of age, to escape the inconveniences of heat and cold, and whatever may in the slightest degree offend the touch, taste, scent—any of the over-refined senses.

I saw a letter the other day written from Cincinnati by a young man to his mother, during the spell of hot weather we have been having of late:—

"There is in every house," he says, "an abundance of ice, great blocks of it, 18 inches long by 6 deep and 6 wide, brought every morning, or oftener if you want it, and one can break off as much as one likes for use at table, &c. Then, at every corner of every street, and in the middle of every street, and between the middle and end of every street, there are ice-cream soda fountains where you can get the greatest variety of ice-cold delicious drinks of all kinds for a trifle of money. These make life worth living."

The devil, then, with his allies, the world and the flesh, is leading us to neglect altogether the old-fashioned, hardy virtues of endurance and self-denial; to shirk everything in the shape of unpleasantness or pain, and to make bodily comfort and exciting amusement the aim of life. You have only to go down one street in a big town to form some idea of the devices of the present day for bringing ease and enjoyment into daily life. Third-class railway carriages, padded in every direction, are more luxurious now than the first were fifty years ago.

"And no wonder, when our blotters, our books, our prayer-books even, are padded!"

Dress, furniture, food—all have unstinted time and the most elaborate care bestowed upon them, that the gratification of our lower nature may be provided for at every turn. Amusement is made the one object in life. There must be a "good time" for boys and girls; "evenings out" for servants; "week-ends" for clerks and shop assistants; motoring, and bridge, and cigarettes for the well-to-do all the week round.

Mind, I am not saying that these things are wrong in themselves. Fresh air, exercise, games, are good things; a dance, a tennis-party, a cigarette, a novel, a play, may all be harmless *as relaxation*. It is when these things are made ends in themselves, and the occupation of life, that they become wrong.

What I want you to notice is the very general neglect nowadays to take life seriously or to remember the strict account we shall have to give of it; to note how the fear of sin and of the judgements of God are banished from the minds of men.

We take precautions when we go into an infected atmosphere, and we must be on our guard when we leave school against imbibing the spirit of the world and gradually falling in with the ideas of the day. Unless a habit of self-control has been formed, unless by serious thought and prayer a girl has grasped the true purpose of life, and made a firm determination to balance amusement by serious duties, she will fritter away her time at home, and duty will be quite lost sight of in pleasure.

The first few months after leaving school test a girl's true worth. *Now* she will "come out." *Now* will be seen the outcome of that multitude of little acts of self-restraint or of self-indulgence, the result of which is—character. The strength and the weakness in her will come out now, and her true self, such as her own self-training has made her, be disclosed. There is a deeper reason than at first sight appears for calling this period of a girl's life her "coming out."

"Don't you think it's awfully hard to make plans and resolutions that, will wear when you get home?"

"And harder still not to care too much for pleasure; to see comfortable, convenient, fashionable things all round and not to get too fond of them? I know girls who look all right in school, but as soon as they were home for good, and 'out,' they seemed to think of nothing but dress and amusement."

"Pleasure is awfully exciting, you know, especially in the evening. You say and do silly things then that you are ashamed of next day, but it's hard to hold yourself in at the time."

It is hard to prevent pleasure running away with us, but it can be done.

"How?"

By fortifying ourselves against it before it gains too strong a hold on us. By trying to bring home to ourselves that short answer to the question of the Catechism: "Why did God make you?" Not merely knowing the answer, there is no difficulty in that, but with the help of serious thought and prayer, feeling the force of it, so that it sinks down into our souls and abides there as a deep conviction.

"Why did God make you?"

"To know Him, love Him, and serve Him in this world and to be happy with Him for ever in the next."

Not a word, notice, about pleasure. Contentment beyond our wildest dreams will be ours if we carry out the end of our creation. But it is not itself the end. If it were, the answer would be:

"God made me to enjoy myself in this world. I must, therefore, seek pleasure in everything, as much, as intense, as prolonged as I can get it."

Had this life been the only one intended for us, and had we been bidden to make enjoyment our object in this world, it would have been our duty to give ourselves to the pursuit of pleasure with steady unremitting application. But there is another life prepared for us, the happiness of which is to be inconceivable and everlasting. Our few years in this world are given simply to prepare ourselves for the blessedness of the world to come, by using all things we find here, or that find their way to us here—pain as well as pleasure, want no less than plenty—as means to eternal life. All are meant to serve this end. Therefore likes and dislikes must not be our rule in dealing with these things. We must not take all the pleasant things and shirk all the disagreeable ones, or we shall not carry out the designs of God, we shall not love and serve Him in this world, we shall not be happy with Him for ever in the next.

One proof that I was not made for the pleasures of this life is, that they do not satisfy me. In moderation they are useful, even necessary, to carry on work of any kind with brightness and perseverance. They are the jam on our bread. But whoever tries to have all jam will find, not only that it does not attain its end, but that the relish of it goes and is succeeded by disgust.

Those who have few pleasures enjoy them keenly when they come. But pleasure palls on those who pursue it eagerly and perpetually, whose lives are a round of gaiety and excitement. "Vanity of vanities and all is vanity," was the cry of Solomon after he had "abounded with delights and enjoyed good things. I made me great works," he says. "I built me houses, and planted vineyards, I made gardens and orchards and set them with trees of all kinds. I got me men-servants and maid-servants, and had a great family; and herds of oxen and great flocks of sheep; I heaped together for myself silver and gold and the wealth of kings; I made me singing men and singing women, cups and vessels to serve to pour out wine. And whatsoever my eyes desired I refused them not; and I withheld not my heart from enjoying every pleasure. And when I turned myself to all the works which my hands had wrought and to the labours wherein I had laboured in vain, I saw in all things vanity and vexation of mind, and that nothing was lasting under the sun. Therefore I was weary of my life when I saw that all things under the sun are vanity."[1]

And hear that other cry fourteen hundred years later: "Our hearts were made for thee, O God, and they can never rest until they rest in Thee."

Solomon and Augustine had given themselves up to a "good time," and both tell us, as the fruit of their experience, that nothing of this earth can satisfy the heart of man.

Let us take one more proof of the truth that pleasure cannot be a worthy object to take as our aim in life. If it were, the pursuit of it would ennoble us. Does it do so? Do we find ourselves admiring those whose one thought is to have a "good time"? No, surely. Sought for its own sake, pleasure spoils all that is good and noble in us. We deteriorate visibly and quickly. Eating and drinking, gossip, and dress, and exciting

---
1 Ecclesiastes ii.

amusement, fill our minds from morning till night, and at last we become almost incapable of generous impulses, of anything in the shape of sacrifice or effort, incapable even of serious thought.

Now a life such as this cannot be an innocent life. We need serious work, real effort taxing the powers of mind or body, to keep us out of harm. We might be sure that if Solomon withheld not his heart from enjoying every pleasure, there would be sin—grave sin before long. Emptyheadedness and frivolity are not far off from sin, and they are part of that worldliness which causes the loss of so many souls.

It is not safe, then, to let our animal nature get the upper hand, to let it shirk labour and whatever interferes with its comfort and ease. Our Lord's invitation to us is to follow Him along the steep and rugged path of self-denial; but He goes first, and with our feet in His footprints, the way is not so rough as it looks.

"Isn't it very easy to drift into frivolity? Because, you know, there does not seem to be so much harm in it at first."

There lies its danger. And when we have gone a certain distance along that easy road, the will and the energy to retrace our steps and climb the higher one, are wanting. We must not think, then, that we can stop at will on the downward path if we once let ourselves go. We must restrain ourselves from the first, refuse resolutely to gratify our senses in every indulgence they cry for, and remember that work is what is expected of us in this world. "*Il faut travailler en ce monde,*" the holy Curé of Ars used to say, "*il faut souffrir et combattre. On aura bien le temps de se reposer toute l'éternité. Il ne faut pas considérer le travail mais la récompense.*"[1]

---

1 "We need to work in this world. It is necessary to suffer and fight. There shall be plenty of time to rest for all of eternity. We must not consider the work but the reward."

"Can one know how much pleasure there ought to be in one's life?"

We differ so much in character, capabilities, and circumstances, that it would not be possible to lay down any rule. Our sense of responsibility must come in here to guide us. It might help us to form a judgement respecting our own case, to consider what advice we should give to another situated as we are. Some persons are capable of much strenuous and sustained effort, and can afford to work longer and harder than would be safe for others. But for all alike, some measure of relaxation and amusement is needful to keep them in good working condition; the bow too much bent will break.

Provided we give ourselves conscientiously to our duties at the appointed times, we need not hesitate to enjoy, and enjoy heartily, the intervals of rest and amusement which the day or circumstances bring. God is not a hard taskmaster. He says, indeed: "Seek first the kingdom of God and His justice," but He adds immediately, "and all these things shall be added unto you." Taken in this way, temperately, as means to an end, pleasure is not only safe and meritorious, but more pleasurable than when sought directly, as an end in itself.

There is one more way of preventing pleasure from getting too strong a hold upon us and filling too large a place in our life!

"I think I know—remembering that our Lord had not much of it in His."

Yes, and that is the best and perhaps the easiest way. You remember those words we say in the Jesus Psalter: "O Jesus, make me always remember Thy blessed example, through how much pain and how little pleasure Thou didst press on to a bitter death, that being the way to a glorious resurrection." And St. Bernard's words: "It would be shameful to be a delicate member under a thorn-crowned head." Our Lord and Master was poor and in labours from His youth, and shall I shirk work and weariness? He "pleased not Himself," and "went about doing good," and shall I be content with a selfish, useless life?

We know He does not wish us to be without pleasure because He Himself had little of it in this world. On the contrary, He arranges in His kindness that there shall be a good deal of it in the life of most of us. But He wants us to use it wisely and moderately lest it should turn us from the road on which we are following Him, and to be ready to part with it resolutely whenever in any shape whatsoever it would separate us from Him.

Pleasure seems to have taken us a long way out of our route, as it has a trick of doing, and we have almost lost sight of that second mode in which our "coming out" may be a trying—that is—a testing time. And yet I hardly like to leave this subject without touching upon one or two others that are somewhat closely allied to it. Let us have a talk about one of them to-morrow.

XVIII

ABOUT A JELLY-FISH

The little ones not coming to-night?

"No. Joan called this morning and carried them off to the seaside."

"Just think of it! As if she had not enough to do with her own tribe, she must needs beg for ours, who, she thinks, would like to be with their cousins. So we have been busy getting them off, and now here we are by ourselves in a comfortable sort of desert. Of course it's horribly selfish to say so, but it really is nice to be quiet sometimes."

Shall we make hay, then, while the sun shines, and talk over one or two things which we have been keeping for a time like this?

"'Responsibility' was one of them."

Let us start with that. If I remember rightly, we did start it once before by noticing that the word implies having to answer to some one for a trust confided to us. We may go on to notice that this responsibility increases with our years, and in proportion to the privileges and emancipation which to some extent the end of school life brings. Privilege and responsibility go together like light and shade, you cannot have one without the other.

School-days for some of us will soon be over. The sowing time is not altogether past, for we sow as long as we are in this world. But the spring time, and therefore the best time, is drawing to a close. It is natural, then, to look back upon it to see what sort of seed has been sown and what kind of crop we may expect to reap.

To do this in detail would take us too long. Let us content ourselves with one test. We may say that provided one seed has been well sown, our spring time has been well employed and we may look forward with confidence to the harvest.

If the sense of our responsibility to God, of the necessity of using aright the grand but dread power of free will, has really come home to us, and produced a firm purpose so to use it as to work out the end for which it was given—school life has done its part in the training of conscience and in the formation of character.

"Do you think all girls or most girls feel like that when they are leaving school?"

It is to be feared that in many cases this sense of responsibility has not been aroused, and that girls look forward merely to a golden age of liberty and pleasure. There is nothing wrong, mind, in a girl enjoying her greater freedom. But this must be rightly understood. Does it mean that from being accountable to this person and that, controlled by one rule here and another there, she has passed into a new order of things, in which she is to be accountable to no one, and to be fettered by no rules? No, certainly. There must be "ordered freedom." Home has its rules and its duties which bind no less strictly than those of school, and a generous nature will subject itself to them all the more willingly that they must be to a certain extent self-enforced, and that the fulfilment of them is a condition of the brightness and happiness of home.

A good deal of liberty there will still be, and this, with the training she has had as to the employment of leisure, she may be trusted to use wisely.

Some school-girls, after a retreat, were asked to say what conviction or what practice they thought most likely to steer them safely through life.

One said: "Fidelity to prayer, morning and night."
Another: "Regular frequentation of the Sacraments."
A third: "A yearly retreat."
A fourth: "Regular work."
A fifth: "The realisation that God loves us."
A sixth: "The remembrance that God will always forgive us when we come back to Him."
And so they went on:
"That we must never give up prayer."
"That we can only live our lives once."
"That nothing matters *very* much if we save our souls."
At last one said:
"I think what we need most is to realise that we must not lean on others as we do here, nor expect to be *led* to what is right, but must look to ourselves and be responsible for ourselves. I mean that we cannot take for granted we may do this or that because others do it, read a book against which we have been warned, because So-and-So sees no harm in it, but we must remember we are answerable for ourselves in all these things."

All the debaters came round to this view, and so the champion of Responsibility carried the day.

You will hear it said that our boys and girls must be brought up to be "self-reliant citizens." If this means that they must be made aware that they have a work to do in this world, a work waiting for them, fitted to their hands and strength and brains, a work which they cannot shirk or throw upon some one else; for which they will have to give a strict account, and on the faithful performance or neglect of which depends their happiness or misery here and hereafter—if, in short, it means that they must be trained to act like those who know they have to answer for a great trust—then self-reliance is the chief duty we have to bring home to every boy and girl, a lesson more important by far than all the others put together which take up so much of their time and attention.

When we are going in for an examination, we look up the papers set in former years in order to form a fair idea of what we may expect. We would give a good deal to know the exact questions that will face us on the examination morning.

"That would be unfair."

In a test of this world, certainly. But in the great examination we have all to face, in which we must pass, because failure would mean a miserable eternity, God lets us know beforehand the questions we shall be asked.

Time, talents, health, sickness, friends, books, money, influence—these are some of the subjects of examination. All these things were given for a purpose; not simply for our enjoyment to be used as we liked, but to be turned to account in our Master's service.

What have we done with our life, and with all that was given with life to help us in the work of saving our own soul and the souls of others? How have we used our memory, understanding, imagination, and will? Was our own gratification—the study how to get most amusement or comfort out of everything within our reach—our main object in life? Or did we use in God's service all He had so liberally given?

If we are wise we shall prepare in time our answers to these questions.

In childhood, when your character was unformed and your will weak, you had the leading-strings of rules and the watchful eye of others to keep you on the right road. But little by little these checks and reminders are removed that you may have the opportunity and the merit of using your freewill properly by choosing what you know to be right.

There is less and less of compulsion from without, but you are taught that, so far from having outgrown rules or restraint when school life is left behind, you will have to be more careful than ever lest you should misuse your freedom. The responsibility which to a large extent has rested hitherto on your parents and teachers must now be borne by yourself. You will no longer be reminded as before of your duties; the monitor must be your own conscience. It has had its time of training, and is ready, or ought to be ready, for its work of steering you safely to the end of your course.

The main thing, then, to be brought home to a girl when school time is over, and she is launched into life, whether it be amid the rush of a London season, or the quiet of a country home, is this sense of responsibility. She is not to be led blindly here and there. She must learn to hold her own and remember that she is accountable, not to men, but to God. À Kempis bids us recollect that "He who beholds us is God, of whom we ought to stand exceedingly in awe, wherever we are, and like Angels walk pure in His sight." This conviction trains to seriousness and prudence on the one hand, and to liberty on the other.

A very superior woman, whose enlightened views and deft handling of her charges has much impressed me, says her great concern is to awaken the sense of responsibility, and to form a character.

"I show you what is right," she said to one of her pupils, "now I leave you, my work is done, you must choose your course and take the responsibility of it."

Madame's work of training in this instance was not an easy one. At the age of sixteen the girl was absolutely without character, principles, or self-control, at the mercy of every passing whim or influence under which she happened to come.

"If you were a rock I could hammer you," her governess would say, "but you are a jelly-fish."

By slow degrees, however, a character was developed. To make her feel herself a responsible person, some light charges were given her—to open certain windows at fixed times, have the garments she had undertaken to make for the Needlework Guild ready for the appointed day, take down the hours of lectures and remind her governess of them, and so on. Habits of order were formed by insisting that whatever belonged to her should be kept in its place, and that her appearance and dress should be properly cared for. To train her to unselfishness, she was taught to look after the comfort of others in company, to sacrifice her own tastes when they clashed with those of others, and be glad to make her companions happy even at the price of cost to herself.

The girl responded to the efforts made in her behalf. There was much to be done in the way of overcoming idleness, human respect, vanity, and an excessive love of pleasure. But little by little the work was done. Unsuspected gifts were brought to light; habits of industry, of self-control, and of noble independence took firm root; and I doubt if you will now find many Catholics more reliable, zealous, and self-sacrificing when good work is to be done, than the girl who started life as a jelly-fish.

XIX

"Trade Till I Come"[1]

"Of course the jelly-fish lived happily ever after?"

Most happily, after her battle and victory. No one can expect to be happy till the enemy is routed, hence the old proverb: "If you want peace, prepare for war."

This girl is a signal example of the joyousness that comes of a hard fight with Self, crowned with success at last. The recollection of what she has achieved in many directions by means of very ordinary gifts, brings me to the talk I want to have to-night about the responsibility we are all under of cultivating the talents confided to us. Some of us have many, some fewer, some brilliant gifts, others more homely ones, according to God's designs over us and the work given to each to do for Him. À Kempis warns us against envying those who are more enriched than ourselves, and a little thought will show us that to do so would be foolish as well as wrong. Does the cricketer covet the colour-box of the artist, or the athlete grudge the angler his tackle and flies?

"No, but each one wants to have the best that can be got in his own line—the best baits and rods, or bats and leg-guards."

Exactly, and this is what I was coming to. The best that can be got in our own line is what we must all try to secure, not

[1] Luke xix.

for our own honour and glory, to make a figure, or to eclipse others, but for the glory of God and the furthering of His interests. St. Thomas Aquinas tells us that whatever excellence a man has, is given to him for the service of his fellow-men. Hence we are bound to cultivate by strenuous labour the gifts which will ensure our leading a useful life, and fit us for the special work to which the Providence of God will guide us if we render ourselves worthy of it.

Yes, labour is the word. There must be hard mental effort if we are to get the best out of ourselves and develop fully what is given to us but in germ. In every one of us there are unsuspected powers, just as in the field of the Gospel there was a treasure hidden, that only after hard toil and diligent search was brought to light. This is the reason why we open up the ground in many directions, apply our mind to such various subjects, and widen its interests by exercising it all round.

"But we shall never want half the things we have to learn—mathematics, for instance, or Latin."

Apart altogether from the information given, these subjects have a value of their own. Labour itself, as we have seen, is good for us. The concentration of mind, habit of exact reasoning, wrestling with and mastering of difficulties, that are called for by the study of Euclid, or of a foreign language, are moral as well as mental training. "By enforcing accuracy you brace character," we are told.

Speaking of a woman's education, Ruskin says:—

"Let her practice in all accomplishments be accurate and thorough, so as to enable her to understand more than she accomplishes. A woman in any rank of life, ought to know whatever her husband is likely to know, but to know it in a different way. His command of it should be foundational and progressive, hers, general and accomplished for daily and helpful use…so far as may enable her to sympathise in her husband's pleasures, and in those of his best friends. Yet, observe, with exquisite accuracy as far as she reaches. There is a wide difference between elementary knowledge and superficial knowledge—between a firm beginning and a feeble smattering. A woman may always help her husband by what she knows, however little; by what she half-knows, or misknows, she will only teaze him."[1]

We may say in some measure of the cultivation of our gifts what St. Ignatius says of fidelity to our graces: "Few men understand how far God's grace would take them if they would but follow its lead." And few of us realise the possibilities for good that diligent trading with our talents would bring within our reach. Strain is not called for in this matter or in any other, but conscientious labour is. And if as time goes on some special talent should show itself, it should be developed as far as opportunity allows, for besides the resource thus provided for our leisure hours, such a talent may point to that sphere of usefulness in the future for which God destines us and for which we must be preparing.

Time is a talent—and what a precious one, every moment of it able to purchase us a fresh degree of never-ending happiness in Heaven! Yet is there anything more ruthlessly wasted? People talk of killing time as if it were an enemy. They let it slip away haphazard, going through the day without plan or order, taking up and leaving one pursuit after another as the fancy of the moment dictates, looking out for pleasure everywhere, and as for duties, leaving them for odd moments where there is no room for them.

Danger lurks in leisure hours unless we have some definite design in the employment of them. Hard work, physical or mental, and hard play too, is a shield against evil, but to be <u>doing nothing</u>, or nothing that actively employs the powers

[1] "Sesame and Lilies."

of soul and body, is to lay oneself open to the attacks of the enemy. How often, perhaps, have we learned to our cost that "an idle brain is the devil's workshop." We must call ourselves to account for the use of our hours of leisure and solitude. Coventry Patmore, who at one time held an official position in the British Museum, presented the Trustees in later life with some valuable books as compensation for the time which his conscience led him to think he might have wasted when in their service. We too shall one day be reviewing our service and bitterly regretting any waste in it—but where will be *our* opportunity of compensation? Let us guard against those spaces between duties which, like joints in armour, invite the shafts of the enemy; it is just there a dart may pierce through and wound. "Be never altogether idle," says à Kempis.

You remember the traitor at home who is more to be feared than all our outside enemies put together; how this traitor, the body, has to be watched and controlled and denied what would favour its evil tendencies. Now the atmosphere in which these thrive is idleness. They need nothing but a fit of indolence to come out of their hiding-places and overwhelm us almost before we are aware of their presence. We have to keep them down by living in another atmosphere in which they do not flourish. The energy which throws itself into hard work, physical or mental—into the solving of a problem or the bodily activity of a game—this is fatal to them.

Our mind is an ever-grinding mill; memory and understanding, imagination and will are always at work upon something, but it depends to a great extent upon ourselves what they shall work upon. Our education, physical, literary, scientific, or artistic, besides, as we have just seen, training us to self-discipline, and being in this way invaluable in the formation of character, has this further advantage, that it affords abundant grist for the mill, employing mind and body on what is good and ennobling, or at least harmless, thus crowding out evil that would harm us.

"Our minds, like our bodies, need rest at times."

Undoubtedly. But the rest must be taken wisely and temperately in the case of both, not from a motive of self-indulgence, but to make them fitter for application afterwards. Rest for the mind is found in a change of work, not in doing nothing. To see whether you have used it wisely, ask yourself if you go back to work refreshed and strengthened. The light novel or the comfortable lounge does not always serve the true purpose of relaxation and rest.

There is not one of us who can afford to lay aside vigilance in our hours of leisure. But those who know themselves to be inclined to habits of indolence and self-indulgence must be doubly watchful.

"It seems to me that persons who are naturally indolent are much worse off than others. Their faults may not be so striking and disagreeable as those of peppery people, but they have not the energy to fight themselves that these have."

Could *anything* be more exciting than television?

I am not sure that the peppery folk who have to bear up against the disappointment and discouragement that come of frequent failure, would altogether agree with you. But however that may be, both classes have Self to fight in one form or another, and both must strive with the help of prayer and the Sacraments to acquire those habits of self-discipline which will lead to victory in the end.

Indolence, which rebels against the irksomeness of regularity and whatever calls for vigorous exertion whether of mind or body, is, I grant you, a foe hard to fight, but with the grace of God and patient determination it can be overcome.

There are matters in which the habit of shirking trouble and putting off unpleasant duties may have grave results. It takes trouble to say our morning and night prayers, to examine our conscience at night and before confession, to make a good act of contrition and purpose of amendment, to be in time for a Mass of obligation—in a word, to fulfil duties to which we are strictly obliged. Therefore we must rouse ourselves to exertion, and resolutely pull ourselves together when trouble has to be faced in the fulfilment of duty. Every little victory in this direction helps to replace a bad habit by a good one; "custom is overcome by custom," as à Kempis reminds us, and our will grows stronger every time that we conquer ourselves.

The conviction that comes of serious thought and prayer, supplies motives that little by little strengthen the will to act resolutely in matters that should have a fixed time and not be left to the whim of the moment—such are the hours for rising and going to bed, for prayer, meals, reading or practising, house duties, our daily walk, and the like. Regularity, we are told, is the only way of killing sloth. To oblige ourselves to punctuality in these points, to order in the arrangement of things under our charge, to concentration of mind upon the duty of the moment, and to painstaking effort in all we do, especially in what is not to our liking—these practices persevered in will conquer indolence at last.

And here I cannot refrain from urging on you the importance of having a hobby to which you can always turn in your leisure time, some pursuit of your own choice that really interests you, and develops originality by calling into play your special gifts. A good hobby is a most valuable resource, serving at once the purposes of work and play. Gardening, cookery, needlework, carving, photography, making collections, reading, music, sketching—there are enough to meet every variety of taste. We can choose from among them; but something we must take up if we are to keep out of idleness—*and sin*. From how much foolish castle-building, unkind gossip, and unwholesome reading—to say nothing of other invaders of the leisure hour—does a good hobby save us!

"The cultivation of hobbies is one of the most valuable of all arts. Next to religion, and a sense of humour, it is chiefly hobbies which help us along in the pilgrimage of life; and a good seat on hobbies, as on other horses, can only be acquired in youth. Only in youth, also, can we give those warning words about riding gracefully, and not riding a hobby to death, which we sometimes silently wish to give to more elderly riders!"[1]

Dr. Creighton, late Bishop of London, said that the main business of education is, not to enable people to get on, but to enable them to use well the time when they are not getting on; in other words, the real test of our education is the use we make of our leisure. Few things are a better index of character than our favourite pursuits in those intervals of relaxation necessary to rest mind and body, and ensure the vigour and freshness essential to all good work. Variety is the essence of happiness in work; "all good work," Buskin tells us, "is done with joy."

---
[1] Miss Soulsby, "Stray Thoughts on Character."

Here is a nurse's testimony to the value of a hobby:—

"Ever since I became a Queen's Nurse I have been so glad that I did not give up all my music. The old 'chronics'—and I have a good many of them—do so enjoy the violin."[1] This energetic nurse also runs a convalescent library, organises lectures, and takes patients for drives on Saturday afternoons.

"Mustn't it be delightful for the patients to have a nurse whose whole heart is in her work like that, and whose hours off as well as hours on, are so devoted to them!"

I was wondering if you would notice that—the variety of ways in which she spends herself in the service she has chosen as her life's work. Hours on duty and leisure hours, equally filled, and with a heartiness about it all that is quite delightful.

---

1 *British Journal of Nursing*, May 14, 1904.

XX

"Lord, When did we see Thee Hungry?"[1]

We were saying the other day that to help us in the terrible examination we have all to face one day, our Lord lets us know the subjects beforehand:—
"And when the Son of Man shall come in His majesty, and all the Angels with Him, then shall He sit upon the seat of His majesty. And all nations shall be gathered together before Him, and He shall separate them one from another, as the shepherd separateth the sheep from the goats: and He shall set the sheep on His right hand, but the goats on his left.

"Then shall the King say to them that shall be on His right hand: Come, ye blessed of my Father, possess you the kingdom prepared for you from the foundation of the world. For I was hungry, and you gave Me to eat: I was thirsty, and you gave Me to drink: I was a stranger, and you took Me in: naked, and you covered Me: sick, and you visited Me: I was in prison, and you came to Me.

"Then shall the just answer Him, saying: Lord, when did we see Thee hungry, and fed Thee; thirsty, and gave Thee drink? And when did we see Thee a stranger, and took Thee in? or naked, and covered Thee? Or when did we see Thee sick or in prison, and came to Thee?

---

1 Matt. xxv

"And the King answering, shall say to them: Amen I say to you, as long as you did it to one of these My least brethren, you did it to Me.

"Then shall He say to them also that shall be on His left hand: Depart from Me, you cursed, into everlasting fire which was prepared for the devil and his angels. For I was hungry, and you gave Me not to eat: I was thirsty, and you gave Me not to drink. I was a stranger, and you took me not in: naked, and you covered Me not: sick and in prison, and you did not visit Me.

"Then they also shall answer Him, saying: Lord, when did we see Thee hungry or thirsty, or a stranger, or naked, or sick, or in prison, and did not minister to Thee?

"Then He shall answer them saying: Amen I say to you, as long as you did it not to one of these least, neither did you do it to Me.

"And these shall go into everlasting punishment, but the just into life everlasting."

I have given you our Lord's own words in a somewhat long quotation because of their extreme importance. What can be more important or concern us more than those two sentences of His, one of which we shall hear from His lips some day?

They show us that if we want our Judge to be merciful to us on that dreadful Day, we must be merciful to Him now in the person of those whom He puts in His own place. We must be ready to deny ourselves for their sakes by giving some part of the money we have at our disposal to relieve their wants.

And we cannot begin too early. This is curious about money, that the more we have, the less disposed we are, as a rule, to part with it. The poor are wonderfully generous in sharing the little they have with those who are poorer than themselves. But we, too many of us, hoard up our money to spend it in purely selfish enjoyment. We must be strict with ourselves in this matter whilst we are young and our hearts are tender. Once let them harden towards the poor, and it will take almost a miracle of grace to soften them. Dives[1] saw Lazarus at his gate every time he went in and out without ever being touched by his misery—and our Lord tells us the result.

In the Old Law the Jews were obliged to set apart a fixed portion of what they had for the relief of the needy amongst them. We, under the Law of Love, have no strict obligation to do this. But we have our Divine Master who is to be our Judge, urging us by some of the weightiest words that came from His sacred lips to be kind to those whom He has left in His place. We are not obliged to give them a certain proportion of any money we get, but this is an excellent way of securing our duty of almsgiving against forgetfulness and selfishness. You see we cannot afford to be selfish or to forget. Dives did not dare to say, those on the left hand of the Judge at the Last Day will not dare to say: "Lord, we did not mean to be unkind to the poor, but we never thought about them."

We must think. We must learn to interest ourselves in the sufferings of the poor, to make sacrifices for them, and to cut down wasteful and extravagant expenditure on pleasures and amusements, that a due proportion of what we have, may be at our disposal for charitable uses.

"What would you call a due proportion?"

Opinions on that point would vary considerably, and our own conscience must finally decide. One who has had much experience in the training of girls, says:

"You ought to give away one shilling out of every half-sovereign[2] you spend on yourself…You must dress according

---

[1] Dives is the name often given to the rich man in the parable of Lazarus and the rich man, found in Luke Chapter 16—*dives* being the Latin word for "rich man."

[2] A half-sovereign was worth 10 shillings; thus she is recommending a 10% tithe.

to your station[1]; you must not give in alms what was meant for suitable dressing, any more than you may spend it on sweets…A girl should feel from the first, that money means not only pleasure but also responsibility. She should never have money unless it has some of the duties of property attached to it. She should have enough to feel that her own charities and some amount of sensible spending can be fairly expected from her…It is just as clear a duty to plan our money as to plan our time. Perhaps you do neither. But if so, you can hardly be a faithful steward."[2]

This involves the keeping of accounts, and makes us spend money, not casually, as the whim of the moment prompts us, but on a plan. Remember that first among your duties in this respect comes the payment of debts. Some workpeople, a poor dressmaker, for instance, often need their money badly, but are afraid to ask for it lest they should annoy their customers. You have no right to keep it from them, and should not be required to be asked for it. Till your debts are paid, deny yourself resolutely every self-indulgence in the shape of new things, presents, &c.

"That would make one hurry up, wouldn't it!"

And, whilst I think of it, beware of leaving money about. Many a poor servant has become dishonest through the carelessness of the girls of the household who have left temptation in their way.

Ask yourself what proportion of your money you have given to God this last year, either by putting alms into the poor-box, making clothes for the poor, giving at the offertory, or responding to any of the appeals made from the altar at different seasons of the year.

---

[1] This is not entirely relevant today; see p. 203 for a more detailed discussion of what is intended by this statement.
[2] Miss Soulsby, "Stray Thoughts on Character."

Our Bishops and priests are not rich; they are obliged to meet heavy expenses to keep up their churches, schools, orphanages, &c., and it is only by the help we give that these expenses can be met. They do not like asking. They know, as they tell us, that we are asked often, for the needs are many. But what can they do? Souls must be saved, children taught their Religion, the churches where we hear Mass and receive the Sacraments kept up. What can they do but ask us to come to their help? Ought we not to be glad to do so, to put by something of our own—not applying to father or mother for what we want—but giving out of our own little store? And giving at some cost to ourselves, going without something we want that we may have its price to give away in charity. Do not say when you hear some urgent appeal: "That is for the 'grown-ups,' and does not concern me." It concerns you very much; you can give a little now, and so train yourself to take an interest in Catholic charities which will make you give more when you have more to give. Remember that charity is a duty, that you are growing up, and that the kind of "grown-up" you will be later will depend very much on the way you are training yourself now. Your father or mother may point out to you the duty of almsgiving, but they will not oblige you to give. You know the subjects for examination on the last dreadful Day; it rests with you to prepare yourself for it.

The misery on every side of us is appalling. Close to luxurious homes, are hovels where the poor are herded together in want and wretchedness beyond description. Many are forced to spend weeks without doing a stroke of work. And it is the children especially who suffer in consequence. They are ill-fed and ill-clad, often having nothing but what might be called rags on their feet; without fire by day or warm bed-clothing at night. Gifts of boots, blankets, sheets, and clothes of every kind are needed by those who visit and try to relieve them. When winter comes, help is asked to provide Christmas dinners, food, clothing, and fuel. Those who can do it are invited to visit them in their dull homes and in the monotony of the workhouse, taking with them tea, sugar, snuff, toys, sweets, pictures—anything that will help to make a merry Christmas for those who are easily pleased and who will reward their donors with their blessings and prayers.

"I should like to do that sort of thing, but I don't care to give in church or put into the poor-box. There is a satisfaction, you know, in dressing a child, and hearing the grateful thanks of the poor people. One likes to see what one gives appreciated, it is only natural."

Quite so, and because it is "only natural," we must take care to supernaturalise our giving, or it will not be the Christian charity required of us and deserving reward. Our Lord will say on the Great Day: 'You did it *to Me*; come, blessed of My Father." There must be some sort of reference to Him in what we do or give to lift our almsgiving above mere philanthropy and make it Christian charity.

"Isn't that rather a selfish way of looking at it? The main thing, surely, in giving is to relieve the needs of others, not to earn reward for oneself. If one can get reward too, so much the better. But what one has to see to chiefly is to help; *the reason why* you help doesn't make any difference to the poor provided you do help."

Not badly put for a philanthropist, but not the correct view for a Christian. The "reason why" makes all the difference, not to the helper only but to the helped. For not only is the supernatural intention needed to make the good work deserving of everlasting reward, but it is necessary here and now to the character and continuance of the work itself. Take away the Christian charity that sees Christ suffering in the person of the poor, and you will find philanthropy unable to do its work either acceptably or perseveringly. Natural benevolence can do something, but it is not strong enough to bear up against monotony, failure, ingratitude, persistent self-sacrifice.

Philanthropy could not welcome slavery, to redeem a widow's son; or leprosy, to lighten the lot of lepers. Nature breaks down under long-continued strain, but charity such as burned in the heart of Vincent de Paul, or of Father Damian, "beareth all things, endureth all things, never falleth away." It can do all things in Him who strengthens it, and for His sake.

And Christian charity differs from mere philanthropy, not only in its power to do and to endure great things, but in its whole character. There is a humility and a reverence, a gracefulness, a tenderness in its dealings with the suffering members of Christ, that can only come from Faith. And it is in these things that the charm and acceptability of our service lies. The poor are sensitive, the appearance of condescension hurts them. Those who know them best and help them most, are taught by charity all manner of innocent devices for sparing their feelings and enabling them to accept relief without prejudice to their self-respect and without pain. It is faith and charity that tell us the poor, however rough and even repulsive at times, are our brothers and sisters, children of the same Father, redeemed by the same price, destined to live together for ever in the same Home.

"Therefore from the beginning the follower of Christ has been taught to see Christ in the poor and the needy. The Church has always put aside a substantial part of her revenues for the poor, because to her the poor represented her Lord and Master. The monk, in his rule, receives the poor man who knocketh at the door even as Christ. The Bishop washes the feet of the poor to make some return to Christ for having washed the feet of the first pastors. Kings and queens who believed in the Gospel, have fed the poor at their tables and ministered to them, seeing well, in their intelligence of Christ's word, who it was that all the time received their pious duty. Saints have kissed the feet of the poor and pressed their lips with burning countenance upon their wounds, because they realised the vivid presence of their crucified Lord. This is the spirit of the Gospel. Extinguish that spirit, and you may comfort men and women by your charitable work, but it will not draw either you or them nearer to God."[1]

I saw a picture once that has often helped me as I passed the poor-box. It was not one of the great Masters—oh dear no! but a very indifferent print, showing a hand dropping a coin into the box; and within, the Infant Jesus receiving it and clothing Himself with the little robe it gave Him. You may smile, but that print has made a difference in my almsgiving, and that, after all, was the object of the designer, I suspect.

English charity in Catholic days was beautifully homely in its fashion of giving, as when the mother of St. Thomas à

---
1 Bishop Hedley.

Becket weighed against her little son, laid in one scale, food and clothes for the poor, put into the other.

"How the poor must have prayed to see him grow big and heavy!"

The homely ways, thank God, have not quite died out amongst us.

A priest, visiting in a Catholic family, tells how, on the Feast of the Epiphany, the household assembled to witness the children's offerings at the Crib. The tapers around being lit, the function commenced by a hymn, after which the two little girls, and then the son and heir, a boy of seven, went up in turn and laid their offering, a shilling, at the feet of the Holy Child—their own savings, mind you, the outcome of self-denial in the shape of sweets and other luxuries. Considering, no doubt, that public prayer would befit the solemnity of the occasion, the boy said aloud as he made his offering:

"Dear Infant Jesus, I give You a shilling for the poor. Please buy something cheap with it, that it may go further."

"He will have heard his mother discussing ways and means for the Christmas charities."

What she thought of his views on the subject of Domestic Economy, I do not know, but that he should have had any at all, spoke well for the children's training.

We must not forget the spiritual works of mercy, as far above the corporal as the soul excels the body. I should like to have a talk about these too, but it must not be to-night.

XXI
"God's Coadjutors"[1]

"A girl I know never has anything to spare for charities. She says she really hasn't it to give, and that once you let yourself get interested in the poor, giving becomes a perfect craze, driving you to the most ridiculous lengths, so that you never know where to stop."

"Oh blessed craze!" I should be inclined to answer, "that never knows where to stop in giving to Christ."

Bunyan tells us of a young woman whose name was "Dull." She would be no great acquisition, perhaps, to our evening talks, yet I would rather have her and the whole family of the Dulls than a young person whose name is "Perversity," a first cousin to that "Mary, Mary, quite contrary," of whom we learned in our nursery days. She is never happy without a difficulty or a grievance. It soothes her to know there are spots in the sun, discords in music, eccentricities in Nature, and imperfections in Art; in all things except articles of Faith and the multiplication table, abundant room for protest and dissent. She twists your words out of all shape, strains your similes till they snap, promptly sets her foot on anything like enthusiasm, and is always ready to show you the mischievousness of what appeals to others. Had she been here when we were speaking

---

1 1 Cor. iii.

of the necessity of curbing our love of pleasure, she would have objected:—

"Are we never, then, to enjoy ourselves, but go off all of us into a desert, like St. John?"

Had she heard us last night speaking of the necessity of denying ourselves for the sake of the poor, she would have broken in with:—

"Must we wait, then, till every beggar in the world is comfortably off before we can buy a new hat? Or are we to give all our new things to the poor and keep the rags for ourselves?"

"The provoking creature! But really I shouldn't know how to answer her last objection. It is a difficulty, isn't it, to know how far charity should go?"

The charity of Christ presses us in varying degrees—much charity, much generosity; little charity, little generosity; no charity, no generosity. The heroism of charity is not for all, but let us at least admire what we have not the courage to imitate. "Admiration is the delighted recognition of something superior to oneself." It is the outcome of humility, unselfishness, and the nobility of mind that cherishes high ideals. And all these it fosters in us. Hence admiration is a thing to cultivate. Let it go out freely to what is lofty and beautiful—to the heroism of self-sacrifice above all, and even though our own attainments in this direction may never go beyond mediocrity, the maintenance of a high standard will keep our practice far above the level that low ideals can reach.

"'Perversity' was speaking of dress. That is a difficulty with many girls, I imagine; I mean, to know what is right to spend on oneself."

I should say, let your dress be in good taste, modest, and suitable to your age and position. Beware of three defects respecting it: (1) Of anything unworthy of a Christian girl and a child of Mary Immaculate—such as slovenliness on the one hand, and on the other, the vanity and vulgarity betrayed in unseemly display, or in the adoption of extremes in the matter of fashion: (2) Of giving too much time and thought to the subject of dress: (3) Of ordering what you cannot pay for within a reasonable time. Let me remind you once more, because of its extreme importance, that not to pay debts quickly when money is wanted is dishonesty and cruelty. If girls would bear in mind that of the four sins crying to Heaven for vengeance, two of them are sins of this class,[1] would not the fear of God's judgements—failing other motives—prevent the thoughtlessness which brings distress, and at times utter ruin, on those whom they employ?

"What about the spiritual works of mercy we were to have to-day?"

We must content ourselves with the first of them, that glorious work of instruction, of which the Scripture says, that those who practise it "shall shine as stars for all eternity." St. Denis tells us that "of all divine works the most divine is to co-operate with God in the salvation of souls." "We are God's coadjutors," St. Paul says (i Cor. iii). Surely words such as these should fire our zeal and make us seize every opportunity of deepening our knowledge of our Religion, that we may fit ourselves for the occasions which are sure to come of helping some soul in need.

"But it is not in their line, some would say, to go about giving instruction, and they don't believe in interfering in their neighbours' affairs."

Not in their line! And pray, what right has one set of Catholics to go about with their hands in their pockets, whilst others are straining every nerve to be of service to souls? If it is

---

[1] These two sins are *oppression of the poor* and *defrauding the worker of his wages*. If we consider that the other two are *willful murder* and the *sin of Sodom*, we gain a true sense of how very serious these sins are.

not in our line to go out of ourselves when good is to be done, the sooner we make it our line the better.

Only, do let us remember that it is *trained help* we want in these days. We need a firm grip of truth ourselves if we are to be of use to others, or even to hold our own amid the infidelity all around. But with thorough knowledge of our Religion and prudent zeal, we shall do much.

Some years ago a large pleasure steamer going down the Thames, collided with a boat larger than itself, and in a few moments hundreds of excursionists were struggling in the water. Little help was at hand, but a man in a small rowing-boat pulled up to the scene of the disaster. On every side were men, women, and children fighting for dear life, clutching hold of the swimmers and dragging them down to destruction with themselves. Skirting carefully the struggling mass, the man picked up as many as his boat could carry with safety—alas, how few they were compared with those he had to abandon to their fate! As he pulled slowly off, agonised cries came to him to save "just one more." It was told by one of the rescued how the poor fellow, choking with emotion, sobbed out as he pulled away at his oar, "Would God I had a larger boat!" It was an awful thing to go away with the few and leave the many. But at least the man did what he could. What should we have thought of him had he passed by that frightful scene and made no effort to save!

And we Catholics, who have had every advantage in the way of religious instruction—can we see souls around us going to their ruin or groping in the darkness of heresy, and hold out no hand to help?

Do what you can, what comes nearest to hand. Do not wait for great opportunities to come in search of you, but seize the little ones that crowd about you every day. And do not pick and choose. The soul of a crossing-sweeper or of a workhouse child is as precious in God's sight as the soul of a princess. To teach one child its Catechism or prepare it for its first confession, is a work Angels might envy. Take a Catechism class, or read or tell the Life of Christ to some poor old body who cannot read.

"I should not dare to instruct any one. I should be afraid of teaching them wrong."

And are you not afraid to bury your talent and be reproached as a slothful servant? "Freely you have received," our Lord says, "freely give." Beware by all means of doing the work of God negligently; make yourself fit for it, don't be afraid of the work of preparation and of taking pains. And then rely upon the help of God. He does not leave His coadjutors in the lurch, but stands by them and puts the right words on their lips, and the right grace into the hearts of their hearers. I think I have told you before of a young lieutenant in the army, who had had none but the most meagre instruction, but was full of zeal. How he found out at a dance that his partner was dissatisfied with her position in the Church of England, and did his best to help her to the truth as they waltzed round the room together. And how he followed up his work by taking her to those who could finish what he had begun.

"A young man like that was too good for this world."

Perhaps he was. He died soon after in South Africa. He had not been long a Catholic, and from the time of his reception into the Church his one thought seemed to be to bring others to the truth.

Is it want of will, want of energy, want of heart, rather than want of ability that ties our hands and brings excuses to our lips? "Would God I had a larger boat!" the man cried as he pushed off with the few and left the many to perish. Oh, would to God we had larger hearts that we might take more into them and save more!

There is a way of helping souls on a large scale admirably suited to the needs of those who deplore their inability to instruct, and dread responsibility. You all know that Association, with a world-wide organisation, and branches in almost every country, for the spread of the Catholic Faith in heathen and non-Catholic countries. The conditions of membership are not heavy—(1) The daily recitation of one *Our Father* and one *Hail Mary*, with the invocation *St. Francis Xavier, pray for us*: and (2) The annual contribution of 2s. 2d. yearly, or one halfpenny weekly.

If we could see what the missioners in pagan lands see constantly, how eager we should be to help them in their grand work. They tell us that there are parts of Africa where the devil reigns supreme; he has his temples, his altars, his priests, his human sacrifices. In one place when the king dies, all his slaves are put to death—sent to wait upon him in the other world! In the slave-markets hundreds of human beings, some covered with wounds and sores, others dying of starvation, are huddled together, to be bought and sold like cattle—fathers and mothers, their little children clinging to their necks, to be separated from them presently by the various purchasers. If these poor creatures knew anything of the sufferings of our Divine Redeemer and of the reward in store for those who suffer patiently for His sake, they would be comforted in their misery. But they know nothing of this. They are miserable slaves here, and believe they will be nothing better in the world to come.

When the missioners are able—that is, when the alms sent them are sufficient—they establish mission-houses and schools where the children are baptized and brought up happily, and the old people are cared for and prepared for a happy death.

Read the *Annals of the Propagation of the Faith*, or any of the magazines which tell of the spread of the Faith among the heathen. Little by little these accounts will interest you. The knowledge of what others are doing and sacrificing in order to make Jesus Christ known to the multitudes who have never heard His Name, will fill you with a generous sympathy. It will make you eager to show your gratitude for the gift of Faith by putting aside something from your pocket-money for the help of the Foreign Missions. If this entails now and then the giving up of what was to have been spent on pleasure to yourself—so much the better!

By contributing towards this great work, the Association for the Propagation of the Faith, you share in the merits of the missioner—his labours, hardships, and suffering; you help to secure the happiness of many souls, not for a few years but for all eternity, and make many friends for yourself in Heaven. They will not forget you there. Could you but save one soul, that happy soul will be mindful of you and pray for you when you too will stand in need of prayer, and your friends on earth have perhaps forgotten you. Best of all, you will rejoice the Sacred Heart of Jesus by becoming His coadjutor in the work of saving the souls for whom He died. Oh would to God we had larger hearts! We should give, and count it a privilege to give, and *to feel the cost* of giving, and so share in the happiness of those who have given all, even life itself!

There is another Association, the Society of the Holy Childhood, the object of which is to procure Baptism in heathen lands for infants in danger of death, and to buy those that can be saved, and bring them up in Catholic schools. This Association children have all to themselves. Its members are children. Two Masses a month are said for these members, particularly for those who have not yet made their First Communion. The subscription is one halfpenny a month or sixpence a year. Is there any Baptized child who would not willingly set aside sixpence a year to procure Baptism for the poor little pagan children, who are left to die by thousands every year, and who if they die without Baptism can never see God? With every half-crown that is sent to China an infant may be bought and brought up a Christian.

I remember a young Trappist monk from South Africa being over here in England some years ago, sent to beg alms for the mission dependent on his Order in its extreme need. He told me of the reception that met him in not a few wealthy Catholic homes; of the "extreme regret of being unable to help in such a work owing to the pressure of local claims," &c. One lady, on hearing of the poverty of the mission and the inability of the Fathers to provide for its urgent needs, was "really *so* sorry to hear of such dreadful distress and would have been *so* glad to help, but"—with a despairing look round the luxuriously furnished drawing-room, every table covered with expensive and elegant knick-knacks—"the exigencies of society nowadays were so exacting, a perfect slavery, in fact, that it was quite impossible to do all one would wish in the way of charity."

"I hope he told her she might gratify her charitable wishes by giving him one of the 'exigencies' lying about. He could have sold it for the mission."

"Or that he did, like Father Ignatius Spencer, who took out his pocket-book and asked the lady who was '*so* sorry for him' how much she was sorry—half-a-crown or ten shillings sorry?"

No, the young monk did neither of these things. His eyes sorrowfully followed hers round the extravagantly furnished room. He thought of the difference to his little fund that even one of those elegant gimcracks would make. But he said nothing. He had himself left father, mother, and home for the sake of the souls for which Christ died, and for a moment the memory of his own sacrifice rushed to his mind and bitter words to his lips. But all was resolutely checked. He thought of his meek Master before the great ones of this world, and bowing his head—he could not trust himself to speak—quietly withdrew.

Of course I see there is another side to this. For, after all, there *must be* gimcracks and there must be limits to objects of charity. Who can say how much jewellery ought to be possessed by a great lady when none of it is exactly necessary? But whilst we allow that there is something to be said for this side of the question, let us be careful not to lose sight of the other side. Let us never forget that some amount of self-sacrifice in this direction is certainly called for, and that in proportion to the necessities of our suffering brethren, "the charity of Christ presses us."

About the time the Trappist was over in England, there died in France a worthy tradesman whose one thought seemed to be the propagation of the Faith among the heathen. All around him he saw men working hard to lay up money for years to come that they might be able to rest at last and enjoy the comforts money can bring. He worked hard too. But it was not to lay up money for himself, or to lay it up at all. People called him a miser, for they knew him to be a fairly prosperous man, and that money must be somewhere. His well-worn coat and frugal table showed it was not spent on himself, so of course it must be hoarded up against a rainy day. Only a few knew that far away, out in Asia, and Australia, and Africa, and America, was his treasure—the precious souls for which Christ died—and that his heart was there. Every year a large sum was sent to the Association for the Propagation of the Faith. Nothing was laid by. God would take care of him, he used to say when his friends expostulated, but he really could not spare anything for the "rainy day" which might never come. At last he was struck down by sickness, and in a few days was brought to death's door. He had no family, and rejoiced to be able to make over all he had to his pet work. Again prudent friends remonstrated. He might recover; it was foolish to give all away yet. But he could not wait. All that he could turn into money he did turn, and a cheque for a very considerable sum was sent to the Directors of the Association. And then he waited in peace and joy for the end.

But the end was not yet.

"Oh, poor man, what did he do?"

He recovered, and how many fingers were shaken at him you may imagine! But, of course, he would make known his recovery to the Directors of the great work whose benefactor he had been for so many years, and they would restore his generous gift or provide for him handsomely till his death. He would do nothing of the kind. He would not hear of the Directors being told. He began to work again for his livelihood, this time as a poor man indeed. His earnings sufficed for his simple wants. He kept his secret to himself during the few years of toil that remained to him. And then the end came. How do you think our Lord met him at the Judgement?

"And all the souls he had helped to save!"

"They will all have gone out to meet him. What a fuss there must have been bringing him into Heaven!"

You say you like the satisfaction of seeing the good you do, of hearing grateful thanks. So did the Saints, for they had the same human nature that we have. Yet we find them giving in secret, and praying not to have their reward in this life, because what gratifies nature is so apt to take from the merit of our good works. It may even spoil them altogether. "Much of the so-called charity of the present day is purely selfish, regarding as much the personal gratification of the giver, as the relief of the sufferer."[1] The poor-box saves us from this danger, and keeps the whole reward for His hand who seeth in secret. A penny dropped into the box is at once an act of faith, hope, and charity, and, like prayer for the Souls in Purgatory, does good that is all the safer for being unseen by the doer.

It does more, by ensuring the relief of deserving cases only. You may prefer to give to the beggar in rags, but you will not always act wisely in so doing; and, as the means of most of us are sadly limited, it is best to place them, as the thoughtful little boy said, where they will "go farthest."

Girls should learn from the first that charity is a real claim on each one of us, not to be met by a penny from the mother's purse for the offertory, and, in later life, spasmodic giving when the feelings are roused by some specially sad case.

"That feeling which relieves your own feelings at the moment, is not nearly so helpful to the character as the steady setting aside of a tenth, or whatever proportion of your money you feel to be right. It wonderfully clears your ideas as to what is *necessary* in personal spending and possible in charitable spending, if, from the first, you feel that this tenth is simply not yours to touch.…All of you who value steady habit and the acting on principle, will appreciate the character-training involved in the *tithe*, as contrasted with the indulgence of that emotion, which is a fire, sometimes lighted from above, and sometimes from below, and always a very wavering guide."[2]

We must bring well home to ourselves this truth that "advantages of fortune are responsibilities, things to use with fear, not fuel for vanity and instruments of self-indulgence. 'To whomsoever much is given, much shall be required of

---
[1] Archbishop Bourne.
[2] Miss Soulsby, "Stray Thoughts on Character."

him'(Luke xii). A long purse is like a long examination paper; no one is ever vain of that, but rather afraid. God will examine me on the whole matter of my possessions; how shall I answer His questions?"[1]

---

[1] "Ye are Christ's." Fr. Joseph Rickaby, S.J.

XXII
About a Bishop and a Time-Table

Now let us go back to the other set of girls who on "coming out" find home life trying or testing, not from the superabundance of exciting amusement which it provides, but from its monotony.

"Monotony! Home monotonous!"

Yes. *Couleur de rose* has a tendency to fade after a while into an unmistakable grey, not through any fault of persons or circumstances, but from the very nature of things. And this the home-comer must be prepared for. Being home for the holidays and being home "for good," are quite different matters, and it is her business to see that her settling down into the home circle is distinctly for good—her own good and the good of all around her.

To secure this, two convictions must have firm hold of her—that she has a work to do in her home, a noble work, worthy of her best efforts to carry on successfully, and, secondly, that it can only be a success at the cost of a good deal of cheerful self-sacrifice.

There must be order in her life, or it will be aimless and useless—there must be the observance of home rules, on which the peace, comfort, and happiness of the household depend; and of her own private rule, that outcome of her sense of responsibility which will make her eager to find a safeguard amid the difficulties of a new life.

The change from school discipline to comparative liberty is a critical phase in every life, and much depends on the way in which from the very beginning you use your liberty. You have now to take care of yourself, depend on yourself, lighten the burdens of others instead of being an additional burden and anxiety to those about you. Hence you must have yourself well in hand. A Rule, or Time-table, carefully drawn up and faithfully though not rigidly adhered to, will make your life an orderly one, and protect you against your own humours and waywardness.

"What sort of Rule should one make?"

That depends on many things. It should be the result of self-knowledge, careful foresight, and prayer. Make it out for yourself, bearing in mind your own duties, circumstances, and special needs. Do not make it too rigid, or it will not work smoothly: nor let it interfere with home duties, nor in the part you ought to take in home pleasures, which are duties as well. You must not fill the day so full that there is no margin for the unforeseen occurrences which are a part of home life; nor must you consider every detail of your Rule of such paramount importance that everything is to give way before it. À Kempis has a word of guidance for us here as in most needs: "If for piety's sake, or for the profit of our brother, we sometimes omit our accustomed exercise, it may afterwards be easily recovered; but if through a loathing of mind or negligence it be lightly let alone, it is no small fault and will prove hurtful."

The great Bishop of Orleans, Mgr. Dupanloup, who, amidst public work of many kinds, found time to watch over and direct young girls just entering upon life, insisted very much on the duty of planning the details of one's daily life, and not allowing time to slip away haphazard.

"Whenever he had the charge of a young girl at that critical moment when childhood disappears to give place to womanhood, he made the most strenuous efforts to fix that young soul definitely in the best path. Here is one of his letters:—

"'My child, what a sad thing it would be if all the noble faculties God has given you were allowed to be lost in the frivolities of the world in which you are about to enter…This is a time of real trial for your character, a time when vanity, dissipation, admiration, and all the rest, will be all about and in you, and tempt you to give up many of your good resolutions…I like to think of you, on the contrary, as standing firmly and courageously by your Rule of life, knowing how to say *No* when necessary; though lending yourself sweetly and amiably to all that your kind parents propose for you and that God does not forbid: gay, unselfish, kind, and thoughtful towards all; but never forgetting that modesty and reserve in dress and manners which a Christian maiden should observe, remembering that God's eye is ever upon her…I write now, before the hour of trial comes, that you may be prepared!'

"He recommended to persons in the world what Fénélon and St. Francis de Sales advised men about the Court to follow in the reigns of Henry IV and Louis XIV: 'A little meditation in the morning; a short spiritual reading in the afternoon or evening, and daily Mass when possible. This is all they advise' he said, 'to a soul that wishes to love and serve God. But of course the efficacy of these measures depends on the way in which they are done.' And to facilitate this interior life, he writes to his intimate friend M. de Montalembert, 'you must jealously guard that precious hour in the morning exclusively consecrated to God. Read no letters, no newspapers, and receive no visits before that. Newspapers especially distract the mind, and take away from it all freshness and brightness. Reserve all that for work in the day. But to keep such a resolution requires some firmness and energy which are not wanting in you.

"'When we are faithful to the daily practices of piety our Rule prescribes,' he used to say, 'we receive in return for this fidelity a host of graces, for God is never outdone in generosity.' Still, while exacting fidelity to the Rule of life, he did not wish to trammel souls, or interfere with their liberty. 'My child,' he wrote to one of his spiritual children, 'although I wish you to follow the practices I have marked out for you, I do not wish you to render me slavish obedience. It may happen that on certain days, either from duty to your relations or charity to your neighbour, you may not be able to keep to the Rule; or you might yourself wish for a little relaxation, and might say to our Lord: "I want to have more liberty to-day, and as Thou art Goodness itself I feel Thou wilt permit it." But when you write to me, you will tell me, will you not, if you have often made these little compacts?'"

"He catches her cleverly there!"

"You will think, perhaps, that the Bishop contented himself with prescribing the spiritual duties of the day. Nothing of the sort. He speaks to one of his penitents of the care she must take of her servants, of the regularity and accuracy with which she must keep the house accounts, of her duty to the poor, &c. She seems to have complained to him of her busy life, for he says: 'I like running better than stagnant water, there are fewer toads.... The multitude of occupations of which you complain is the running water in which our Lord wishes you to live, and He prefers that to an indolent life in a stagnant pool. But learn in the midst of your work to preserve your soul in peace and patience.'

"One great resource, both to avoid idleness and to prevent a woman being too much absorbed by household cares, was intellectual occupation, and this he always strongly recommended. 'I am delighted to hear of your determination to study,' he wrote to one great lady. 'It will occupy your mind, fortify your soul, and in the end become the joy of your life.... Take notes as you read, it is far more idle to read than to write. Without omitting any duty to your family, I think you might set apart an hour or two in the day to work of this sort...there are so many moments wasted for want of such occupation.' Those in whom he found the capacity he always encouraged to work for the public. His greatest satisfaction was to see a wife helping her husband in his literary or political career, and becoming in that way a real helpmate to him."[1]

Much of the Bishop's advice will apply to any girl who has more or less the control of her day in her own hands. With regard to your spiritual duties, you could not do better than follow the advice of St. Francis de Sales to let them interfere as little as possible with other duties, so that they may not annoy those with whom you live. They might perhaps be:—

(1) Morning Prayers before leaving your room.
(2) Daily Mass when within ten minutes' walk of church.
(3) Meditation for a quarter of an hour, or ten minutes of thoughtful spiritual reading.
(4) The Rosary, five decades.
(5) Night Prayers and examination of conscience.
(6) Benediction when within easy reach of church.
(7) Confession weekly.
(8) Communion—What can we say when the Holy Father is so urgent for frequent, even daily Communion where this is possible!

Let me urge you very earnestly to be regular in going to the Sacraments. It will entail self-denial, but the grace you will receive will be out of all proportion to any sacrifice. The

---

1 "Life of Mgr. Dupanloup." By Mgr. F. Lagrange.

Sacraments are the springs of our spiritual life. Where they work freely, there will be the light, strength, and solid happiness that comes of union with God.

If you foresee that you will be prevented from going to Confession on your usual day, anticipate, if possible, rather than defer it. Weekly Confession is easy, provided our nightly examination of conscience is earnestly made. In your preparation, which for a weekly confession need not take more than a quarter of an hour, give most time and care to contrition for the two or three sins of the week—as well as for the sin of your past life—which you are going to confess and about which your purpose of amendment is made.

"Remember that it is a confessor's business, not merely to hear sins and absolve from them, but to hear difficulties and advise about them."[1]

With regard to the frequency of our Communions, we shall be guided of course by the advice of our confessor, but this advice will be determined to a large extent by our own wishes. If we are eager for our "daily Bread," he is not likely to withhold it from us.

There can be no doubt as to our Lord's desire to come to us, after the earnest words of His Vicar to all the faithful at large. "The Master is here and calleth for thee," is said to us all. We should not let feelings be our guide in this matter. Holy Communion is not a reward of virtue, as the Jansenists would make out. It is the visit of the Physician to the weak and failing; if we go to Him for help and strength, we shall most certainly find both.

There are two most important daily acts—getting up, and going to bed—which might almost be included in our spiritual duties, so nearly do they concern our soul's welfare,

---

[1] "Ye are Christ's." Fr. Jos. Rickaby, S. J.

and influence our lives. Have a fixed time for both, and keep to it unless a reasonable cause calls for deviation, such as having been up late at a dance and not been in bed till two or three. "Even so," says one whose opinion is worth quoting, "for those who will do it, there will be less physical harm in getting up for an eight o'clock Mass, than in lying in bed till late on in the morning."

The practice of talking in one's room to a friend, or inviting friends into one's room at that time, is acknowledged on all hands to be most undesirable. Some say it is so enjoyable and has become so general a custom in modern society, that it would be useless to interfere with it. Others think it should be kept down and discountenanced as far as circumstances will allow. Girls at this time indulge in confidences they regret next morning.

What a loss it is to Catholic households that the custom of family prayer at night has gone out of general use! Could it be revived, would it not bring a special blessing on our homes?

"We must train ourselves to rise at the right time as a matter of duty and obedience to conscience. Self-control in rising, washing, eating, and lessons, are the great though indirect means of conquering our lower nature."[1]

Were we to think when we wake in the morning: "God grants me another day to live; another day to serve Him; another day for rising higher"—should we not find strength for that morning sacrifice, the offering or withholding of which, as experience has taught us, affects the whole day?

As to occupations, "see what house duties you will be able and allowed to take upon yourself and be responsible for; if there are any little ones to be helped with lessons, if there is anything in the shape of needlework, mending, &c., in which

---

1 Miss Soulsby, "Stray Thoughts on Character."

you ought to help. Whatever duties will naturally devolve on you now, or that you undertake of your own accord, stick to them, and account yourself responsible for their being conscientiously done. Don't wait for them to be suggested to you. Look round and see what there is to be done, where you can lighten your mother's work, in what way you can be a pleasure to your father,"[1] a help to brothers or sisters.

Can you be of use at the church with the altar linen, flowers, or choir? Or is there any lonely invalid to whom you can be kind? In whatever you undertake to do, or to promise in the shape of assistance, visits, and the like, show yourself reliable. Do not suppose because the poor bedridden old woman or the sick child cannot urge any actual claim upon you, you can break a promise or disappoint them whenever your engagement clashes with your own pleasure or convenience.

Try to secure an hour a day for self-improvement in one shape or another by the cultivation of your mind. It is a mistake only possible to those who have not worked seriously at school, to suppose that education ends with school life. It may rather be said to begin then. School will have done much for us if it has shown us how to use the powers of our mind, and given us a love for intellectual work and sensible reading, and, by introducing us to several branches of study, enabled us to find out which suits us and which we will follow up later.

The desire of every Catholic girl ought to be to utilise to the utmost the opportunities for good that life will bring her. Now, the measure in which she will be able to do this will depend upon the way in which she has cultivated her gifts. Every gift, as we have said before, is at once a privilege and a responsibility. We have to trade with and increase it as far as

---

[1] Miss Soulsby, "Stray Thoughts on Character."

circumstances allow, all our life through. "Trade till I come," is our Lord's injunction to us, one by one.

We must set ourselves earnestly, then, to the task of cultivating our minds; we must put out effort if we are to be ready for the duties devolving on us in these days, and for the opportunities that will surely come even to the most unlikely of us.

The level of intelligence in girls of the present day is a high one. Catholic girls must rise to it if they are to answer the expectation of the Church and the need of the souls they will influence on their way through life. They should rouse themselves to a noble enthusiasm for the work to which they are called. It is a work reserved *for them*. They must do it, or it will be left undone. Priests may do much, laymen may do much, but unless our Catholic women—not here and there, but as a body—are what they ought to be, physically, intellectually, and spiritually, the cause of the Church in this country will be lost. It is not too much to say that its future depends on them, and therefore on our Catholic girls. If the child is father to the man, in the school-girl you can see the woman. A silly, selfish, aimless girl will develop into an empty-headed, frivolous, pleasure-loving woman, whose influence on all who come in contact with her will bear the impress of her self-centred and useless life.

Do not for a moment suppose that all the serious-minded girls go into convents, or that there is no vocation outside convent walls. Every one of you has a vocation; for every one there is a grand task in life waiting. Go out to meet it bravely.

"Of course, clever girls and those in the front ranks can do a lot of good, but others have not the same chance—those in a quiet home like ours, for instance."

All can do something; you are needed every one, first in your own family, then, to a greater or less extent, outside. But if you want to be of service you must not grudge preparation. God will not use those who have not thought it worth their while to get themselves ready. It is the eager ones He looks for, those who cry out to Him with the prophet of old: "Here am I, send me!" For these He will surely have a work, arduous enough, far-reaching enough to satisfy even the most devoted.

Some of you, I believe, saw the mystery play called "Eager Heart" when it was performed in London, and you will remember that it was not rank or wealth that determined the king's choice of his quarters for the night. He went to Eager Heart because she so earnestly desired to have him for her guest, and had done her best to make ready her cottage for him in case he should condescend to seek her hospitality.

All through the history of the Church we see the same choice of His. It is to the Eager Hearts of all time that He betakes Himself when He has work to be done. Labour for Him, toil and expenditure of all one has in His service, is a boon to be craved for. He gives it as a mark of favour and of confidence, but—do note this—it will not come the way of the indifferent. The Eager Hearts will get it, who have toiled long and patiently at their preparation.

If, then, you want God to use you, fit yourself as far as you can for His hand. Would you offer the Holy Father to be used for words of blessing a pen that was greasy, rusty, or in any way unfit for presentation? "God has no need of human learning," a popular preacher objected. "He has still less need of human ignorance" was the wise rejoinder.

"Yet we know what was used for a grand piece of service on Palm Sunday—a young, untrained ass, wasn't it?"

Prepared by the disciples, though, who laid their garments on it, as we are expressly told.

Yes, young, untrained colts, unless they submit to preparation, stand a poor chance of being used for any glorious service.

"But with it even an ass can be made something of, it seems; there's comfort in that."

"But how is one to prepare? We shall not want to talk Mathematics or Logic to whoever takes us in to dinner, and, though it's nice of course to be able to read and speak French and German, we may never want them, and learning them takes a lot of time and bother."

It is quite possible we may not need pure Mathematics and formal Logic—that is to say, what school gave us—exactly in the shape in which it was given. But, as we have already seen, there is a value in what we learn, over and above the actual information gained. Neither Mathematics nor Logic may be called for when you are on a visit, but if they have made you accurate and painstaking, able to follow a chain of reasoning, and to resist the tendency to jump at conclusions, will you consider them useless?

To be of service to those with whom we come in contact, we must be able to see things from other points of view than our own. History, Geography, and Languages help us here by widening our outlook upon men and things, and engaging our interest and our sympathy—which are too apt to be centred on self—for the multitude of persons and things outside that have a claim upon them. This brings us naturally to the subject of books. We were speaking about them some time ago when the little ones were with us. But it would have been talking rather over their heads to have said then all I want to say. So I hope you will forgive me if I go back upon the subject even at the risk of repeating myself. The subject is so important that it will bear some repetition. Let us have another talk about it to-morrow.

XXIII

Books Again

As soon as school-days are over, you will find yourselves ushered into a world of books all urging their claims on your consideration. You will be face to face with great opportunities and—with great responsibilities. For the books you make your companions will surely mould you into their likeness. You are at a very impressionable age when influences whether for good or for evil will tell upon you with a force they will not have later. You are answerable for the effect they will have upon your mind; take care, then, how you use them; exercise self-control; remember that a taste for frivolous reading is soon acquired and is not without great difficulty broken through.

If you have not already got a taste for sensible reading, set yourself to get it now. It is the most useful of all tastes, for it cultivates our minds, forms our judgement, strengthens our principles, and builds up our character. You are sure to have a certain amount of leisure in the day; secure it for useful reading instead of wasting it in lounging about or in idle gossip.

A love of reading staves off many a temptation, helps us in many an hour of over-strain, or illness, or sorrow. It has been well said that, "It is hard for a person who does not like reading to talk without sinning....Towards afternoon one who has nothing to do drifts rapidly away from God. To sit down in a chair without an object is to jump into a thicket of temptation. A vacant hour is always the devil's hour. Then a book is a strong tower, nay, a very church, with angels lurking among the leaves."

Needless to say, not all reading, not even all harmless reading, secures these ends. It is a custom sadly too common, to devote all one's time for reading to newspapers and magazines. There is no surer way to ruin the taste for reading that is really educating.

"Father often makes us read the newspaper aloud in the evening. He says we ought to keep up with what is going on in the world, to know how the country is being governed, and to understand the wants of the nation."

"Yes, but he always tells us what we are to read, and trusts us not to look at other things."

I should be the last to discourage such reading of the newspapers as will give you an intelligent interest in the affairs of the country. But I would warn you against making such reading and the devouring of magazines your chief mental food. This would most certainly do you harm.

"What harm?"

What harm would it be to make the staple of our food consist of the lightest or richest confectionery?

"Well, it wouldn't feed us for one thing. And we should be good for nothing, and get ill—very ill perhaps."

The same will happen to us spiritually unless we feed our mind on solid food. If we neglect to do this, the powers of our mind become gradually weakened, till at length they are incapable of relishing anything but a ceaseless round of novels, or those mischievous "Tit-Bits," which are the ruin of mental digestion.

For the building up of our higher selves, we need reading of a more solid character. "To use books rightly," Ruskin tells us, "is to go to them for help; to appeal to them when our own knowledge and power of thought fails; to be led by them into wider sight, purer conception than our own; and receive from them the united sentence of the judges and councils of all time against our solitary and unstable opinions."[1]

"Suppose you don't like the books you ought to like; suppose they bore instead of interesting you. You can't make yourself care for things, you know."

But you can. A taste for the best books does not come naturally; we have to train ourselves to it. If you find an author dull whom good judges admire, you may be sure that the fault is on your side. Go on, then, with your book though it does bore you. Try to bring yourself up to its level. Read on patiently, trying to see what others see. You will be repaid if you persevere. One of you learned from your mother the beauties to be found in a peaty pool. Beauties come out by degrees as our mind becomes trained. Likes and dislikes must not be the sole guide of our reading; we must train ourselves to like the best books.

"It is a good thing to keep a sensible book always on hand, and, alternately with books you fancy, to read every day something a little above you; to take up some special subject every three or six months, and read several books on it."[2]

"What about novels? We have not read anything yet but Scott and Dickens, but I am looking forward tremendously to reading others, and—well, to tell the truth, I'm rather afraid I shall get too fond of light reading."

You must keep yourself well in hand, then. Remember that, like other forms of recreation, they must not become the occupation of life, but be used as means to an end. It is a wise counsel to read no novels in the morning. Keep your mind

---

1 Ruskin, "Sesame and Lilies."
2 Miss Soulsby.

for serious reading whilst it is fresh. Have a fixed time in the afternoon that you will give to lighter reading, and show your self-control by closing your book at an exciting part when the right moment comes.

Don't let yourself be the slave of any book. Watch its influence upon your mind. If, when you put it down, you turn to your daily life again with a disgust for its commonplace scenes and humdrum duties, with feelings of pity for yourself and of irritation with others, be quite sure that book is doing you harm. Instead of invigorating your mind by a wholesome change of scenery, and sending you back to work refreshed and braced, it is making you discontented, feeble, selfish. Put it away.

"Very easily said, but not so easily done."

I agree with you, but it has to be done nevertheless. Would you go on sipping what you knew to be poison because it happened to be sweet? Show as much concern for the health of your soul as you do for that of the body, and put that book resolutely from you. I say resolutely, because I quite admit it needs a determined will to break away from what is fascinating, even when we know it to be hurtful. We must put out effort, and quickly, before a bad habit is formed.

We may perhaps know some case of a woman who has taken to drink. The terrible craving for what she knows is ruining and killing her has been indulged till it has overmastered and paralysed her will, and drowned all that was noble in her. She has become utterly selfish. No thought of the wretchedness of her home, of husband, and of children moves her now. Nay, no thought of her own soul and of its frightful peril has any effect upon her. She has moments, indeed, when she deplores her state and makes a feeble attempt to rise out of it; but by long indulgence the will has grown so weak that it sinks down unequal to the effort, and at last gives up the struggle. How did this miserable habit come to be formed? Like all others, by isolated acts. There was a time when the mind was keenly alive to the danger, when conscience cried loudly and reproached bitterly. But it was not listened to, and now it has almost ceased to speak.

Let us fear those acts of hurtful self-indulgence which slowly but surely form self-indulgent habits and end in making utterly selfish lives.

"But surely novel reading is not so awful a thing as drunkenness?"

Those who know the effect of novel reading upon persons who make it, not the recreation but the occupation of life, tell us that its effects are alarmingly like those of drink. There is the same deadening of all noble impulses, the same weakening of the will, the same selfish indifference to the call of duty and to the needs and the sorrows of others, the same lethargy in all that concerns the things of the soul and of eternity.

Be careful, then; manage yourselves sensibly in this matter. Use the reading of fiction as a means, not as an end, and watch it to see that it remains a means. I should not advise any of you to read a novel the last thing at night because you heard a bishop say the other day that he reads a chapter of some light book or some pages of Longfellow to help him to get to sleep. A bishop's life is often so full of anxiety and care, that unless he were to divert his mind from them at night he would be unable to get the sleep that is necessary for the discharge of his duties. He finds a few pages of light reading distract him and soothe the brain; he takes them, then, as means to an end.

We have no such motive; sleep comes without difficulty to us. After an examination, on a journey, in illness, and, as I said just now, in moderation as recreation, we may read well-chosen novels. But do let us make it a rule not to waste time over them in the morning when our minds are in good working order. Such reading "prevents the formation of those tastes which are the making, and in later years the solace, of the educated man and woman."[1]

"I never knew it mattered so much what we read."

"Why may grown-up people read newspapers and books that we may not? If we may not harm ourselves with what is bad, why may they?"

The food of the mind is like the food of the body. Just as there are things at table which you would not give to your little brothers and sisters, because they would be bad for them though their elders can take them with safety, so there is reading which might harm you, by disturbing your faith, for

[1] "At the Parting of the ways." Fr. Lucas, S.J.

instance, but which would not hurt, perhaps, more mature and better informed minds, less sensitive to every impression, and to the spell and fascination of evil. A well-behaved child takes at dessert what is given it, and does not feel aggrieved to see other things on the plates of its elders.

But some books are bad for every one—books that ridicule the Catholic faith or distort its doctrines, and books that are called "immoral." Attacks, not on the Catholic Faith alone, but on the fundamental doctrines of Christianity, are now met with in novels and magazines which lie about on every table. Be careful what you take up. And do not be talked into reading them on the ground that one should know both sides, that truth should be able to bear discussion, and the like. Truth can bear any amount of investigation and discussion, and can repel every assault, but we, with our lack of theological training, are not the people to investigate or to rush into conflict.

Do not be deluded, either, into thinking that for the sake of helping others you may read books which attack your Faith. Those whose studies enable them to face dangers in behalf of their neighbour, have a special grace of protection for themselves and of assistance for others. You have neither the training nor the grace which alone could justify you in incurring such risk, and you have the warning of Holy Scripture that those who love danger shall perish in it.

"There is other unwholesome reading that is called 'immoral'—books, and papers, and illustrations, the whole gist, and tendency, and purpose of which is to insinuate and suggest and tacitly recommend sins against purity. From this evilly suggestive literature I should turn aside."[1]

"Shut up at once a book which teaches knowledge of wickedness. Do not read Society novels that make you live with flippant, irreverent, or coarse people, or those who take

---
1 "Ye are Christ's." Fr. Joseph Rickaby, S.J.

sin lightly....Every book you read alters you for good or bad. Your book list is a very great help to self-examination....The animal nature in each of us needs to be disciplined and raised, its lower desires must be stifled, and the higher side, which is feebler and later in development, needs to be fostered. We need to turn away from everything that has a danger signal, everything that jars on our sense of niceness, because of this traitor in the camp, this lower nature which may feed on what at first sight shocks our better instincts. That better nature soon becomes quiescent unless we obey it at once, unless we turn away with some exertion of bodily activity and change of employment from evil thoughts. Unless we put down the book or paper which jars on us, the traitor in the camp will read the passage twice over, or dwell upon the thoughts until they permanently soil our mind...If we once let our eyes dwell on anything bad, we cannot forget it at will; it haunts us for years, and comes back when we most long to be free from it. Bad novels find entrance where bad companions would not, and yet they are the more dangerous of the two; for we more insensibly fall into the tone of the books we read, than of the people we meet, since there is nothing while we are reading to arouse our attention, or that of others, to the gradual change in our standard which is taking place. It is not only downright bad novels which our conscience ought to forbid, not only those which manifestly seek to attract by picturing evil, and which ask our sympathy for sin, and obscure our sense of right and wrong; there are many which do not deserve such censure, but yet which strike us as rather profane, or rather vulgar, or rather coarse when we begin them, though there is nothing positively wrong in them. But if we are to strive after perfection, then it is our clear duty to close such books at once; for nothing is so quickly lost as this vague sense of distaste for what is wrong, and we may accept it as an inevitable judgment that by the time we have read such a book through, we shall for ever have lost that full power of seeing and shrinking from its evil which was ours when we opened it."[1]

A gentleman I know has lost his sight, but, thanks to Braille, he is still a reader. You should see the care he takes of the middle finger of his right hand which is reserved for reading. It is allowed to do no other work, that it may be kept soft and sensitive for that precious communication with other minds which through its touch is still left him. Nothing may come near it; he guards it instinctively as we guard our eyes. So should we prize and protect the sensitiveness of our conscience. Once lost, it can hardly be recovered.

If, till your judgement is formed and your mind and taste trained, you can get safe guidance as to your choice of books, be thankful, and have recourse to it instead of investigating for yourself. Before you read a book find out what sort of opinions the author holds and whether he deserves your respect. Remember that because you can read one book of a certain author, it does not necessarily follow that you can read all.

And beware of curiosity. Surely God knew what was best for Eve when He forbade her to eat of the tree of the knowledge of good and evil! She was perfectly happy. She had the knowledge of good; why should she want the knowledge of evil? But she was curious. She would risk the consequences of self-indulgence. And we know the result, not to herself only, but to all her children to the end of time.

Learn a lesson from her bitter experience. Keep unsound and unwholesome reading of every description far from you. Do not risk the most precious possession of your soul, its faith and its purity, for the sake of some passing gratification against which your conscience warns you.

---

1 Miss Soulsby, "Stray Thoughts on Reading."

"Books against faith are more radically injurious than indecent books. Writings which offend against Christian purity will generally strike a warning note of shame in any averagely modest mind; and this is a safeguard against being surprised into danger. But anti-Catholic or anti-Christian writings, especially if ably penned, appeal to the more intellectual side of our nature, and, by flattering it, lead us into unsuspected peril. Those especially have most to fear from irreligious reading who, destitute of any systematic training in philosophy or theology, indulge their intellectual curiosity or vanity by making themselves acquainted with all the various aberrations of the human mind. The press is being worked just now for all it is worth in order to deliver Rationalistic attacks upon Christianity, whether openly or under cover of so-called science, and Catholics have therefore the greater need to guard their Faith by care in their choice of reading. It is not bravery, but rashness of the most foolish and dangerous type, to expose oneself unnecessarily to catching the plague of unfaith. It is moral cowardice born of human respect, and not courage, to yield to those who taunt us with being 'afraid of considering the other side of the question.' For us Catholics in the matter of religious belief, there is only one side."[1]

The Collect for the Feast of the Epiphany shows the difference of position between those who have *found* and those who are *seeking* for Truth: "O God, who by the leading of a star didst reveal Thine only-begotten Son to the Gentiles, grant that we who already know Thee by Faith may be brought to contemplate the beauty of Thy majesty." We have not to look here and there in weary search for Jesus, but so to utilise our gift of Faith that it may bring us to the unveiled sight of Him in Heaven.

---

[1] "The First Commandment." Fr. M. de Zulucta, S. J.

A party of non-Catholics, on pilgrimage to Fountains Abbey, had been walking in procession among the ruins singing, "Lead, kindly Light." One of them coming upon a Catholic girl asked:

"Why do you leave Newman's beautiful hymn to us? You never use it in your churches."

"We leave it," she answered pleasantly, "to those who need it, and unite our prayers with theirs that the 'kindly Light' for which they ask so often and so fervently, may lead them where it led Newman."

XXIV

"In Him was Life, and the Life was the Light of Men"[1]

But do not let secular reading engross all your interest. Find some time—say a quarter of an hour daily—for such as will bring before you the things of the other life, inform your mind more and more fully on religious subjects, and brace your will to a more faithful following of Christ. We are no longer in the days of the "Garden-of-the-Soul-Catholics,"[2] when a book treating of spiritual matters was a rarity, prized and utilised in proportion to the risk of possessing it. Such books are now multiplied on every side; the difficulty is to choose among them, and to resist the tendency of simply devouring a new book through curiosity, instead of taking it up with a real desire to profit by what we read.

We have seen that we should train ourselves to like the best books. Foremost among these are surely the Lives of the Saints. Nothing, perhaps, does more to fire us with an enthusiastic

---

1 John i.
2 *Garden of the Soul* was an immensely popular book of prayers and devotions compiled in 1740 by Bishop Richard Challoner, best known for his revision of the Douay-Rheims Bible. Due to the persecution of Catholics in England during this period, such books were difficult to obtain and dangerous to keep. It remained a favorite until the early 20th century, though subsequent editions bear little resemblance to the original.

devotion to the Church, to make us recognise her claim to be the Church Catholic, the Church of all ages and of all nations, than to come face to face with the proofs of her power to sanctify souls. We see the long line of her heroes of all nations, and tribes, and peoples, and tongues, stretching from the first Christians of Apostolic times down to those of our own day. Different in every outward circumstance, we recognise them all as members of one family by the same characteristics—the same close following of Christ and intimacy with Him; the same power of intercession; the same miraculous gifts; the same sanctification through her unfailing Sacraments, and the duties and trials of daily life. Whether it is the founder of a religious Order, or a soldier in the camp, a village curé, or the head of a State, the Church takes them in hand and turns them out heroes of sanctity, who go, not safely only, but grandly, through the perils of life, and pass on their torch to those who in days like these sorely need its cheering light and warmth.

Do read the Lives of the Saints, the canonised and uncanonised holy ones of our own times in particular. Like the salt breezes from the sea, or the bracing wind of the moors, such reading will fill you with an exhilarating sense of joy and strength. You, too, will put your hand trustfully into the hand of Mother Church, and beg her to lead you whither she has led so many.

But if we are what our reading makes us, if companionship with the Saints of God uplifts, enlightens, and encourages us, what shall we say of His Life from which the Saints have drawn all the virtue that sanctified their own? He would lead a life which brought Him into daily contact with circumstances such as ours, with home interests and sorrows and joys; with work and weariness; disappointment and failure; pain of body and mind, with the sufferings of the poor and the afflicted; with injustice and with sin. The story of how He bore Himself in these various situations is left us in the Holy Gospels for our instruction and comfort, and help—why do we not read it more?

Suppose we had had no Life of Him all this time—only a few facts handed down, as to how He looked and what He said and did. And suppose that it was suddenly announced one day in the morning papers that in an old monastery of the East four undoubtedly genuine histories of Him by eye-witnesses of His daily Life had been brought to light—what would be the eagerness of men to see, and read, and study them!

His enemies and His friends, those who would set themselves to find discrepancies in the records, or a flaw in that spotless Life; and those who would thirst to drink in its every detail that they might make it the model of their own—all would hail the discovery and seek to profit by it. We, His followers, should feel that we had a right to the history of the Life that was lived for us. We should clamour for it, thank God we had lived to see the day when it was given to the world, and—were we so happy as to find a copy translated into our own tongue—read, and re-read, and learn it off, that its virtue might filter through our mind and heart into our lives and bring them into the likeness of His.

"And we do none of these things!"

No, and why not?

"I suppose we think we know the Gospels. But not all of us do. I have heard girls say they have never read the New Testament and do not even follow the Gospel of the Sunday at Mass."

Think of that! And they will read the lives of men and women whose histories are a disgrace to their race. They will pore for days over silly, sensational stories, knowing the harm they are doing themselves. But the Life of Him who loved them unto death—this is insipid, this has no interest for them.

"What can you do if you have read it and it does not make the impression it ought? You know it is no use to pretend to be very much interested when you are not."

No, certainly, pretence never does any good, and you are to be commended for saying what plenty would not have the courage to say.

What are we to do? I should repeat what I said of the reading of authors that are somewhat above your level: Read on patiently; try to see beneath the surface; to see what others have seen, what you, too, will surely see if you read humbly and perseveringly. For this Divine Life, which in the fulness of its beauty is above the comprehension of the most enlightened, is more easily understood by those who wish to understand than are the works of men. Those who read humbly and reverently, praying that our Divine Lord would give them the relish of His Blessed Life, and patient suffering, and gentle ways, will, if they persevere in their search, have a deeper knowledge of Him than keener minds which lack the necessary preparation of heart: "I give Thee thanks, O Father, Lord of Heaven and earth, because Thou hast hid these things from the wise and prudent, and hast revealed them to little ones" (Matt. xi).

Could we not read one incident in our Lord's life daily, read as with Mary's pondering heart, praying Him, by the Divine virtue shining forth in that incident, to make our hearts more like unto His?

XXV
Charity Begins at Home

I am afraid the subject of reading has taken more than its share of our time. There are still several things I want to talk about, but our talks are coming to an end with the holidays.

"Then comes our last term at school, and then—Home for good!"

"I wonder how much of our Time-table will be kept to? One can never be sure of having an hour to oneself at home; something or other is always happening—people call, or some one is ill, or mother or the boys want something."

Never hesitate to sacrifice your leisure when a need has to be met. Indeed, time cannot then be considered as leisure. Have the home interests at heart, and look upon it as your first duty to see that they are properly cared for. I should not say, 'Be always ready to leave everything at your brother's call,' for their claims upon you might not always be valid and reasonable. But if your father or mother wants you, shut up your book at once. Take work and worry off your mother as far as you can. Be on the alert to see where your help would be acceptable. And learn *how* to help. Unless you know the proper way of doing things—how to cut out a blouse, or order a dinner, or entertain a visitor, your interference will only add to her cares.

Put your heart into household duties, appreciate their value as factors in your moral and social training, and above all as being God's will for you at present. This will save you from the silliness of going about your work in a lackadaisical or condescending fashion as if domestic duties were beneath you. No idea could be more absurd, or show more plainly how little school life has done for you.

"Literary education entirely unfits a man for the Force when it puffs him up, makes him conceited, and leads him to think himself too good for his profession." So say the "Rules and Regulations for the Government and Guidance of the Royal Irish Constabulary." The very sensible observation may perhaps serve for the guidance of "peace-officers" at home!

To say nothing of bills, it makes all the difference to a household when there is a "valiant woman" at the head of it, with, we may well add, a valiant daughter as her right hand. "The ways of the house" will then be well looked to. Servants work in quite a different spirit when they find that those who give directions know how they should be carried out, and in case of need can lend a helping hand themselves. One who knows how a house should be kept, how a dinner should be cooked, and a dress made, has immense advantages over another who has no practical knowledge of these matters. A lady once told me that she owed a great deal to her resolution as a girl, never to miss an opportunity of learning anything useful that came in her way—lessons in dressmaking, bookbinding, carving; hints as to the management of a dairy, of a garden, of poultry, of children—all had been of service.

Remember that "home for holidays" and "home for good" are two different things. Those whose anxiety hitherto has been to forestall *your* wishes now expect you to conform to *theirs*, to take up cheerfully the small duties and responsibilities of home life, and to enter into its pleasures. To do this steadily will require the conquest of self in many ways. It takes energy and generosity to throw oneself into little tiresome duties, into amusements which do not amuse us personally, into the hundred and one miscellaneous occupations that make up life at home.

Set yourself resolutely against the prevailing spirit of independence, self-assertion, and criticism, which makes girls nowadays chafe under the discipline of home, and resent interference and control. They will not stand a word of remonstrance, much less of reproof, and show a complete disregard of the honour, as well as for the obedience to parents, required by the Fourth Commandment.

The tendency of a right-minded girl is to believe that her elders know better than she does, and that even if their views are not up to the latest lights, it is not for her to bring this home to them by her tone of voice, depreciating remarks, or huffiness of manner whenever their opinions or wishes run counter to her own.

Among your home responsibilities, none is greater than your influence over your brothers. You cannot escape from this responsibility. It is impossible that you should not help or hinder them greatly, that you should not give them high ideals—or the opposite. You are "your brother's keeper," and to be able to influence him as you ought, you must make yourself acceptable to him. Do not think it waste of time to consult his tastes and lay yourself out to meet them even at a considerable cost of time and inconvenience to yourself.

In a home I know, where there are three grownup brothers, the wardrobe of each is given into the charge of one of his three sisters as soon as she leaves school. It is pleasant to see the zest with which the girls discharge their duties, and the pride they take in their brothers. Young men have their weaknesses in matters of dress and comfort no less than the weaker sex, and the question of neck-ties, studs, and cuffs, is the subject for grave consultation between them and their respective *chargées-d'affaires*, whose sympathy and devotedness have resulted in a mutual trust that bids fair to have a far-reaching influence for good in the graver concerns of after life.

> "For there is no friend like a sister
> In calm or stormy weather;
> To cheer one on the tedious way,
> To fetch one if one goes astray,
> To lift one if one totters down,
> To strengthen whilst one stands."[1]

Above all, be on the alert in the evening to see that things go well. Count among your most important duties whatever will make home happier for your father and brothers, whose evenings will depend for their brightness very much upon your readiness to fall in with their tastes, and be disengaged for bridge, billiards, whatever is wanted. If there are friends to entertain and music is called for, do not go through the affectation of excuses before you can be prevailed upon to play or sing. One of your brothers is an inveterate chessplayer, and wants a game. Get out the board briskly, instead of refusing on the ground that you have no chance against him. There are so many of you, that tact is required at times to make all go smoothly; to notice when people are tired and out of sorts; to parry skilfully a home-thrust; to draw into a conversation that will interest him some one who is a bit cranky or downhearted; to turn into a safer channel a discussion that was beginning to get warm.

Remember that your business as homemakers is carried on mainly in the evenings; then you must be at your best, and put aside resolutely, to a more seasonable hour, private pursuits and worries that would prevent you being a joy-giver all round.

---

1 "Goblin Market." Christina Rossetti.

"That means, do you know, any amount of real, solid self-denial."

I know it perfectly, and am glad to see that you realise it beforehand. It is half the battle when girls coming "home for good" know to what they are coming: it is to a training school where all they have learned—and, let us hope, begun to practise—as to obedience, deference to elders, self-control and unselfishness—will be put to the proof.

We have seen that, whether home life provides a large amount of liberty and pleasure, or a generous allowance of rubs and contradictions, it is in either case a searching test of a girl's worth. If she is one of those to whom the end of school life means simply "a good time coming," this reminder of the necessity of self-denial will exasperate her. But if she comes home with the determination to put duty first and take pleasure by the way, as it comes; to carry out heartily the regular routine of a well-ordered household whether it falls in with her ideas or not; to share as far as she is allowed her mother's responsibilities, and to brighten home for her father and brothers, she will understand that this can only be done at the price of steady and cheerful self-denial. Yet—paradox though it seems—there will be happiness in it all, and happiness in proportion to her generosity.

"You will think me very mercenary, but do you mean *real* happiness? I know that yielding to others, and all that sort of thing *ought* to make one happy—people say it does. But is it what we girls should call happiness?"

You do not see how the pain of going against self is compatible with what *you* call happiness?

"I confess I don't."

Look at it this way. In an Eastern mine a traveller has come across a magnificent diamond, but so thickly crusted with earth that only a feeble glitter reveals its worth to the connoisseur. In its actual state it is quite unattractive, but, put into the hands of a skilful lapidary and suitably set, it will be fit for the crown of a king. Now supposing the owner objects to the process of removing the crust, on the ground of the labour, expense, possible injury to the stone, &c.; what follows?

"Why, the beauty of the gem will never be brought to light."

And what would you say should he complain that, so far from being a pleasure to him, his treasure did but cause him trouble and expense?

"I should tell him to have a little patience and to go in for trouble that would be so well repaid."

Exactly. But in our case it is not a question of payment in the future only. Here and now we begin to get our reward. Take another example.

The faster you fly from your shadow, the quicker it follows you. The more selfishness seeks to shake itself free from everything in the shape of discomfort, the more relentlessly do these things fasten upon it and torment it. Over and over again in these talks we have come back to the truth, that the way to be happy here and now is to accustom ourselves to do without many things that we like, and to put up with things we do not like. We have each of us two selves, a higher and a lower. Our only road to real happiness lies in freeing the nobler self from the tyranny of the inferior. The motto of the one is: "What I want; at any cost;" that of the other: "What God wants, not what I want." To live up to the last, costs; it cannot be done without persistent effort and self-denial. But in proportion as the higher self gains strength, we find in ourselves a solid contentment and joy: that rest to our souls which our Lord has promised. It is not excitement, nor exuberance of spirits, but more, much more than this—a deep peace, a quiet gladness which *even you* would call happiness.

And we have not to wait for a full victory to reap these fruits. Our first efforts are rewarded—try and you will find it so. Instead of giving way to ill temper and making all around you suffer when you feel crossgrained and upset, go out of yourself by doing a kindness to some one. It may be nothing more than listening kindly to some trivial trouble, writing a note for your mother, or going out with your brother when you want to finish your book, but it will do its work and let sunshine into your soul.

You have often heard me speak of Père de Ravignan. His was a nature that needed strenuous and repeated efforts before self-mastery could be attained. "How did you gain it?" a friend once asked him.

"There were two of us," he answered. "I threw one out of window, and—I remained."

XXVI

Home-makers and their Difficulties

The Holy Home at Nazareth is the model of Christian homes, at least as to the dispositions of its inmates—no comforts or conveniences, no excitement or change; everything clean, but poor in the extreme; daily privations, and a monotonous round of hard and homely labour—this was the life there.

Yet nowhere in all the world has there ever been so happy and so peaceful a home.

"Of course. But look at the Three who lived there—all perfect: no want of consideration, no teasing ways to put up with; in spite of its privations, life there must have been delightful."

You are right in maintaining that the home-makers in our case are sadly unlike those at Nazareth. But we must do our best to make ourselves less unlike.

"I was thinking not of oneself, but of other people who make home trying at times."

Would it not be wiser to leave out of consideration the "other people" whom probably we cannot alter, and turn our attention to the one person whom we can mend because her character is still in process of formation and is of our own making? Each member of the Holy Household of Nazareth loved the others with a self-forgetting affection; shared the daily toil and cares, and gave a special contribution to the peace and happiness of the little place. If, in outward conditions, our home is not modelled after the cottage of Nazareth, we can try to make at least one of its members less unlike the holy Three whose presence rendered Nazareth a Paradise.

The contact with others in home life, like that in a railway carriage, is sometimes too close to be pleasant, and, as is the case on a journey, there is no remedy but patience. Our fellow-travellers in the train are trying in various ways. One insists on closed windows, and suffocates us; or on an open one, unmindful of our neuralgia. This girl annoys us by her fidgety ways with her luggage; that youth by the rustling of his paper; that man by his cough; that woman by her unrefined interest in her luncheon basket. What can we do but bear all with meekness and as little advertence as may to the cause of our discomfort? It is just possible that when we get out at our station there will be a sigh of relief all round at the exit of the traveller whose ill-suppressed signs of annoyance, and ignorance of the conditions of railway travelling, had been a severe tax on their powers of endurance.

Neither charity nor dutifulness requires us to believe every one perfect. All at home have their failings, ourselves among the rest. Were it otherwise, we should probably have finished our course and been removed from this place of training. It is much more conducive to our peace to allow as necessary the state of things we find here, than to be surprised at it. Patients in a hospital ward are not surprised to discover ailments, some of them very unpleasant ones, on every side. Even in the most model home we must school ourselves from the first to take things as we find them, and make the best, not the worst of them.

Let us bear in mind, too, that the need of patience is not all on our side. Those who come in contact with us require it, perhaps, as sorely as ourselves. Home knows us pretty well. The eyes there are too keen, and scan us too closely and too constantly to be easily deceived. And often it is the young eyes that see best.

A young home ruler and his baby sister were sitting side by side in an infant school, making acquaintance with subtraction.

"See, Madge," said the teacher, "if Johnnie has three sweets and gives you one, how many will he have left?"

"Free."

"No, he gives you two—see, one, two—now how many has he?"

"Free."

"Try again; he gives you these two; now he has only one, hasn't he?"

"No, 'cos he wouldn't have enough for his very own self."

This was conclusive. "His very own self" was the sole consideration when Johnnie was concerned, as Madge knew well. As to the arithmetic, it must take its chance—facts were facts.

A Catholic father, whose intercourse with his children reminds us of St. Thomas More's with the happy household at Chelsea, had few things more at heart than to make them grow up unselfish and thoughtful for others. "He was never weary of inculcating that the greatest of pleasures was giving pleasure. His desire to instil into his children an unselfish aim, led to rather an original institution in the family for birthdays. The child whose natal day approached received a liberal sum to spend in presents for every one in the house, from the Serjeant himself down to the little scullery-maid, with a balance for the poor. It was a grand success, a death-blow to selfishness, and proved out and out the value of his kind and generous teaching."[1]

We learn consideration for others by changing places with them and trying to see things from their point of view. Why should we consider our train as the most important one of the day, and complain with such indignation because the porter, who often has to reckon and remember his trains by the hundred instead of by a unit, makes some slight mistake in directing us, especially at holiday seasons when many "specials" are on and "ordinaries" are off? A poor, aggrieved porter said: "We ought to eat a Bradshaw[2] for breakfast to be able to remember all the information we're asked to give."

Learn to manage your conversation well. The father of whom we were speaking just now, wrote thus to his daughter Mary:—

---

1 "Memorials of Mr. Serjeant Bellasis." By E. Bellasis.
2 George Bradshaw created the first comprehensive listing of railway timetables in the 1840s, and for over a century thereafter, any such railway table was referred to as a *Bradshaw*, regardless of its actual publisher.

"Do not form opinions of people or things hastily, but reserve your thoughts to talk them over with those you love; it will delight them, and save you from misconception.

"Do not be too ready to believe anything you hear to another's disadvantage. Of such stories the greater part are wholly untrue, or greatly exaggerated, therefore *mistrust* them all.

"Never express your opinion in a positive manner especially to those older than yourself. The habit of doing so is called 'forwardness' and is most unpleasing. If you have occasion to express your opinion, do it modestly, and as if you were not quite sure of it.

"Do not be too ready to make objections to the opinions you may hear expressed. This habit is called captiousness, and is always offensive. It may be you are obliged to disagree; if so, do it with gentleness, and, if possible, in the form of a question. Learn to take a pleasure in acquiescing when the subject is indifferent. It is a sure way of pleasing, whilst a habit of disagreeing is very objectionable.

"Avoid a critical spirit; in other words, do not find fault with individuals or things. There are few things which will not admit of criticism, but remember, a critical spirit is often ill-natured and indicative of a commonplace understanding.

"Never trust yourself to criticise Catholic religious practices or habits, at home or abroad; most likely you misapprehend them, but to find fault with them is to act in a Protestant spirit.

"Ask the opinion of others as often as you please, but give your own as seldom as possible, unless you are asked; and then give it diffidently."[1]

Does this advice sound very much behind the times? Let us answer the question by another: "Would it be any advantage

---
1 "Memorials of Mr. Serjeant Bellasis." By E. Bellasis.

to our boys and girls and to the company in which they find themselves, if it were kept in mind and acted upon?"

When you can control conversation, lead upwards rather than downwards. Some girls have a way of raising the tone of the conversation into which they are thrown; others as surely depress it.

"What would depress it?"

A large amount of tittle-tattle, flippant or unkind talk; making dress or appearance the main subject of conversation; a habit of seeing the ridiculous side of everything—mind, I say *of everything*—this is quite different from the sense of humour which adds so much to the brightness of life. Perpetual banter is very wearying and objectionable; know when to be serious.

Be careful how you speak of the absent. Train yourself to hate and to fear detraction for the harm it does, not only to the person to whom you speak, who is not there to defend himself, but also to those who hear you, and to yourself. Think sometimes, as you hear yourself talk, of the words: "Thy speech doth betray thee." Let us be like St. Teresa, of whom it used to be said, that in her presence the good name of the absent was always safe. Stop detraction whenever you can, by defending or excusing the absent. If you cannot stop it, refrain from listening or showing interest by asking questions. You cannot check your elders, but you can be silent and irresponsive. Draw attention to people's good points rather than to their failings; invite admiration instead of criticism. Above all, do not criticise priests. By a disparaging remark you may do more harm and prevent more good than you will ever know in this world, injuring not the priest only, but others whom, but for your thoughtless words, he might have helped.

We should refrain from drawing the attention of people to words or things likely to irritate them, and never pass on remarks that hurt. And we must watch our own words and tone of voice when little misunderstandings occur, as they will do from time to time in every home. Be the first to make up a quarrel, and don't be afraid of owning yourself to have been in the wrong. It is a good saying, that he who never made a mistake never made anything.

Take slights and annoyances in a large-minded way; don't think they were meant, and if they were, don't fret and worry over them: *Laissez tomber, laissez passer*, is a useful motto for home life, whilst touchiness and resentment are fatal to its happiness and peace.

For the safe conveyance of any inflammable body, the Railway Companies take special precautions. In the "Rule Book" of the North-Eastern Company we find:

"On each side of any vehicle containing explosive matter, there will be affixed in conspicuous characters, by means of a securely attached label or otherwise, the word 'Explosive.'"

Would it be well for the public safety if some of us were to be labelled thus?

XXVII

Home: The First Field of Work

"Isn't it rather hard, don't you think, to be blamed by one set of people for having no purpose in life and frittering it away in trifles; and, if you have a purpose, to be told by another set that one's vocation lies in one's own home, and that the desire for outside work is mere craving for excitement and independence?"

Put in that way, it certainly does seem something of a hardship. But let us examine the charges separately.

You will own that we are quite unjustifiable if there is any ground for the first. No girl ought to be content with an empty, aimless life. Every one is bound to work hard at the formation of her character and the cultivation of her gifts, and to hold herself in readiness to turn to good account later all she has—talents, position, influence—for the cause of God and the Church.

The second charge concerns those, probably, who, neglecting plain duty at home, pine after work outside. They grudge half-an-hour's reading to an invalid mother, but would "simply love" to be a district visitor, cheering up some old woman in the slums. At home they are self-seeking and useless, but in a hospital they flatter themselves they would be models of self-sacrifice, idolised by their fellow nurses and by their patients.

"That is absurd, of course; but when there are no home duties, or not enough to fill one's day, there can be no harm, surely, in looking for work elsewhere?"

You are quite right in maintaining that the energies within us demand a field for their exercise. You feel like the eager youth who knelt at our Lord's feet asking: "Good Master, what good shall I do that I may have life everlasting?" He did not ask what evil he must avoid, but what good he must do. He felt, and felt rightly, that Heaven is a reward to be earned, and wanted to know the conditions. Our Lord spoke to him of good, and, seeing him still unsatisfied, of greater good.

"And Jesus looking upon him, loved him." He loves the earnest heart that asks what it can do with its gifts and its strength; but He bids it be ready for sacrifice as well as for labour. "Many seek themselves in what they do," says à Kempis, "and are not sensible of it." If we honestly wish to know what we *ought* to do, not what we *want* to do, many of us have only to look round us to find, at home, work in abundance waiting to be done.

No girl can say she has no home duties. There may be more for some than for others, but towards all those who make it home, a girl has responsibilities, and all in various ways and degrees have a claim upon her. Human nature, however, is apt to chafe under the commonplaces of daily life, which exact a constant expenditure of physical strength and mental energy, yet leave no mark and apparently achieve nothing. It needs the eye of Faith to see in them anything noble or ennobling. It needs a glance backward upon the smallest of homes in a village street, where the making and mending of rough furniture, fetching water from the well, sweeping the house, obeying orders, was the daily work of the Son of God, who had the preaching of the Gospel, the training of the Apostles, the foundation of the Church, the redemption of mankind before Him, and only three years to do it all.

But He waited patiently for His hour, for the Providence of God to unfold Itself, and in those sacred years of the Hidden Life taught all who were to call themselves His followers not to begrudge to their life's work the time of preparation which is its only secure foundation and the essential condition of its success.

Let us who long to set our hands to great things, begin by little ones. Let us learn the lesson of patient preparation which our Master teaches us at Nazareth; from the humble works which filled His day and which gave to God greater glory than the united worship and service of men and angels, learn that the true worth of any work is not to be measured by its value in the eyes of men, but by its being the fulfilment by us then and there of the Will of God.

What He wants of us by and by He will make known when the time comes. It is His work more than ours; we need not be anxious or think we are losing time; "They also serve who only stand and wait." He cares more for the workman than for the work, and in the interests of the work itself, prepares the workman beforehand, just as is done in every craft and profession among men. Would it not be the greatest mistake for the apprentice to look upon his time of training as lost time?

"But it's just the training we want to get to."

And have got to long ago, and are in the midst of day by day. Get well into your heads that the most valuable training for any work in the future is to be found ready to your hand in the round of daily life at home. It is a thousand pities that girls do not recognise this and understand that there is no demand for untrained workers now.

What is needed for any work you may take up later? Surely the power of self-control, of concentration of mind on details, of self-sacrifice, of being able to sink self, work in concert with others, take criticism and contradiction placidly; the power of loyal obedience to a head, the power of hard work, of perseverance in what we have undertaken, even when uninteresting and monotonous and beset with difficulties.

All these valuable qualities are called for at home. Never mind if the occasions are small, the benefit now and in the future of profiting by them will not be small.

I am not saying that our road in life is never clearly marked out for us as soon as we leave school, but only that, as a rule, there is an interval of time at home which is the immediate preparation for our life's work, and should be used wisely as such. The more fully you know your religion, the better you could take a Catechism class, or help inquiring Protestants, or instruct a convert. The more practical your knowledge of cooking, cutting out, housework, sanitary conditions, the more efficient you will be later for work among the poor, or for managing a household of your own. The more cultivated your mind all round, the more beneficial will be your influence on all with whom you are brought into contact. This thought will give you an object in your occupations and in the pursuit of any hobby you may have taken up; and still more in your choice of books.

We must not expect miracles like the London cabby, who waited patiently on a pouring night at the entrance of the Houses of Parliament, long after all the members had left.

"It's no use waiting there," some one called out at last, "there's no one in."

"My business is not with them that's in but with them as comes out," was the answer. And he waited on.

"The stupid!"

Yet no more stupid than we should be to expect an array of virtues to come trooping out without any trouble on our part, when wanted in after life. Only what is in can come out, and that only is in which we have put there by strenuous effort and diligent practice.

"I thought all the virtues were planted in our souls at Baptism."

They are, but as seeds to be carefully tended, not to be left alone to grow and blossom and bear fruit spontaneously as in the soil of Eden. Unless sustained and fostered, the life that is in this precious seed will perish.

We are almost on the eve of "coming out." *But what is coming?* That which we have been preparing since our baby days; that, whether of good or of evil, to which we have trained ourselves by repeated acts; that which has been visible to the keen eyes of the home and school circles for many a year, and will now be manifested on a wider field; our own handiwork, our own equipment for life—this is coming out.

School life first, and then home life is the training ground in which we are to exercise ourselves in the qualities and virtues we shall need if we are to be the useful, zealous, influential Catholics we want to be and mean to be.

"Influential!"

Certainly. You don't suppose, surely, that the talents and opportunities which have been given us are meant to lie dormant or to be thrown away! Our example, our interest in things Catholic, our self-sacrifice in the cause of Religion, of the rescue, and housing, and education of our poor children, our zeal in seconding the efforts of the clergy as far as our means will allow, in helping with spiritual or temporal alms the needy souls Providence puts in our way, in upholding a high standard of Catholic life and practice before the world—this is what we must freely give who have so freely received. Yes, certainly, we must look to it that our influence shall be of the right sort. Much has been given us, much will be expected of us; let us get ourselves ready.

"How?"

By the quiet exercise of the virtues called for in our daily life at home. They will be needed every one of them on a larger scale later on. Influence goes out unconsciously from a girl who is what she ought to be, as the perfume from the flower. She need not trouble about it. If she tends the flower properly, God will see to its perfume. Far and wide over the field of the Church and beyond, it will go, "the good odour of Jesus Christ," delighting first, and then attracting souls to His love and service.

"Well, only think of *us* being influential Catholics!"

XXVIII

Wider Fields

Your question about outside work has led us far afield. What I have said has not, I hope, in any way discouraged you, but only shown you how useful a preparation for it may be found in your home life.

In the social workers of to-day qualifications are called for which were never dreamed of twenty years ago. The hardships of the poor, arising from drink, from overcrowded, insanitary homes, the poisonous trades at which they have to work, excessive and ill-paid labour, or the want of labour, which means misery and starvation, are evils which are at length engaging the serious attention of the State and being remedied, at least in part, by the law of the land. But much of this misery and wrong continues in spite of Government inspection. The poor are helpless, and are often as ignorant of the laws in their behalf as if these had never been passed. It is for those who visit them to bring the evil before the authorities who can deal with it. But to reap the fruits of recent legislation, the modern district visitor must know what it is, and where to complain and to whom.

"Where can one learn all this?"

The broad outlines of such knowledge may be obtained from a patient study of standard works dealing with what has already been accomplished in the direction of social legislation, from the invaluable data contained in Blue Books, from an intelligent reading of the daily papers, and from the conversation of experienced workers. All this is an education following upon the education of school-days.

"Some people say women should be content to look after their homes and have no business to meddle with politics."

They do. And there are others who ask: Is it our duty to see that a remedy is brought at last to the misery in which so many thousands of our fellow-countrymen are living at a stone's-throw from our doors? If this is a duty, then the means to bring about a remedy is a duty too. And who, they ask, is so fit to improve the home as woman, whose special domain home is? Women sooner or later will do it; they are becoming more and more alive to the need of remedying the appalling evils on every side, and are ready to show that they are able to cope with the evil. Are Catholic women to stand aloof from the movement and allow non-Catholic workers to use all the influence their interest and energy will secure them? Or will they fall in with a movement which they cannot check, bring Catholic influence to bear upon it, train themselves to work at least as efficiently as non-Catholics, and to deal with the social question on Catholic lines?

For many years Catholics were kept apart from the national life through no fault of their own. But those days are gone by. We are free now to make ourselves what we ought to be, a social force in the land. It depends upon our own energy whether we become a force or not. We have to get rid of the feeling of outlawry, and boldly take our place among our fellow-countrymen in private life and in combination with them.

It is the duty of English Catholics, our ecclesiastical superiors tell us, to put themselves in the van of the social movement. We have to arouse in ourselves a conscientious conviction of our personal duty, not merely to those who are of the household of the Faith, but to our fellow-countrymen at large. By throwing ourselves into the political and social life of the nation, we shall insensibly Catholicise the nation, whereas if we stand apart, we shall not only lose an opportunity that may never recur, but betray the trust committed to us, and prove ourselves unworthy of that influence over the destinies of our country which Providence has placed within our reach.

Whilst, therefore, our first and deepest concern will be to promote the cause of the Church in England, we must not stop there, but take a keen interest in the national life of the country, and co-operate as far as we can with all agencies, Catholic or non-Catholic, working for the national good.

"What kind of things can girls do—ordinary girls, you know, not particularly clever, but wanting to do something?"

There is plenty to be done. They could help in a girls' club or in a settlement by taking a Catechism class of little children. They could read at the mothers' meetings, sit down there by the side of the poor and hear their troubles, help to hand round tea to them, or play for a dance. They could get up a game of "musical chairs" or "post" for those who like to play, but force a game on none. The great secret of a successful worker is that she finds out what the women and girls like and does not impose her own fads upon them.

Older workers could instruct converts or help with district visiting, look up cases and report them to the committee. At the girls' clubs they could help to amuse the factory girls, the seamstresses, and the shop girls who come in fagged out with their days work. Without anything undesirable in the shape of familiarity on the one hand, or of condescension—an attitude the poor are quick to detect and resent—on the other, they can let these tired toilers feel that they have the real sympathy of women like themselves. Any trouble, any expenditure of ingenuity and tender kindness, is well bestowed that will bring brightness into the lives of girls which otherwise would be comparatively friendless and not without danger.

But remember that if you take up social work you must be at your post regularly. "Do impress on all who offer help," said an earnest, self-denying worker, "that they must come prepared for self-sacrifice. How discouraging it is after having spent time in putting girls into the way of work, to find them throwing it up after a few weeks. If they do not mean to be regular in their attendance, let them not offer themselves. Let them bind themselves for three months or six, and not send their excuses as soon as they have begun what they have undertaken."

If you want to do something for your Master, be sure that in one shape or another you will find the cross in your work. If you are not prepared for this, get out a novel and sit in an armchair by the fire, or do some fancy work for a bazaar, but do not dream of taking up social work among the poor.

There is so much to be done, that Catholic women should come forward. But it must be with the Apostolic spirit. They must be ready to put up with what is inconvenient and painful and not be too ready to believe they cannot do this or that. Let them try, and they will find that once the love of souls has taken possession of them, and a few victories over selfishness and sensitiveness have been won, they can do and bear what a while ago would have seemed an impossibility. "Through the help of my God I shall go over a wall," said David (Ps. xvii). There are many walls, difficulties of every kind, in work amongst the poor. One zealous worker says:

"There are problems now for every district visitor which can only be met by prayer. It is no matter of simply going out and talking commonplaces. From the morning prayer the right word to be said must come."

It is this purity of intention, this working for God, and looking to Him to bless and prosper what we do, which gives value to and draws down blessing on our acts. In these days of ceaseless activity it is specially necessary for us to remember the importance of our motives. Let me read you what one of our Bishops says as to the motive and aim of Christian charity:

> "There are those amongst us who care not what are the motives of beneficent work, provided humanity is succoured and the world's condition made better. But no Christian can assent to such a view. Therefore from the beginning the follower of Christ has been taught to see Christ in the poor and the needy. The Church has always put aside a substantial part of her revenues for the poor, because to her the poor represented her Lord and Master. The monk in his rule, receives the poor man who knocketh at the door even as Christ. The Bishop washes the feet of the poor to make some return to Christ for having washed the feet of the first pastors. Kings and queens who believed in the Gospel have fed the poor at their tables and ministered to them, seeing well, in their intelligence of Christ's word, who it was that all the time received their pious duty. Saints have kissed the feet of the poor, and pressed their lips with burning countenance upon their wounds, because they realised the vivid presence of their crucified Lord. This is the spirit of the Gospel. Extinguish that spirit, and you may comfort men and women by your charitable work, but it will not draw either you or them any nearer to God."
>
> "And let us observe," the Bishop goes on, "that our Lord not only puts before us Himself as the end and purpose of Christian charity, but also makes it clear that the love of God does not exist without love of one another. It was to be the very mark by which His disciples were to be recognised—that they loved one another. The love of God in a man's heart is demonstrated, and, as it were, certified by kindness to men. For it is very easy for a man to deceive himself as to his real love of God unless he translates his spiritual affections into deeds....Do something, or do not pretend you love God! Try to do some good, or your piety is a sham! Open your purse, or do not flatter yourself that you are a man of prayer! Take an interest in human trouble and suffering, or the Church services you enjoy so much will not bring you any nearer heaven! Be kind, considerate, gentle, and helpful to those in your home and your circle, or the largest number of the most devout prayer-books will be no shield at the judgment, no rampart in the day of visitation."[1]

---

1 Bishop Hedley.

Do something!—this ought to be the cry of our conscience to every one of us. We are not among those to whom the gifts of God in the shape of opportunities of active service have been denied. Our minds have been cultivated, our consciences instructed, our responsibilities brought home to us. All around us work is lying, work we can do. Are we going to waste the talents entrusted to us?

What are we going to do with our life? Fritter it away in the selfish pursuit of pleasure? Is to have "a good time" our highest ambition in this world?

"Once the zeal for souls has been aroused, you said just now, we can do great things. But how can one rouse this zeal?"

A girl once told me that she never knew what zeal for souls meant till she began to read the *Annals of the Propagation of the Faith*. At first she found them dry, but she knew they ought to interest her, and she persevered in the reading. Gradually she came to look forward to them; then she read them eagerly. Then they were not enough to satisfy her, and she got the *Illustrated Catholic Missions* to supplement them. Little by little the souls for which Christ died, more especially the nine hundred millions who have never heard His Name, became her absorbing thought, and nothing would satisfy her but to devote her life to the work of bringing some of them at least to His knowledge and love. She is now working among the natives at Moropai, Bengal.

The Society for the Prevention of Cruelty to Children is another that may well meet with the active sympathy of those who have good homes, and who can scarcely bring themselves to believe that there are little ones in this Christian land who tremble at the name of "father" or "mother."

Here and there a sister's influence may induce a brother to join the Society of St. Vincent de Paul, whose members benefit their own souls as much or more than they alleviate the distress of others.

To make the most of the little we can do, it is well to get into communication with those who can put us in the way of good work and teach us how to set about it. A League of Catholic Women Workers, similar to those which exist abroad, has been started in this country, with the object of bringing Catholic women together, promoting by every available means the improvement of the homes of our poor, better methods for the care and training of children, the diffusion of good books, &c., making known what is being done elsewhere in these directions, and gaining strength by mutual effort and organisation.

The needs to be met are endless. If one is above your capacity to tackle, look out for another. But, for God's sake, *do something*! Do not kneel down morning and night and say "Our Father," if you will not stretch out a hand to your brothers and sisters who in the name of our common Father cry out to you for help. Train yourself without loss of time in that service of God which shows itself in self-denying labour in His cause, in the cheerful sacrifice of time, tastes, money—whatever you have to give. Look around you, and see how you may make a beginning here at home. Watch for opportunities of being kind and neighbourly to those among whom you live. Where a helping hand is wanted, offer it, even at the cost of inconvenience, and perhaps even at the expense of that sense of personal dignity that fears to demean itself by stooping to lowly acts of kindness. A servant is ill or absent; some little delicacy that you could make or carry, is needed by a neighbour's sick child; or the child itself has to be tended or amused for an afternoon; a bundle of poor clothes must be finished for Christmas, or the church has to be decorated, or a letter written for an invalid—there is no lack of work for willing hearts and hands. If, not from love of excitement or independence, but from higher motives, you want to do outside work, bear in mind that the thorough and cheerful discharge of home duties, will not only be excellent service now, but first rate training for wider service later, which it will deserve as its reward.

XXIX
"Noblesse Oblige"

"Our last talk these holidays?"

"Then our last term at school; then Christmas, and then—Home for good!"

It is fortunate the little ones have not been here for our later talks, or they would have been grumbling at their "dryness."

"They are very late—I hope they haven't missed their train; they should have been here half-an-hour ago."

"Well, let us make hay while the sun shines. There is one thing I want to ask. We are always being told to act on principle, to guard against worldly principles, and I'm not sure I know what is meant. What is 'principle'?"

A full answer to that question would be a lengthy one. But let us look into the word and dig out some at least of its meaning.

Dictionaries tell us that the word "Principle" means the cause, source, or origin of anything; the ground of action or motive; a fundamental truth; a settled law; a rule of conduct or action. "Unprincipled"—having no settled principles; destitute of virtue. We might say, then, that in its ethical or moral sense, the word "Principle" stands for a settled law or rule of action, based upon fundamental truth, brought home to the conscience and become matter of intimate conviction.

The word is generally used in a good sense—that is, to denote a right cause of action or rule of conduct.

Father Faber says: "It is of great importance to have well ascertained First Principles. It is astonishing how few have such. An almost incredible amount of excellent efforts comes to nothing because it is at random and by fits and starts, and operating inconsistently with its antecedents. The really powerful man is the man of ascertained principles.... Above all, a man should have ascertained principles of practical religion, if religion is to be the business of life. It is deplorable for the cause of God on earth that such men are so few."

Were I to ask you whether you would rather have the moss rose in the vase there, or the bush from which it was gathered, you would probably choose the bush. Why? Because the cut flower, though so beautiful now, will be dead or dying tomorrow and you cannot depend on one of the buds around it coming out. They may or they may not. But the roses in the garden can be relied on; the buds—a good many at any rate—will be full-blown flowers after a while; in short, the rosebush is something stable, the other is not. Now, what makes the difference?

"Why, the root."

Yes, it is the root, hidden far down in the earth, that bears the plant up, and keeps it steady, and provides it with nourishment, so that we can count upon its flowers even before they appear. Now what the root is to the plant, principle is to us. The word means "beginning," and as the stem and branches spring from the root, so do our actions start from or begin with principle. The root pushes its way through the earth, and gets a firm grasp of it all round. It feeds itself with its juices and sends them up into the stem, and branches, and leaves, and buds, and flowers. The root is the principle or source of all those fair forms, of that brilliant colour, of the delicious perfume. Cut off from the root, your rose must perish. So will fair appearances of piety, resolutions, and good practices, unless they spring from principles that are sound and strong.

We call men and women unprincipled who make their likes and dislikes the motive of all they do. And we say a girl is high principled who acts, not from impulse or routine, or whim, or human respect, but in obedience to her conscience, because to act in such or such a way—*is right*. Without high principles no one can grow up good and happy, and lead a noble and useful life. It is worth while, then, to see how principles come to be formed.

We know that we shall be later what we are making ourselves now. We are framing our character day by day by the way we use our will, not once or twice, but habitually; and the way we use our will depends on our principles. If our mind has taken a strong hold of solid truths, the will will be strengthened to act in the right way, and produce, as it were by habit, the beautiful flowers and fruits of a Christian life. The right acts are often hard to do; they go against our humours, inclinations, and passions; but when the principles are deep and firm, the will is hardy and does hard things bravely.

How different is the poor weak will that is not rooted in good because the mind has not taken the trouble to feed itself on truth. Take an example:—

Two boys make a retreat. Both hear the same words: "God has put me into this world for a little while, to get myself ready for the next, into which I shall have to go very soon. Getting ready means doing His Will, avoiding sin, keeping His Commandments. If I use bad words, if I neglect prayer, if I lead others wrong, I am doing the very opposite of what I was sent here to do, and I must expect to be punished for it."

Boy number one says: "That's all true, and Father looked into the second bench when he said it. That's where it's wanted.

I hope B. heard it, and that it'll make him conquer that beastly temper of his."

Boy number two says: "If all that's true, and I know it is, it will never do for me to go on like this. I must make a change. I must make more effort to overcome my temper and take such and such means of curing myself." The first boy has thrown away words that were meant by God to sink into his soul and feed and strengthen it. If he listens through the retreat like that, and hears sermons through life like that, he will gain nothing at all by these means of grace, or rather he will lay up for himself the punishment of the slothful servant who knew his lord's will and did not do it. For no grace leaves us as it finds us. Either we use it and grow stronger and better, or we throw it away and lose something of what we had before.

Into the heart of the second boy the good seed has sunk. What is wanted now is that it should be helped to grow like the seed that is watered. One such seed if tended has in it the power to make a Saint.

"Tell us some seeds that have made Saints."

"What is this for eternity?" St. Aloysius often asked himself. "I was born for something greater than to be a slave to my body," St. Stanislaus would say often. "Conquer thyself," was a favourite saying of St. Francis Xavier. "The Saints never complain," was often on the lips of the Curé of Ars. "It is not what I like but what God likes that is to be my rule," a holy priest of our own days used to say.

"I like that the best."

Make it your own, then. Dig deep into it to get out all its hidden meaning. See how just and reasonable it is; how useful to take as a guide. Dwell upon it, go back upon it, till it becomes your own intimate conviction, strong enough to lead you to choose God's Will rather than your own when the two come into conflict; to be a principle of conduct with you habitually. Any one who will let such seed as that sink deep into his soul by pondering it till it has worked its way into his mind and feelings, and become as it were part of himself, will grow up a fervent Catholic.

"Do you really mean to say that *one* truth well pondered would have such an effect as that?"

The lives of the Saints show us that it has done this for them. God will never do great things in and by the soul that has but a feeble grasp of truth; but He will do wonders in that soul which has thoroughly got hold of and made its own even one of the fundamental truths of Religion. But His complaint is that men and women will not "think in their hearts."

Yet the need for serious thought and for high principle is greater now than ever. The time has gone by, as we were saying the other day, when young Catholics had no further prospect or hope than to lead a harmless life in comparative retirement, without expectation of taking part in the life of the country. They must plunge now into the battle of life, meeting with and knowing all sorts of evil. To be prepared for this ordeal, they must have learned to hold to principle and to honour—in the Catholic sense—above all things, that is, at any cost.

We see the moral influence exercised by good Protestants. What shame it would be if we Catholics, possessing the Real Presence in our midst, the Mass, the Sacraments, did not do much more, and hold up a higher standard before our neighbours, who expect it of us and are scandalised if they do not find it.

To have the strength of principle necessary for this, we must be penetrated with that sense of Responsibility of which we have already spoken. We must have trained ourselves to stand with God's help *alone*, doing our duty in His sight and before men, *because it is right*; doing it quietly, unassumingly, but without the least compromise; trampling on human respect to the point of saying when asked to abate that principle or to follow bad example: "No, I will not, because it is wrong; I cannot go against my conscience." Only on the Last Day will such a one know how many souls have been deterred from sin by her example.

Danger comes from the temptation to go as far as possible with others in questionable matters, stopping short only of actual sin. The fear of what others will say, the craving to be *à la mode*, to read what every one reads, to see what every one sees; the desire to show your companions that you are not bigoted, that you are not going to judge them or be shocked by what you hear or see, even if it be against God's honour—such a frame of mind insensibly but inevitably leads over the border, with the result, not only of harm to yourself, but of scandal to others, who gather from your example that Catholics are no better than those who have not the high standard *their* religion puts before them. Boys and girls should have learned at school to take their own line for "the Right" whether they are under supervision or not; all the more when there is no one at hand to guard them from evil or to commend them.

There are boys who go for their holidays to a home where both parents are not Catholics, or where they are indifferent Catholics; where the religious observances of school life are ignored—a low Mass on Sunday, and nothing all the week except perhaps dangerous friends and a life of amusement, without an idea of living for anything except success and a cheery time. Their standard gets lowered, and when they go back to school, they look forward to the freedom from restraint and supervision which they will enjoy when they go out into life. They begin to look on their religious exercises as a part of education, right enough for boys, maybe, but to be dropped by *men*, for they do not see it at home, and why should they be different from their home associates? Unless there has been fostered throughout their school life a spirit of manly pride in their religion, in being *allowed* to serve God as Catholics, and a sense of honour which prompts them never to do a shady thing, not because they might be seen, but because *it is wrong*, it will be a miracle if these lads do not turn out as too many do—nominal Catholics and perhaps hardly even that. *Age viriliter*—play the man—is the motto for boys nowadays.

And for girls too, in the sense of making a stand when there is question of God's honour and of right and wrong.

Some girls have not clear ideas on this point. They attach, or appear to attach, more importance to certain devotions and pious practices than to the fundamentals on which these rest. They pass blamelessly through their school course, but have not the stamina in them to stand the shock of the first real difficulties they meet with when school life is over.

On the other hand, there are girls who, with less appearance of goodness, quietly keep to what they know to be right in spite of every one around them. These are the girls who do good, who make others *see* what the Church teaches—girls perfectly straight, never hiding their religion, showing by their manner, more than by their words, that they dislike a questionable story or joke: full of life and fun, and ready to enter into everything going on around them *until* it touches the border of sin, when they quietly show they will go no further.

Is it too much to expect high principle such as this in those who have had the best of instruction, and daily Mass, and frequent Sacraments at their disposal? If these do not start in life with a high standard, with the resolution of fearlessly doing right because it is God's Law, and there is no choice but to adhere to it—to whom are we to look for that example of Catholic life and practice which, as children of the Church, we are bound to give to our non-Catholic neighbours?

A lady said of a young Protestant officer who had just left the regiment her husband commanded: "He will be a great loss; he was always on the side of right; he had such an influence among the other young ones; he was never ashamed of going to church or taking the Sacrament." And of a young sailor, also a Protestant, it was told that, if the other young men were talking in a manner they should not, and he entered the gun-room, one or other would say: "You had better stop that; here is Thomas, and he won't stand that sort of thing."

If I have taken examples of high principle from among Protestants, you will not suppose that there are not plenty of noble instances of such among Catholics—girls as well as boys. But I want to show what a shame it will be if we, with all our graces, fall short of a Protestant standard of practice.

And why should such cases be the exception? Think what it would be if all the boys and girls turned out from our Catholic schools were to set the example required of all, and calling forth admiration when seen in the few! Why, we should have England Catholic again in no time!

Just a word about devotions and pious practices, lest you should have mistaken my meaning, or suppose I would have you undervalue them. Far from it. They are based on the solid foundation of Catholic doctrine respecting the Incarnation, the Real Presence, the honour due to the Blessed Mother of God and to the Saints. They are authorised by the Church, and commended to us in great variety, not that we may encumber ourselves with a multiplicity of them, but that we may choose wisely from among them such as suit us, without criticising such as do not happen to appeal to ourselves but are helpful to others. What I meant to insist on was, that these devotions and practices should come on the top of principles and be the outcome of them, not be a veneer with poor stuff underneath.

We must have a firm hold on foundations, or we shall have no rock to cling to when the winds blow. But with sound principles to steady us, we shall pass safely with God's help through the difficulties that sooner or later must come to us one and all.

Remember that indifference is the danger nowadays. It is the natural result of mixing so much with non-Catholics and working with them, as we shall be more and more called upon to do if we are to secure the representation of Catholic interests and the presence of Catholics on the committees of societies with national or general objects. But in our dealings with non-Catholics we must never allow principle to be sacrificed to expediency. We are expected to hold our own, and we must do it. Faith goes when practice goes.

Do not be taken off your feet by the first shock of finding such numbers differing from you in fundamental questions; by the free discussion of the religious questions now prevalent; by the paganism of modern society in its views and its ways.

And do not be carried away by clever talk, by smart but irreverent words about holy persons and things. Cleverness and power are good or harmful according to the dispositions of those who possess them; the Devil would pass any examination with the highest honours and be a member of all the learned societies of Europe.

"The young should hold fast to what truth they know; they should be suspicious of plausible novelty; they should be able to doubt, to question, to hold back *even when they cannot refute*, and they should be firm and courageous in acting on what they know to be true."[1]

You as Catholics, with your higher tone of morality—that is, truer notions of right and wrong—will at times have to go against what you see and hear around you. Determine not

---

[1] Bishop Hedley.

only *to be*, but, when need requires, to *show yourself to be*, on God's side in the great battle between good and evil. This will cost. Of course it will. And the trial comes just at the age when we are most sensitive to a pitying smile or a clever joke at our expense. Think then that your Good Angel says to you the words once said to Peter: "Thou also wast with Jesus of Nazareth." Think you hear our Lord Himself saying to you: "He that shall confess Me before men, I will also confess him before My Father who is in heaven."

Brace yourself to bear bravely the unpleasant consequences of a straightforward word when your views of right and wrong come into conflict with those of freethinkers or indifferent Catholics; when they would have you accept slippery principles in place of those with which your Faith provides you. Not that you will be called upon to force your convictions upon others in season and out of season. This would do more harm than good. But when God's honour or your neighbour's good calls for a fearless avowal of principles, then the manly Catholic will courageously confess the Faith that is in him. This manly action will always influence others for good and ensure you their respect whatever they may say or do. Often enough by the courageous showing of her colours at the outset, a girl has won a position that has not only secured her against further molestation, but made her very presence a power for good and a guarantee for propriety in any company in which she may find herself.

"I wish I could feel that I shall do all that when the time comes, but I feel that I should give way at once like a bit of wet paper, as the Curé of Ars said."

Say rather with David: "With the help of my God I will go over a wall," and with St. Paul: "I can do all things in Him who strengtheneth me. Not I, but the grace of God with me." Do your part now to form sound principles by serious thought and earnest prayer, and God will take care of you when the time comes.

"What serious thoughts, for example?"

About the end for which God made us and sent us into this world...

The folly, the ingratitude, the hatefulness of sin; the stupidity of behaving ourselves in this world as if we were to stay here always; of using time, health, position, money, gifts of body or mind, as ends in themselves, instead of means to the salvation of our soul...

The love of God as shown in Creation, the Incarnation, the Passion, the Eucharist, the easy forgiveness of sin, the promises attached to prayer...

The love of God to us personally, and the duty as well as the need of our hearts to make Him some return...

The truth that nothing happens in this world but by the Will or permission of God, and that He makes all things, all things without exception, work together for the good of those who love Him...

The truth that God is always at hand to help, and that He will never let us be tried beyond our strength...

The thought of Death and Judgement coming soon...

And Hell or Heaven for ever, depending on the state in which we are found at Death.

Any one of these thoughts pondered seriously, and helped by prayer, will slowly but surely work a change in your mind and heart. You will feel yourself strengthened to act upon your convictions in small occasions; and when bigger ones come in your way, God will be there—as your father by the awkward stile the other day—and with the help of His hand you will be over, not safely only, but easily.

"You will say I belong to the family of Mr. Ready-to-halt or Mrs. Feeblemind, but it does seem to me much more difficult to serve God and save one's soul in these days than it was in—well, the Middle Ages, for example, when girls sat over their embroidery all their lives. Not that I should have liked it, mind; I should simply have hated it, it must have been so awfully stupid and slow. All the same, I think it must have been ever so much easier."

To unite the education, the aspirations, the social duties and amusements, the "go" of the modern girl with those qualities which are the characteristics of true womanhood, is a difficulty, no doubt. Yet that it is no impossibility, can be shown by Catholic girls and women of our own time, who as truly and as closely follow in the footsteps of the Maiden-Mother, the type of perfect womanhood, as the most simple and secluded of her daughters of other days. She is the model for all times and conditions, but she must be studied if her example is to tell upon us.

We may admire the humility of her self-effacement in the Visitation; her quick and practical sympathy at the Marriage of Cana; her marvellous fortitude on Calvary. But of all the helpful and attractive virtues we may study in her, none, perhaps, is more suited to our modern requirements than her prudence.

There is nothing feeble in this highest and finished type of womanhood. She is at once the Lily of Israel and the Tower of David. Her complete self-possession at all times and under all circumstances, teaches us the lesson of self-control over our memory and imagination and affections, over our thoughts and our words, our looks and our gestures, so necessary in days when girls are inclined to "let themselves go," to an extent undreamed of in your Middle Ages.

If you want a picture of Mary to study, you will hardly find a lovelier one than that painted by the master hand of Cardinal Newman:—

"Her holiness was such, that if we saw her, and heard her, we should not be able to tell to those who asked us anything about her except simply that she was angelic and heavenly.

"Of course her face was most beautiful; but we should not be able to recollect whether it was beautiful or not; we should not recollect any of her features, because it was her beautiful sinless soul, which looked through her eyes, and spoke through her mouth, and was heard in her voice, and compassed her all about; when she was still, or when she walked, whether she smiled, or was sad, her sinless soul, this it was which would draw all those to her who had any grace in them, any remains of grace, any love of holy things. There was a divine music in all she said and did—in her mien, her air, her deportment, that charmed every true heart that came near her. Her innocence, her humility and modesty, her simplicity, sincerity, and truthfulness, her unselfishness, her unaffected interest in every one who came to her, her purity—it was these qualities which made her so lovable; and were we to see her now, neither our first thought nor our second thought would be, what she could do for us with her Son (though she can do so much), but our first thought would be, 'Oh, how beautiful!' and our second thought would be, 'Oh, what ugly hateful creatures are we!'

"It must be recollected that she is not only the great instance of the contemplative life, but also of the practical; and the practical life is at once a life of penance and of prudence, if it is to be well discharged. Now Mary was as full of external work and hard service as any Sister of Charity at this day. Of course her duties varied according to the seasons of her life, as a young maiden, as a wife, as a mother, and as a widow; but still her life was full of duties day by day and hour by hour. As a stranger in Egypt, she had duties among the poor heathen among whom she was thrown. As a dweller in Nazareth, she had her duties towards her kinsfolk and neighbours. She had her duties, though unrecorded, during those years in which our Lord was preaching and proclaiming His Kingdom. After He had left this earth, she had her duties towards the Apostles, and especially towards the Evangelists. She had duties towards the Martyrs, and to the Confessors in prison; to the sick, to the ignorant, and to the poor. Afterwards she had to seek with St. John another and a heathen country, where her happy death took place.

But before that death, how much must she have suffered in her life amid an idolatrous population! Doubtless the Angels screened her eyes from the worst crimes there committed. Still, she was full of duties there—and in consequence she was full of merit. All her acts were perfect, all were the best that could be done. Now, always to be awake, guarded, fervent, so as to be able to act not only without sin, but in the best possible way, in the varying circumstances of each day, denotes a life of untiring mindfulness. But of such a life, Prudence is the presiding virtue. It is, then, through the pains and sorrows of her earthly pilgrimage that we are able to invoke her as the *Virgo prudentissima.*" [1]

To have some such picture as this in our minds as the beads of our Rosary slip through our fingers—this is to study Mary. And the simple study, mind, like the exposure of the sensitised plate to its object, imprints the likeness there. "Our Lady's children should be ladylike," was the keynote of a retreat given to girls—a thought worth working out. If you will study Mary in your Rosary, you will grow like her. You will be like her above all in that virtue of heavenly Prudence which is specially needed by us in these days of rush and excitement, of complex duties, and difficult problems, and perilous situations.

We hear much in these days of the Rights of Women, but not enough of the tremendous Responsibilities upon which they are entering, and which, no less than prerogative and privilege, enter into the idea of Rights. But if Mary be our Helper, says St. Bernard, we shall not falter; under Mary's protection we shall walk securely, giving to God the service of a full, and rich, and active life, a life that will deserve at the end His word of joyful commendation: "Well done, good and faithful servant, enter into the joy of thy Lord!"

Catholic Girls, there is nothing you may not hope for if you will only wake up to a sense of your importance, of the place you hold in the destiny of those dear to you, and of your

1 "Meditations and Devotions." Cardinal Newman.

native land. Do not throw away in frivolity and selfishness the lives that can do so much. If you have any ambition, any desire to be true to yourselves and worthy of your name of Catholics, open your minds and your hearts to the future that lies before you, and fit yourselves to meet it!

Hark! Yes, here they are, and no mistake. Listen to the feet and the voices making for our room.... Well, here you are at last!

"Oh, we've had such a glorious time!"

"And we've brought back such lots of things—starfish, and eels, and shells."

"And such a queer creature—even the fishermen said they had never seen anything like it."

"And once we were nearly drowned. We went a long way off from Joan into a dangerous place, and we were playing at pirates in a cave, and the tide came in suddenly, and we had to come out through the sea and tear for our life, with the waves tearing after us."

"And they nearly caught us. Oh, it *was* fun!"

"And Joan was as white as a sheet, and tried to be cross."

Well, you shall tell us all about it to-morrow; now we must get you some supper and see you off to bed.

"And to-morrow we'll show you all we've brought. Have you missed us all this time?"

Indeed we have; it has not been like the same thing without you.

"We knew you would; but never mind, we shall be here for Christmas."

"Oh, but it *has* been fun; we wish you had been there. And see how brown we are!"

"Well, good night, everybody!"

"Good night!"

Alphabetical Index

Accomplishments, 157-8, 221, 241
Anchorets, 2
Almsgiving, 194-5

Bible, the, 60
Body, the, 14, 124-5
Books, 79, 112-122, 225-239
Brothers, 242

Catechism, necessity of knowing, 62
Catholic Women Workers, League of, 266
Catholics, duties of, 135, 261, 272
Character, 108, 184
Charity, Christian, 198, 203, 264
Church, the, 84, 94
  Infallibility of, 82-84
Comfort, love of, 171
Communion, 218-9
Confession, 50, 219
  not for conversation, 109-10
Contrition, perfect, 47
Conversation, 250-1

Dangers, 57, 79, 172-3, 273, 276
Debts, 196
Detraction, 252
Devil, the, 38, 129

Devotions, 275
Difficulties, 60, 101
District visiting, 262
Dress, 203
Drink, 229

Education, true object of, 135-6
Examinations, public, 158

Faith, 64, 71, 80, 100
Friends, 104

Getting up, 219
Gifts, obligation of cultivating, 139
Going to bed, 219, 230
Guild, an Irish, 148

Happiness, 244
Hobbies, 45-6, 191
Holy Childhood, Society of, 208
Home duties, 157, 169, 254

Idleness, 45, 174, 188
Independence, spirit of, 242
Indifference, danger of, 276
Instruction, the work of, 204
Intention, value of, 151, 263

Jesus Christ, 8, 81
Juliana of Norwich, Mother, 1

LEISURE, employment of, 189
Life of Jesus Christ, 237
Lives of the Saints, 236

MONEY, use and abuse, 194

NAZARETH, the Home of, 247
Non-Catholics, dealings with, 78
Novels, 115, 227

OUR LADY, 279-281

PASSIONS, 126-7
Parents, duty to, 159
Philanthropy, 198-9
Pleasure, its use and abuse, 171
Politics, interest of women in, 261
Poor, duties towards, 195, 266
Preparation for life, 222-3
Prevention of Cruelty to Children,
    Society for, 265
Principles, 108, 268, 272
Propagation of the Faith,
    Association for, 208, 265
Providence, 88
Prudence, 280-1
Purpose in life, 139, 174, 265

READING, 79, 117, 227
Reason, the light of, 10, 67
Religion, interest in, 136-7
    study of a duty, 82-3
Responsibility, 10, 179, 272
Revelation, 61
Roads, 22-3

SAINTS, 14, 127
School treats, 144
Science, 60, 76
Selfishness, 156, 158
Self-control, 115, 120, 173
Self-improvement, 157
Self-love, 129

Self-sacrifice, 145, 151, 263
Sin, 30-1
Social work, 261
Soul, the, 8, 20
Standard, a high, 274, 276
Standards, Christ's vs. Satan's, 56
State of life, 140
Study, 157, 186, 221

TALENTS, 139
Tastes, cultivation of, 118, 140
Temptation, 38
Time-table, importance of, 215
Training, need of, 256

UNSELFISHNESS, 146, 152

VIGILANCE, need of, 57
Vocation, 140

WORK in life, 139
    a duty for all, 134
    social, 260
World, the, 54
Worldliness, 55, 155, 171, 176

Additional titles available from

St. Augustine Academy Press

Books for the Traditional Catholic

Titles by Mother Mary Loyola:

Blessed are they that Mourn
Confession and Communion
Coram Sanctissimo (Before the Most Holy)
First Communion
First Confession
Forgive us our Trespasses
Hail! Full of Grace
Heavenwards
Holy Mass/How to Help the Sick and Dying
Home for Good
Jesus of Nazareth: The Story of His Life Written for Children
The Child of God: What comes of our Baptism
The Children's Charter
The Little Children's Prayer Book
The Soldier of Christ: Talks before Confirmation
Welcome! Holy Communion Before and After

Tales of the Saints:

A Child's Book of Saints by William Canton
A Child's Book of Warriors by William Canton
Illustrated Life of the Blessed Virgin by Rev. B. Rohner, O.S.B.
Legends & Stories of Italy by Amy Steedman
Mary, Help of Christians by Rev. Bonaventure Hammer
The Book of Saints and Heroes by Lenora Lang
Saint Patrick: Apostle of Ireland
The Story of St. Elizabeth of Hungary by William Canton

Check our Website for more:

www.staugustineacademypress.com